THE
ROYAL NAVY
IN WORLD
WAR II

THE
ROYAL NAVY
IN WORLD
WAR II

ROBERT JACKSON

Airlife
England

Copyright © 1997 Robert Jackson

First published in the UK in 1997
by Airlife Publishing Ltd

British Library Cataloguing-in-Publication Data
    A catalogue record for this book
    is available from the British Library

ISBN 1 85310 714 X

Typeset by Servis Filmsetting Ltd, Manchester
Printed in England by Butler & Tanner Ltd, Frome & London.

Airlife Publishing Ltd

101 Longden Road, Shrewsbury SY3 9EB, England

Contents

Acknowledgements

I am indebted to three people in particular for supplying the bulk of the photographs which appear in this book. They are Mrs Fay Robertson, whose husband took part in the attacks on the *Tirpitz* in 1944; John McVittie, an old friend who flew Swordfish in the Arctic and the Indian Ocean; and Bill Coley, who served on escort carriers and witnessed the savage battles that attended the Russian convoys.

I make no apology for the fact that the illustrations are biased towards naval aviation. The Second World War proved that without offensive and defensive air support, a modern fleet might just as well stay in port. The lesson has been underlined several times since, off Korea, at Suez and – most notably – in the Falklands.

Robert Jackson
Darlington, England.

Introduction

As the New Year of 1939 dawned, it was clear to the British Chiefs of Staff that war with Nazi Germany – and possibly also with Germany's Axis partner, Italy – was inevitable. The signs had been obvious since 1936, when German troops marched into the Rhineland and set a pattern of expansion and aggression which, faced only with appeasement on the part of the British and French Governments, had resulted two years later in the unopposed annexation of Austria.

The occupation of the Rhineland had set in motion plans for the expansion of all three of Britain's fighting services. In the case of the Royal Navy, a supplementary naval estimate introduced into the House of Commons in 1936 called for the building of two new battleships, an aircraft carrier and a variety of smaller vessels. In 1937 a revised estimate included three more battleships, two more aircraft carriers, seven cruisers and a substantial increase in smaller craft, notably destroyers.

Welcome though it was, this increase in Britain's maritime strength could at best be described as modest, and it came too late to provide the Royal Navy with the assets it so badly needed to confront German and Italian fleets which, although a good deal smaller, were in many respects far more modern in terms of equipment. Although four new battleships of the King George V class were building at the start of 1939, none would be ready for at least eighteen months; and of the fifteen existing capital ships, only two, the *Nelson* and the *Rodney*, had been built since 1918.

At the end of the First World War the Royal Navy had 44 capital ships, plus one more building. By 1920 this total had been reduced to 29, a figure generally accepted as being the minimum number needed to defend Britain's worldwide interests and to maintain parity with the rapidly growing naval forces of the United States and Japan. But on 6 February 1922, the number of capital ships available to the Royal Navy was reduced still further with the signing of the Washington Naval Treaty.

The principal aim of the Washington Treaty, which was engineered by the United States and which in effect was the first disarmament treaty in history, was to limit the size of the navies of the five principal maritime powers, which at that time were Britain, the U.S.A., France, Italy and Japan. For Britain, this meant a reduction in capital ship assets to twenty by scrapping existing warships and dropping new projects; however, because her capital ships were older and less heavily armed than those of the United States, she would be permitted to build two new vessels as replacements for existing ones. The other nations would also be permitted to build new capital ships to replace vessels that were twenty years old. This arrangement would allow France and Italy to lay down new warships in 1927, while Britain, the U.S.A. and Japan would not need to do so until 1931. No new capital ship was to exceed 35,000 tons, nor mount guns larger than 16-inch. No existing capital ship was to be rebuilt, although an increase in deck armour against air attack was allowed, as were the addition of anti-torpedo bulges, provided these modifications did not exceed a total of 3,000 tons.

The Washington Treaty also limited the tonnage of aircraft carriers. Each signatory nation was allowed to build two vessels of up to 33,000 tons; the remainder were limited to 27,000 tons, and the total aircraft carrier tonnage in the case of Britain and the U.S.A. was not to exceed 135,000 tons. Japan was allowed 81,000 tons, while France and Italy were permitted 60,000 tons each. None of the carriers was allowed an armament in excess of eight 8-inch guns, nor might they be replaced until they were twenty years old. No other warships were to be built in excess of 10,000 tons, nor have guns larger than 8-inch.

Naval aviation, in which the Royal Navy had established a commanding lead by the end of the First World War, had stagnated in the years since; by 1930, because of the nation's fluctuating political fortunes, with all three services fighting for survival in the midst of the worst economic crisis in Britain's history and the politicians' fool's paradise of disarmament, nothing at all had been done to authorise even the modest expansion of the Fleet Air Arm that the Admiralty wanted. The upshot was that of the six aircraft carriers in service at the beginning of 1939, only one, the *Ark Royal* – laid down in 1935 and in the process of completing her trials – was a modern, purpose-built ship. Four of the others were conversions from battleship or battlecruiser hulls and the fifth, H.M.S. *Furious*, was too small to be of much use. Five new 23,000-ton fleet carriers were either under construction or planned; again, it would be eighteen months before the first of these was ready for commissioning. As for the first-line aircraft at the Fleet Air Arm's disposal at the beginning of 1939 – the Fairey Swordfish torpedo-bomber, the Blackburn Skua fighter/dive-bomber and the Gloster Sea Gladiator fighter – all were obsolescent.

One predictable result of the Washington Treaty was that all five major maritime powers built cruisers right up to the agreed limit of 10,000 tons, and with the heaviest armament allowed. Britain, for example, laid down seven Kent class ships of 9,880 tons, mounting eight 8-inch guns, followed by six similar London class ships. A destroyer replacement programme of nine vessels a year, each displacing 1,350 tons and mounting four 4.7-inch guns and eight torpedo tubes, was also started in 1929. In addition, the decision was taken to give Britain's ageing submarine force a shot in the arm by building nine O class vessels and six P class boats.

By 1930, the strength of the Royal Navy stood at sixteen battleships, four battlecruisers, six aircraft carriers, twenty cruisers with 7.5-inch or 8-inch armament (with three more building), 40

other cruisers, 146 destroyers (ten more building) and 50 submarines (ten more building). Meanwhile, all the construction programmes of the maritime powers had been severely affected by economic constraints, the world being in the grip of a savage depression. With the exception of Japan, all the maritime nations were eager to escape the cost of building replacement capital ships, as permitted by the Washington Treaty, and on 22 April a new treaty, signed in London by the five principal powers, made fresh provisions. Britain, Japan and the U.S.A. agreed that they would lay down no new capital ships before 1936, while France and Italy decided to lay down only the two they were already allowed. Furthermore, Britain, Japan and the United States agreed to make further reductions in existing assets; Britain would reduce her force of capital ships to fifteen by scrapping H.M.S. *Tiger* and three Iron Duke class vessels, and relegating the old *Iron Duke* herself to the role of training and depot ship. The United States and Japan also agreed to reduce their capital ship assets to fifteen and nine respectively.

Within three years, the Treaties of Washington and London had been torn to shreds by the march of international events. First of all, in 1933, Japan invaded Manchuria, giving notice to the world that she intended to establish domination of the Far East, and then withdrew from the League of Nations. She quickly followed this step with a notice to end her adherence to the Washington and London Treaties, her intention being to establish naval parity with Britain and the U.S.A. France, increasingly alarmed by the growing hostility of fascist Italy, followed suit early in 1935. Also in 1935, and in defiance of the League of Nations, Italy embarked upon a campaign of aggression in Abyssinia; and in 1936 Nazi Germany, having repudiated the Treaty of Versailles, seized the Rhineland.

Faced not only with a potential threat to her possessions in the Far East, but also with threats much closer to home from a revitalised and increasingly aggressive Germany and an ambitious Ialy, Britain began to rearm. Five King George V class fast battleships of 35,000 tons were laid down, each armed with ten 14-inch guns and sixteen 5.25-inch dual-purpose (D.P.) guns. These were followed, after Japan had abandoned the Treaty limits, by four Lion class ships of 40,000 tons mounting nine 16-inch guns, although those were later cancelled. At the same time, existing British capital ships were modernized with the provision of extra armour and improved armament.

The cruiser force also underwent substantial upgrading. Eight Leander class vessels of 7,000 tons, armed with eight six-inch guns were built, followed by four 5,220-ton Arethusas with six; this kept the cruiser tonnage within the limits imposed by the London Treaty, but the subsequent crash rearmament programme produced eight Southamptons of 9,100 tons mounting twelve 6-inch guns, followed by two slightly larger Edinburghs and eleven Fiji class of 8,800 tons, with the same armament. Eleven Dido class vessels were also laid down; these were 5,770-ton ships with an armament of ten 5.25-inch D.P. guns, their primary role being to counter air attack. As well as these new warships, the older 8-inch cruisers of postwar vintage were retained in service, as were 23 C, D and E class vessels. Six of these were rearmed with eight 4-inch A.A. guns as anti-aircraft cruisers. There were also three surviving Hawkins class cruisers, one of which, H.M.S. *Effingham*, was rearmed with nine 6-inch guns.

Destroyers, too, were key participants in the maritime arms race. In order to keep pace with destroyer developments in other countries, Britain laid down sixteen big Tribal class vessels of 1,870 tons, armed with eight 4.7-inch guns and four torpedo tubes, followed by the 1,690-ton J and K classes with six 4.7-inch guns and eight torpedo tubes. An entirely new design of small, fast destroyer (900 tons and 32 knots) was also introduced; this was the Hunt class, 20 of which were on the stocks at the outbreak of war. Although of limited endurance, they were to perform excellent service in home waters.

To bolster trade protection, the Admiralty ordered more vessels of the type known as sloops, which displaced between 1,000 and 1,250 tons and which, although slow, had a good endurance. By 1939, 53 were in service. Finally, a completely new type of small long-endurance vessel, designed on the lines of the whale-catcher and called a corvette, began to be introduced from 1939.

So much for the material available to the Admiralty as the spectre of war loomed in the summer of 1939. As to planning and strategy, the Royal Navy, because of Great Britain's global responsibilities, faced far more problems than any other major maritime power.

It was the Royal Navy which, when war came, would bear the main responsibility for maritime operations in the North Sea and the Atlantic, although it was envisaged that the French Navy would have an important part to play in convoy protection on the more southerly Atlantic routes and in hunting down enemy commerce raiders. As to the Mediterranean, this area of operations would be divided between Britain and France, the French being responsible for the western part, the British for the eastern, although there were plans for some French warships to operate under the command of the British Mediterranean Fleet. The Italian Navy, the *Regia Marina*, was seen as a formidable threat; it possessed modern battleships and cruisers, a force of over 100 submarines, and was backed up by large numbers of bombers belonging to the *Regia Aeronautica*, the Italian Air Force. In the face of this threat, the British and French Admiralties took the joint decision that in the event of war the Mediterranean would be closed to all mercantile traffic bound for the Middle East; this would be diverted round the Cape of Good Hope, an 11,000-mile haul necessitating the rapid establishment of shore bases on the east and west coasts of Africa.

The British and French naval planners had little doubt that their combined navies would be more than a match for the *Regia Marina*, even though its fighting capability was an unknown quantity – for the simple reason that neither the British nor the French had ever fought against it. What was also unknown was the true state of the Japanese Navy and its associated maritime air power, on which intelligence was almost completely lacking. In 1939 Japan was adopting an increasingly belligerent stance towards Britain and the United States, but ships could not be spared to bolster the existing force of cruisers and escort vessels – elderly ships, for the most part – responsible for the defence of British interests in the Far East. Japan had not yet allied herself with Germany and Italy, which had concluded a joint offensive–defensive pact known as the Berlin–Rome Axis on 22 May 1939, but there were indications that she might be persuaded to do so; in that event, a plan existed to reinforce the Eastern Fleet by despatching the bulk of the Mediterranean Fleet to Singapore, leaving operations in the Mediterranean entirely to the French.

Such, in broad outline, was the state of the Royal Navy in August 1939 in terms of material and overall strategy. And then there was the Navy's greatest asset: its manpower. On 1 January 1939, there were 10,000 regular officers and 109,000 men, together with 12,400 officers and men of the Royal Marines. In addition to these were 73,000 officers and men of the Royal Naval Reserve and 6,000 Royal Naval Volunteer Reservists. Together, they formed the best trained and most dedicated cadre of naval personnel in the world.

The tragedy was that, at the outbreak of the Second World War, their training and dedication were not matched by the standard of the ships available to them; and in the first grim years of battle, many lives would be wasted as a consequence.

CHAPTER ONE

The North Sea and Atlantic, September 1939 – April 1940

In August 1939, with the invasion of Poland imminent, the German Naval Staff lost no time in deploying units of the *Kriegsmarine* to their war stations in the Atlantic, ready to begin an immediate offensive against Allied shipping. On 19 August, fourteen U-boats were dispatched from Wilhelmshaven and Kiel, and two days later the 13,000-ton pocket battleship *Admiral Graf Spee* also sailed from Wilhelmshaven, under cover of darkness and unobserved, to make rendezvous with her supply ship, the fleet tanker *Altmark*, in the South Atlantic. She was followed on 24 August by a second pocket battleship, the *Deutschland*, which sailed for her war station south of Greenland, to be joined later by her own replenishment vessel, the fleet tanker *Westerwald*. Within the next 24 hours, signals had been dispatched to all German merchant vessels, ordering them to make for home, friendly or neutral ports with all possible speed.

If the German Naval Staff was determined to bring home the bulk of its merchant fleet, many of whose vessels were carrying raw materials vital to the German war effort, the British Admiralty was equally determined to seize them – in particular the German mercantile flagship, the fast Atlantic liner *Bremen*. From 31 August, Admiral Sir Charles Forbes, C.-in-C. Home Fleet, deployed the battleships *Nelson*, *Ramillies*, *Rodney*, *Royal Oak* and *Royal Sovereign*, the battlecruisers *Hood* and *Repulse*, the aircraft carrier *Ark Royal*, twelve cruisers and sixteen destroyers in a blocking screen across the Iceland–Faeroes–UK gap, combing those high-latitude waters for the elusive merchantmen.

On 3 September, following the declaration of war by Britain and France, the light cruiser H.M.S. *Ajax* drew first blood – not in northern

Fairey Swordfish flying past the cruiser H.M.S. Ajax. *Famous for the River Plate action, she spent most of her subsequent war service in the Mediterranean*

waters but in the South Atlantic, where she intercepted two German freighters. Their captains ordered the ships to be scuttled in order to avoid capture. Also on this day, the U-boats struck their first blow when the U-30 (*Leutnant* Lemp) torpedoed and sank the British passenger liner *Athenia* south of the Rockall Bank. About 1,300 survivors were rescued by the destroyers *Electra* and *Escort*, assisted by some foreign vessels, but 112 people lost their lives. Although the story was put out that Lemp had mistaken the liner for an armed merchant cruiser, it seems more likely that he had misconstrued his orders and believed such attacks to be permitted by the German government; whatever the truth, the British Admiralty took the sinking as evidence that unrestricted submarine warfare was in force, a belief that was to lead to the early establishment of a full convoy system for the protection of mercantile trade. In fact, the first convoy sailed on 6 September, from the Firth of Forth to the Thames Estuary, and the next day three escorted Atlantic convoys were also dispatched to Gibraltar, Halifax and Sierra Leone.

Victim of the U-boat war: a British merchant ship goes down in the Western Approaches

(**ABOVE**) *An early victim of the mercantile war was the tramp steamer* Kensington Court, *sunk by a U-boat 70 miles west of the Scillies on 18 September 1939. A Sunderland flying boat circles over survivors*

H.M. Submarine Sturgeon *operated with the 2nd Flotilla in the North Sea from the beginning of the war. Transferred to the Royal Netherlands Navy in 1943 as the* Zeehond, *she survived the war*

Although the liner *Bremen* escaped the attentions of the Home Fleet on her homeward run from New York – she had already found refuge in Murmansk – the British naval blockade enjoyed considerable success during September, the warships intercepting 108 merchant vessels and escorting 28 of them to Kirkwall, Orkney, for inspection. British submarines deployed in a screen between the Shetlands and Norway, and off the north German coast, were less successful, the only damage being done to their own side. On 10 September, the submarine *Triton* sank another British submarine, H.M. Submarine *Oxley*, on the surface in a tragic case of misidentification that left only two survivors; four days later, H.M. Submarine *Swordfish* almost suffered the same fate in a torpedo attack by H.M. Submarine *Sturgeon*; and on 17 September H.M. Submarine *Seahorse* survived a bombing attack by an Avro Anson of R.A.F. Coastal Command.

While the Home Fleet continued its northern patrol – moving its main operating base from Scapa Flow to Loch Ewe on the Clyde during September for fear of air attack, the Orkney base being very poorly defended at this time – two hunting groups, each consisting of an aircraft carrier and four destroyers, had been formed to operate against U-boats in the Western Approaches and the Channel area. Minelaying accounted for a good deal of U-boat activity, and in fact mines were responsible for the sinking of a high proportion of the 25 merchant vessels lost in this area during September. Operations to the west of the British Isles were undertaken by eleven submarines of the 2nd U-boat Flotilla. During the same period, eleven more submarines of the 6th and 7th U-boat Flotillas, operating in the Atlantic west of the Bay of Biscay and off the Iberian Peninsula, sank seven merchant ships and captured two more.

On 14 September, the U-boats missed their chance to deal a telling blow to the Royal Navy when the U-39 fired a salvo of torpedoes at the fleet carrier H.M.S. *Ark Royal* west of the Hebrides. Luckily for the carrier, the torpedoes – a new type fitted with magnetic pistols – detonated prematurely and the submarine was sunk by the escorting destroyers *Faulknor*, *Foxhound* and *Firedrake*, her crew being taken prisoner.

Three days later, the Royal Navy's luck ran out.

On 17 September, the fleet carrier *Courageous* (22,500 tons, 48 aircraft) was hit by three torpedoes from the U-29 west of the English Channel. She went down with the loss of 515 crew. An immediate result was the withdrawal of aircraft carriers from anti-submarine operations. On 22 September, the Navy's destroyers enjoyed a revenge of sorts when the U-27 (*Kapitänleutnant* Franz) was sunk off the west coast of Scotland by H.M.S. *Fortuna* and H.M.S. *Forester*.

On 25 September, the Royal Navy fought its first air action of the war when a Dornier Do 18 maritime reconnaissance aircraft was shot down by Blackburn Skuas of No. 803 Squadron, Fleet Air Arm, from H.M.S. *Ark Royal*, led by Lieutenant C. L. G. Evans. The next day, the *Ark Royal* – part of a Home Fleet force, dispatched to cover ships of the 2nd Cruiser Squadron engaged in recovering the submarine *Spearfish*, badly damaged in the central North Sea – was attacked and near-missed by Ju 88s of I/K.G. 30. One bomb hit the battlecruiser *Hood*, but bounced off. Nine He 111s of I/K.G. 26 were also dispatched to attack the 2nd Cruiser Squadron, but failed to locate the warships.

By 21 September, British Naval Intelligence was aware that two powerful German commerce raiders, the *Graf Spee* and the *Deutschland*, were at sea, and the Admiralty was compelled to deploy substantial numbers of ships – including some detached from the Mediterranean – to search for them. On 7 October, the German Naval Staff, concerned about the mounting pressure on the pocket battleships, ordered units of the German Fleet to make a sortie towards the southern coast of Norway; the force comprised the battlecruiser

The armed trawler H.M.S. Syringa (formerly Cape Kanin*) was typical of the many auxiliary vessels that rendered sterling service throughout the war. Unlike over a thousand others, she survived*

H.M.S. Syringa's *ship's company, 1940*

The cruiser H.M.S. Sheffield was in action throughout the war, serving with the Home Fleet and with Force H in the Mediterranean

Scharnhorst, the light cruiser *Köln* and nine destroyers, the intention being to draw the Home Fleet across a concentration of four U-boats and within range of the *Luftwaffe*. The German warships were sighted on the following day by a patrolling Lockheed Hudson of No. 224 Squadron, R.A.F. Coastal Command.

As soon as Admiral Forbes learned that the enemy was out he stationed his main units – the battleships *Nelson* and *Rodney*, the battlecruisers *Hood* and *Repulse*, the cruisers *Aurora*, *Sheffield* and *Newcastle*, and the carrier *Furious*, accompanied by twelve destroyers – north-east of the Shetlands, where they could cover the exit to the Atlantic. At the same time, he despatched the Humber Force, comprising the light cruisers *Edinburgh*, *Glasgow* and *Southampton*, to search for the German ships. The operation was fruitless, and bombers dispatched by both sides failed to find their targets. On 9 October, after dark, the German force reversed its course and returned to Kiel, and by 11 October the main units of the Home Fleet were back in Loch Ewe and the light cruisers were back in the Humber.

There was an exception. One of Forbes's battleships had been detached from the main force to guard the Fair Isle Channel, between the Shetland and Orkney Islands, and when the threat receded she made her way to the anchorage at Scapa Flow. She was the *Royal Oak*.

On the night of 13/14 October, the German submarine U-47, commanded by *Kapitänleutnant* Gunther Prien, penetrated the defences of Scapa Flow and sank the *Royal Oak* with three torpedo hits. The attack, in which 833 lives were lost, was carried out with great coolness, skill and daring, and came as a severe shock to Britain.

Two days after this tragedy, Ju 88 bombers of K.G. 30 carried out an attack on warships of the Home Fleet in the Firth of Forth, H.M.S. *Hood* being the main target. The attack was unsuccessful, the bombers inflicting only light damage on the cruisers *Southampton* and *Edinburgh* and the destroyer *Mohawk*. Two Ju 88s were shot down by

Spitfires. The next day, K.G. 30 also attacked Scapa Flow, but apart from the depot ship *Iron Duke*, which was damaged by a near miss, the nest was empty.

Enemy mines continued to be the main threat to British shipping in home waters, and for a time the Germans enjoyed a definite advantage through the use of the magnetic mine, which was detonated by the magnetic field of a vessel passing over it. Such mines accounted for 59,027 tons of British coastal shipping in September and October 1939, and to compound the problem the entire British minesweeping service was equipped to deal only with moored contact mines.

Minelaying operations by U-boats and destroyers intensified during November, the submarines being active in the Straits of Dover, the Firth of Forth, off Cromarty and in the Home Fleet's new refuge of Loch Ewe. On 21 November, the cruiser *Belfast* was damaged by a mine in the Firth of Forth, and on 4 December the battleship *Nelson* was also damaged by a mine laid by the U-31 in Loch Ewe.

Meanwhile, on 21 November, the battlecruisers *Scharnhorst* and *Gneisenau* had sailed from Wilhelmshaven for the North Atlantic, the purpose of their sortie being to divert attention away from the operations of the pocket battleship *Admiral Graf Spee* in the South Atlantic. Passing undetected to the north of the Shetlands and Faeroes, the warships were sighted on the 23rd by the Armed Merchant Cruiser *Rawalpindi* (Captain E. C. Kennedy), which engaged them in a gallant but one-sided duel. She had time to radio their presence to Scapa Flow before she was sunk by the *Scharnhorst*. Admiral Sir Charles Forbes at once ordered the entire Home Fleet to sea in a bid to intercept the battlecruisers. They were in fact sighted by the cruiser *Newcastle*, which had been patrolling in the vicinity, as they picked up survivors from the *Rawalpindi*, but they avoided her in a rain squall and withdrew to a waiting position inside the Arctic Circle.

On the 26th, the German battlecruisers came south once more, passed through the cruiser and destroyer patrol lines which Admiral Forbes had established off Norway, and regained

Wilhelmshaven the next day. No fewer than 60 warships – six battleships (three French), two battlecruisers, 20 cruisers (two French), 28 destroyers (eight French), three submarines and an aircraft carrier – had been redeployed to various positions in the North Atlantic and North Sea to hunt the *Scharnhorst* and the *Gneisenau*. The Germans had eluded the lot. As a diversionary tactic, it had certainly worked.

The search for the enemy battlecruisers, abortive though it was, illustrated the close cooperation that existed at this time between the Royal Navy and French Navy. On 5 October, the Admiralty, in conjunction with the French Navy, had formed eight Atlantic 'hunting groups' of aircraft carriers and cruisers for the defence of the trade routes against surface raiders. Three were under the orders of the Commander-in-Chief, South Atlantic, whose headquarters were at Freetown, Sierra Leone; one of them, Group G, comprising the heavy cruisers *Exeter* and *Cumberland* and reinforced later by the light cruisers *Ajax* and *Achilles*, the latter belonging to the Royal New Zealand Navy, were responsible for the waters off the east coast of South America – and it was there that the *Admiral Graf Spee*'s rampage at last came to an end.

The pocket battleship sank her first merchantman off Pernambuco on 30 September, and between 5 and 12 October she sank four more before breaking off to replenish from her supply ship, the *Altmark*. She turned up again on 15 November, when she sank a small tanker in the Mozambique Channel. There was no further news of her until 2 December, when she sank the freighters *Doric Star* and *Tairoa* between St Helena and South Africa.

On receiving intelligence of these sinkings, the C.-in-C. South Atlantic, Vice-Admiral d'Oyly Lyon, ordered Force H, with the cruisers *Shropshire* and *Sussex*, to proceed to the area between Cape Town and St Helena, while Force K, comprising the battlecruiser *Renown*, the aircraft carrier *Ark Royal* and the cruiser *Neptune*, was dispatched to search along a line from Freetown to the central South Atlantic. Force G (as Group G was now designated) meanwhile assembled off the River Plate with the cruisers

Achilles and *Ajax*, and *Exeter* and *Cumberland* having been detached to cover the Falkland Islands. There was plenty of mercantile traffic around the estuary of the River Plate, and Force G's senior officer, Commodore H. Harwood, reasoned that Langsdorff, the captain of the *Graf Spee* would be attracted there sooner or later. He was right.

After sinking two more ships in mid-ocean, *Kapitän* Langsdorff elected to steer directly for the Plate estuary, where she was sighted at 06.08 on 13 December. The three British cruisers were soon in action against her, opening fire from different directions. Langsdorff at first divided his armament, but then concentrated his fire on the *Exeter*, his 11-inch shells inflicting heavy damage on the cruiser. Despite this, Captain F. S. Bell continued to engage the enemy throughout the night, at the end of which the *Exeter* had only one turret left in action and was ablaze. Langsdorff could easily have finished her off; instead, he made smoke and turned west, allowing *Exeter* to pull away to the south-east to make repairs, with 61 of her crew dead and 23 wounded.

The pocket battleship now steered for the coast of Uruguay, under fire all the while from the light cruisers *Ajax* and *Achilles*. At 07.25 an 11-inch shell hit *Ajax* and put both her after turrets out of action, but again Langsdorff failed to take the opportunity to finish off one of his adversaries, whose remaining guns were now barely superior to his own secondary armament. The two cruisers continued to shadow the *Graf Spee*, which fired salvoes at them from time to time, until the battleship entered the estuary; Commodore Harwood then called off the pursuit and set up a patrol line, aware that he was in a very parlous position if Langsdorff chose to fight his way out to the open sea.

Langsdorff, his ship damaged – she had taken some 70 hits and 36 of her crew were dead, with another 60 wounded – had decided to make for a neutral port where he could effect temporary repairs before attempting a breakout into the North Atlantic and a run back to Germany. He was also short of ammunition. The *Graf Spee* reached Montevideo on the evening of 14 December, and there now began a prolonged

diplomatic effort to remain in port beyond the legal limit of 72 hours, since the necessary repairs would take an estimated two weeks to complete. British propaganda, meanwhile, went all out to create the impression that a large British fleet was lying in wait to ambush the *Graf Spee* as soon as she re-emerged from the La Plata estuary. The aircraft carrier *Ark Royal* and the battlecruiser *Renown* were reported to be at Rio de Janeiro; in fact, they were 2,500 miles away, and the cruiser force had been reinforced by only one more ship, another cruiser, H.M.S. *Cumberland*.

Langsdorff fell for it. On 16 December he sent the following signal to Berlin:

1. Strategic position off Montevideo: Besides the cruisers and destroyers, *Ark Royal* and *Renown*. Close blockade at night. Escape into open sea and breakthrough to home waters hopeless.
2. Propose putting out as far as neutral boundary. If it is possible to fight our way through to Buenos Aires, using remaining ammunition, this will be attempted.
3. If a breakthrough would result in certain destruction of *Graf Spee* without opportunity of damaging enemy, request decision on whether the ship should be scuttled in spite of insufficient depth in the estuary of the La Plata, or whether internment is to be preferred.

The reply that came back from Berlin was unequivocal. There was to be no question of internment. The authority was given to scuttle the ship, should the German envoy in Montevideo fail to gain an extension of the time limit in neutral waters. By nightfall on 17 December, it was plain that no such extension was to be permitted by the Uruguayan authorities.

On the following morning, watched by a vast crowd of sightseers, *Graf Spee* put to sea. The British warships cleared for action, but before they could engage the enemy, their spotter aircraft reported that the *Graf Spee* had been scuttled and blown up by her own crew. Within a short time, it was learned that *Kapitän* Langsdorff had committed suicide.

The *Graf Spee*'s crew were later transferred to Argentina, where they were interned. They remained there until February 1946, when 900 (some having chosen to stay in South America) were repatriated to Germany on the liner *Highland Monarch* – escorted, in a nice touch of irony, by H.M.S. *Ajax*.

The destruction of the *Graf Spee* was a major coup for the Royal Navy; another was the recovery, on 23 November 1939, of two German magnetic mines from the mud flats at Shoeburyness. Defused and made safe by a very gallant Royal Navy team (Lt-Cdrs Ouvry and Lewis, C. P. O. Baldwin and A. B. Vearncombe) they were transported to Portsmouth for detailed examination. Once the magnetic mine's secrets were unlocked, the Admiralty initiated all technical measures to combat it. Before long, a research team under Rear-Admiral W. F. Wake-Walker had devised effective countermeasures in the form of a so-called degaussing girdle, an electric cable fitted to the hulls of ships to demagnetize them. Degaussing girdles were also fitted to modified Vickers Wellingtons of No. 1 General

Vickers Wellington fitted with a degaussing girdle for magnetic mine countermeasures

Reconnaissance Unit, R.A.F. Coastal Command, whose task it was to fly low over the sea and detonate the mines by triggering their detonators through the generation of an electromagnetic field.

These developments came just in time. In November 1939, enemy minelaying became so intensive that only a single channel into the Thames remained open. In that month, mines accounted for 27 ships totalling 120,958 tons. As the official naval historian Captain S. W. Roskill later wrote:

While awaiting the arrival of the new sweep many extemporised measures were adopted, and together they just succeeded in keeping the east coast traffic moving. Though losses continued on a considerable scale in the New Year, and in the first seven months of war no less than 128 ships totalling 429,899 tons fell victims to mines, we never again had to face as serious a crisis as that of the first autumn.

In December 1939, the Royal Navy, in co-operation with R.A.F. Coastal Command, steadily tightened its blockade of German maritime traffic in the North Atlantic and the North Sea. During this period, British submarines scored some

The German supply ship Altmark *photographed in a Norwegian fjord shortly before the Royal Navy liberated her prisoners*

notable successes. In the Heligoland Bight, H.M.S. *Salmon* (Lt-Cdr Bickford) sank the U-36, and on 12 December Bickford almost succeeded in intercepting the passenger liner *Bremen*, homeward bound from the Kola Inlet, only to be thwarted by the appearance overhead of a Do 18 patrol aircraft. The next day, Bickford sighted a force of three light cruisers, escorting five destroyers which had been out on a minelaying sortie, and launched a salvo of torpedoes; the *Leipzig* took a severe hit amidships and the *Nürnberg* was hit in the bow. The enemy force was then attacked by H.M.S. *Ursula* (Lt-Cdr Phillips) which sank the escort vessel F9.

These successes were tempered, in January 1940, by the loss of three British submarines in rapid succession. The *Undine* and *Starfish* were both forced to the surface by depth-charge attacks and had to scuttle themselves, while the *Seahorse* was sunk. These losses brought an abrupt halt to Home Fleet submarine operations in the inner Heligoland Bight.

In the early weeks of 1940, with the Baltic remaining icebound for an unusually long period, the Germans made increasing use of the alternative route via the north Norwegian port of Narvik to ship Swedish iron ore, a commodity vital to Germany's war industries. The British Admiralty laid plans to extend its blockade to enemy merchant shipping making the long sea passage down Norway's coastline, but this was difficult to implement; for most of the route, the cargo vessels were able to remain inside Norwegian territorial waters by using the narrow passages between the mainland and the offshore islands known as the Inner Leads. The use of Norwegian ports by enemy blockade runners was also a sore point, and matters in this respect came to a head when, on 14 February 1940, the tanker *Altmark* – the *Graf Spee*'s supply ship, carrying some 300 merchant seamen from vessels sunk by the pocket battleship – sought refuge in Trondheim under Norwegian protection.

The *Altmark*'s *Kapitän* Dau had ignored *Kapitän* Langsdorff's order to land his captives at a neutral port, and instead had remained in the South Atlantic until a signal from Berlin advised him that it was safe to run for home. Passing through the Denmark Strait and entering Norwegian territorial waters, the *Altmark* had been intercepted by a Norwegian torpedo-boat, but Dau had refused to allow his ship to be searched.

On 15 February, Admiral Sir Charles Forbes learned that the *Altmark* was off Bergen, and instructed Captain Q. D. Graham of the cruiser *Arethusa*, returning with five destroyers from a sortie into the Skagerrak, to intercept her. She was sighted the next day, steaming down the Leads, but attempts by the British destroyers to close with her were frustrated by Norwegian torpedo-boats steaming close alongside. Darkness found the enemy tanker in Jösenfjord, where she was followed by Captain P. L. Vian in the destroyer *Cossack*. Informing the senior Norwegian officer that there were British prisoners on the *Altmark*, Vian demanded the right to search for them; the Norwegian replied that his orders were to resist, and trained his torpedo tubes on the destroyer.

Faced with this delicate situation, Vian withdrew and sought the Admiralty's instructions.

Three hours later, they came through, and the signal was penned by the resolute hand of Winston Churchill, then First Lord of the Admiralty.

Unless Norwegian torpedo-boat undertakes to convoy *Altmark* to Bergen with a joint Anglo-Norwegian guard on board, and a joint escort, you should board *Altmark*, liberate the prisoners, and take possession of the ship pending further instructions. If Norwegian torpedo-boat interferes, you should warn her to stand off. If she fires upon you, you should not reply unless attack is serious, in which case you should defend yourself, using no more force than is necessary, and ceasing fire when she desists.

For the equally resolute Vian, it was enough. Persuading the Norwegian vessels to withdraw, he took the *Cossack* into Jösenfjord and went alongsde the *Altmark*, evading an attempt by Dau to ram him, and sent over an armed boarding party. Six German guards were killed and six more wounded before they escaped ashore, leaving the British sailors free to break open the *Altmark*'s hatches. Someone asked if there were any British below, and a tremendous yell assured him that the prisoners were all British. The words that followed have become a firm part of British naval tradition: 'Come on up, then – the Navy's here!'

CHAPTER TWO
Norway, 1940

On 9 April 1940, the period that had become known as the Phoney War, came to a violent end when German forces invaded Norway and Denmark. The decision to occupy Norway was not entirely to do with securing the vital iron-ore route; the German naval C.-in-C., *Grossadmiral* Erich Raeder, had learned an important lesson from history, or rather from a book published in 1929 entitled *Maritime Strategy of the Great War*. Its author, *Vizeadmiral* Wegener, had pointed out that if Germany had occupied Norway in 1914, the High Seas Fleet, using Norwegian harbours, would have been free to operate against Britain's North Atlantic convoys instead of remaining blockaded in the North German ports by the Royal Navy's Home Fleet based at Scapa Flow.

There had been plenty of warning of Germany's intention to invade Norway. For several days early in April, the British Government had been receiving intelligence reports of unusual German activity in the Baltic ports, and had interpreted this as a sign that heavy units of the German Fleet were preparing to break out into the Atlantic. As it happened, this interpretation was wrong.

The bulk of the enemy invasion force was already at sea on 7 April, steaming northwards through savage weather. This part of the invasion force was divided into three Task Groups. Group One, with Narvik as its objective, had the farthest distance to travel – roughly 1,000 miles – and was heavily escorted by the battlecruisers *Scharnhorst* and *Gneisenau*, together with ten destroyers; Group Two, bound for Trondheim, was guarded by the cruiser *Admiral Hipper* and four destroyers, while Group Three, heading for Bergen, was protected by the cruisers *Köln* and *Königsberg*, screened by torpedo boats. Groups Four and Five, assigned to Kristiansand and Oslo, did not have to sail so early. The plan was that all five groups would reach their objectives at more or less the same time.

Meanwhile, the British War Cabinet, responding at last to pressure from the First Lord of the Admiralty, Winston Churchill, had agreed that minelaying operations in the Leads would begin on 8 April. Mines (some of them dummies) would be laid at three key points off the Norwegian coast, and on 5 April two minelaying forces set sail to carry out the operation, code-named *Wilfred*. One force was recalled, but the other, consisting of the minelaying destroyers *Esk*, *Icarus*, *Impulsive* and *Ivanhoe*, escorted by the destroyers *Hardy*, *Havock*, *Hotspur* and *Hunter*, laid a mine barrage off Bodo on 8 April.

The covering force comprised the battlecruiser *Renown* and the destroyers *Hyperion*, *Hero*, *Greyhound* and *Glowworm*, and it was the latter that made the first contact with the German ships. Detached to make a vain search for a seaman swept overboard from *Renown* in the murky dawn of 8 April, she sighted the warships of Task Group Two, bound for Trondheim. H.M.S. *Glowworm* fired two salvoes at an enemy destroyer before the latter was lost to sight in heavy seas and fog; a few minutes later a second destroyer came into view and *Glowworm* gave chase, the two warships exchanging shot for shot. The larger German vessel increased speed in an attempt to shake off her adversary but her bow ploughed under, forcing her to slow down. *Glowworm* closed in, her captain, Lt-Cdr G. B. Roope, trying to get into position for a shot with torpedoes.

Some distance ahead, a great, dark shape burst from a fog bank. For a few seconds the men on *Glowworm*'s bridge were elated, believing the ship to be H.M.S. *Renown*. Then a salvo of heavy shells struck the British destroyer, setting her on fire. The newcomer was the *Admiral Hipper*.

Roope sheered off for long enough to radio a report, then turned back towards the German cruiser in the hope of torpedoing her. When this proved impossible he headed his burning ship straight for the *Hipper*, ramming her starboard bow, tearing off 130 feet of the *Hipper*'s armour belt and wrenching away her starboard torpedo tubes. The cruiser's captain, H. Heye, ordered his guns to hold their fire as the *Glowworm* fell away, ablaze and doomed. A few minutes later, at 09.00, she blew up.

Kapitän Heye ordered his ship's crew to search for survivors. They plucked 38 from the sea. Lt-Cdr Roope himself reached the cruiser's side, but was too exhausted to hold on to the rope German sailors threw to him, and was drowned. His matchless courage earned him a posthumous Victoria Cross, the first to be won by the Royal Navy in the Second World War.

Meanwhile, in consultation with its French and Polish allies, the British Government had made plans to transport 18,000 British, French and Polish troops to reinforce the Norwegian garrisons of Stavanger, Bergen, Trondheim and Narvik as soon as there was clear evidence that the Germans intended to invade Norway. The cruisers *Devonshire*, *Berwick*, *York* and *Glasgow*, together with six destroyers, were dispatched to Rosyth to embark garrison troops. This was on 6 April; on the following day, Admiral Forbes ordered all his available ships (the battleships *Rodney* and *Valiant*, the battlecruiser *Repulse*, the cruisers *Penelope* and *Sheffield*, and ten destroyers, plus the French cruiser *Emile Bertin* and two French destroyers) to leave Scapa Flow and head north, while the cruisers *Arethusa* and *Galatea* with eight destroyers headed for Stavanger. A troop convoy bound for Bergen was recalled, and its escorts – the cruisers *Manchester* and *Southampton*, and four destroyers – ordered north to join the main body of the Home Fleet, as were the destroyers that had been covering the minelayers. As an additional measure, Vice-Admiral Sir Max Horton deployed 26 of his submarines to the operational area.

On 8 April, having received H.M.S. *Glowworm*'s enemy-sighting report and distress signal, Admiral Forbes ordered the warships at Rosyth to disembark their troops and put to sea, at the same time detaching the *Repulse*, *Penelope* and four destroyers to join *Renown* and her destroyers. That evening, the Admiralty instructed Forbes that his primary objective was the interception of the *Scharnhorst* and the *Gneisenau*, still in the belief that a major breakout into the Atlantic was in the offing. Further apparent evidence that this was the Germans' intention had come in the afternoon, when a R.A.F. reconnaissance aircraft reported an enemy battlecruiser and two cruisers off Trondheim, steaming west; in fact, the ships were the *Hipper* and her accompanying destroyers, covering the Group Two invasion force.

Yet the Germans' true intention had already been laid bare on that afternoon of 8 April, when the Polish submarine *Orzel* – part of Sir Max Horton's screen – torpedoed and sank the troop transport *Rio de Janeiro* off Lillesand, on the south coast of Norway. Norwegian fishermen rescued about a hundred survivors, some of whom, when interrogated by the military authorities, revealed that they had been on their way to Bergen 'to protect Norway against English invaders'. The military authorities at once called for the full mobilisation of Norway's small armed forces, and the mining of the approaches to Norwegian harbours. The pacifist Norwegian Government, fearful of provoking Nazi Germany even at this late hour, did nothing.

It was not until 19.00 on 8 April that the Admiralty, following an assessment of further intelligence reports on the movements of German vessels (including one from H.M. Submarine *Trident*, which made an unsuccessful torpedo attack on the battleship *Lützow* as the latter headed for Oslofjord), decided that an invasion was underway. However, the possibility of a simultaneous breakout into the Atlantic was not discounted. A signal was flashed to the commander of the northernmost group of British warships, Vice-Admiral William Whitworth, in H.M.S. *Renown*. 'Most immediate. The force under your orders is to concentrate on preventing any German force proceeding to Narvik.'

It was too late. Before midnight, the German invasion forces were already entering the fjords that led to their objectives. At 03.37 on 9 April, however, *Renown*, positioned 50 miles off the entrance to Vestfjord, sighted the *Scharnhorst* and *Gneisenau*, heading north-west to prevent any British interference with the Narvik assault group. Mistaking one of the enemy ships for the cruiser *Hipper*, the British battlecruiser opened fire at 19,000 yards and got three heavy hits on the *Gneisenau*. The German warships returned fire with their eighteen 11-inch guns, hitting *Renown* twice but causing little damage, and then turned away to the north-east; the German commander, Admiral Lütjens, had decided not to take unnecessary risks against what he believed to be the battleship *Repulse*. It was perhaps lucky for the *Renown* that one of her shells put the *Gneisenau's* *Seetakt* ranging radar and its associated gunnery control system out of action; *Renown* herself, at this stage, was not equipped with radar. In fact, only eight Royal Navy warships – *Rodney, Valiant, Sheffield, Suffolk, Curlew, Carlisle* and *Curacao* – were fitted with radar at the start of the Norwegian campaign, and this was mainly anti-aircraft equipment which proved to have severe limitations when operating close inshore in the vicinity of high cliffs.

Admiral Forbes's plan to attack enemy forces at Bergen with four cruisers and seven destroyers early on 9 April might have proved a damaging blow to the enemy. However, this was frustrated when it was cancelled by the Admiralty following receipt of an air reconnaissance report that two German cruisers were in the harbour.

During the afternoon of 9 April, units of the Home Fleet were attacked almost without pause for three hours by 41 He 111s of K.G. 26 and forty-seven Ju 88s of K.G. 30. The battleship *Rodney* received a direct hit from a 500 kg bomb which splintered her armoured deck but failed to explode; the cruisers *Devonshire, Southampton* and *Glasgow* were damaged by near misses, and the destroyer *Gurkha* was sunk west of Stavanger. The Germans lost four Ju 88s. During this first encounter, the Royal Navy had learned to its cost what it meant to operate within range of enemy land-based bombers without fighter cover. The aircraft carrier *Furious* had in fact been ordered from the Clyde to join the Fleet, but she had left in

such a hurry that there had been no time to embark her aircraft. Realising that she could contribute nothing to the safety of his ships, Admiral Forbes ordered her to stay out of range until she had flown on her air group. In the late afternoon of the 9th, he took his main force westward to meet the carrier and the battleship *Warspite* north of the Shetlands.

By nightfall on 9 April, the German invasion forces had secured their main objectives, but the operation had not been accomplished without cost. On the approach to Oslo, the new heavy cruiser *Blücher* was crippled by gunfire from a Norwegian fort and finished off with torpedoes, taking over 1,000 men to the bottom with her, while the light cruiser *Karlsruhe* was torpedoed by H.M. Submarine *Truant* and so badly damaged that she had to be sunk in the Kattegat by a German torpedo-boat. Other warships, including the *Lützow* and the light cruiser *Königsberg*, were damaged by shellfire from Norwegian coastal defences.

Meanwhile, Group One of the German invasion force – ten destroyers under *Kommodore* Friedrich Bonte, carrying 2,000 men of General Dietl's 3rd Mountain Division – had made an unopposed passage through the narrow waterway between the Lofoten Islands and the Norwegian mainland. As they entered Ofotfjord on the approach to Narvik, Bonte detached seven destroyers: three to deal with Norwegian forts said to be defending the Ramnes Narrows (in fact there were none), and four to occupy the township of Elvegaard in Herjangsfjord. The remaining three – Bonte's flagship the *Wilhelm Heidkamp*, followed by the *Berndt von Arnim* and *Georg Thiele* – pressed on to Narvik, sinking the Norwegian defence vessels *Eidsvold* and *Norge* as they entered the harbour. The small Norwegian garrison was quickly overwhelmed and Bonte redeployed his destroyers, bringing the *Anton Schmitt, Diether von Roeder* and *Hans Ludemann* into Narvik after they had disembarked their troops. The destroyers ought to have made the return passage to Germany at high speed once their troops were ashore, but before they could do so they needed fuel and only one of the expected tankers had turned up. Bonte therefore decided to delay the voyage home until the next day, while his destroyers took it in turns to take on fuel. He was not expecting any trouble; the submarine U-51 had reported sighting five British destroyers in Vestfjord at 20.22, but had signalled that they were steering south-west, away from the entrance of Ofotfjord.

In fact, the British destroyers were already making for Narvik, with orders to 'make certain that no enemy troops land', in the words of the Admiralty's instructions, or if they had already landed 'to sink or capture enemy ships and land forces if you think you can recapture Narvik from number of enemy present'.

The destroyers, under the command of Captain B.A. Warburton-Lee, were the *Hardy*, *Hunter*, *Havock*, *Hotspur* and *Hostile* of the 2nd Destroyer Flotilla. Signalling his intention to attack at dawn high water, which would give him the advantage of surprise and enable his ships to pass safely over any mines, Warburton-Lee led his ships slowly in line ahead through Ofotfjord, in visibility reduced by falling snow, and reached the entrance to Narvik harbour without being detected by the enemy. Detaching *Hotspur* and *Hostile* to watch for and neutralise any shore batteries, he took *Hardy* into the harbour at 04.30 and launched seven torpedoes at shipping in the anchorage.

One torpedo ripped through the *Heidkamp's* plating and exploded in her after magazine, killing Bonte and most of his sleeping crew. Two more torpedoes destroyed the *Anton Schmitt*; the other four struck merchant vessels, or missed their targets to explode on the rocky shore.

Hardy swung round in a tight circle, her 4.7-inch guns firing, as *Hunter* and *Havock* entered the anchorage in turn. Their torpedoes set the *Hans Ludemann* ablaze and then they turned on the *Diether von Roeder*, assisted by *Hotspur* and *Hostile*, which had found no shore batteries to engage, and reduced her to a burning wreck that just managed to reach the shore, where her captain beached her. Only one German destroyer, the *Hermann Kunne*, escaped the attack, and even then she was disabled, her engines damaged by the explosions of the torpedoes which sank the *Schmitt*.

The British destroyers withdrew from the harbour and made their way down Ofotfjord at 15 knots, still with plenty of ammunition left. As they passed Herangsfjord to starboard, the German destroyers *Wolfgang Zenker*, *Erich Giese* and *Erich Koellner* were seen emerging from it, and both sides opened fire, the British ships increasing speed to 30 knots. Ahead of them, two more German destroyers, the *Georg Thiele* and *Berndt von Arnim*, crept out of Ballangenfjord into the British warships' path, trapping them between two forces. In the savage fight that ensued, H.M.S. *Hardy* received the full weight of fire from the *Thiele* and *Arnim*. With her captain mortally wounded and her steering-gear shattered, she grounded on some rocks 300 yards from shore. About 170 of her crew struggled ashore, taking Warburton-Lee with them, lashed to a Carley Float. He died just as they pulled him from the water.

Lieutenant-Commander L. de Villiers in H.M.S. *Hunter* now led the British line. Raked by shells and burning, *Hunter* rapidly lost way, wallowing to a stop. Close behind her, Lt-Cdr H. F. Layman in H.M.S. *Hotspur* gave urgent orders to take avoiding action, but at that moment a German shell cut the steering controls and *Hotspur's* bow ripped into the helpless destroyer in front. Both ships now came under heavy fire. With shells bursting all around, Layman managed to make his way from the bridge to the after steering position and after much effort succeeded in extricating his badly damaged ship from the sinking *Hunter*. The other two British destroyers, *Havock* and *Hostile*, came to *Hotspur's* rescue, engaging the *Thiele* and *Arnim* as the latter ran down the fjord in the opposite direction, both seriously damaged. The German vessels vanished in the murk, leaving the British warships free to continue their dash for the open sea. Of the *Hunter's* crew of nearly two hundred, fifty men were rescued from the freezing waters by the Germans.

It was not quite over. As the British destroyers headed seawards, they sighted a large German merchant ship, the *Rauenfels*, entering the fjord. Two shells compelled her crew to abandon ship; two more caused her to blow up. The Germans

might still be in possession of Narvik, but their surviving destroyers could no longer depend on fresh supplies of ammunition with which to replenish their dwindling stocks.

So ended the action that came to be known as the First Battle of Narvik. It had left the Germans with two destroyers sunk, three so badly damaged as to be unseaworthy, one (the *Ludemann*) with a flooded magazine and another with her engines out of action. Set against the loss of two British destroyers, it was a notable victory, and one that earned Captain Warburton-Lee the award of a posthumous Victoria Cross.

The exploit of Warburton-Lee's destroyers was not the only British success of 10 April. Early that morning, sixteen Blackburn Skua dive-bombers of the Fleet Air Arm – seven of No. 800 Squadron led by Lt W. P. Lucy, R.N. and nine of No. 803 led by Capt R. T. Partridge, Royal Marines – took off from Hatston, north of Kirkwall in he Orkneys, each aircraft carrying a 500 lb bomb. Their target was the German naval force at Bergen, which included the light cruisers *Königsberg* and *Köln*

French troops inspecting a Fleet Air Arm Blackburn Skua in Norway, April 1940. An excellent dive-bomber, the Skua might have been used to better advantage

and the gunnery training ship *Bremse*. The ships had already been attacked by Hampdens of R.A.F. Bomber Command during the night, but without success.

After a gruelling 300-mile flight in darkness, the Skuas – their number reduced to fifteen after one aircraft returned with engine trouble – made landfall on the Norwegian coast just as the sun was coming up and climbed to 8,000 feet, making their dive-bombing attack on the *Königsberg* in line astern. The bombing was highly accurate and the cruiser, having suffered three direct hits and a dozen near misses, exploded and sank. She was the first major warship to be sunk by air attack in war. One Skua was shot down by A.A. fire, which was quite heavy once the Germans had got over their initial surprise, and two more were damaged. It was unfortunate that the *Köln* was no longer in Bergen harbour when the Skuas made their attack; together with the *Bremse* and some smaller craft, she had put to sea earlier on the orders of *Konteradmiral* Schmundt, commanding the Bergen task group.

Admiral Sir Max Horton's submarine screen, meanwhile, had been enjoying mixed success. The sinking of the *Karlsruhe* by H.M. Submarine *Truant* (which escaped only after being mercilessly depth-charged for several hours) has already been mentioned. In the early days of the campaign the submarines sank a dozen enemy transports, the U-boat U-1 and a tanker, a success tempered by the loss of three of their own number: *Thistle* (11 April, by the U-4); *Tarpon* (14 April) and *Sterlet* (18 April), both by depth-charge attack.

One major success was registered by H.M. Submarine *Spearfish* (Lt-Cdr J. G. Forbes). Early on 11 April, she was on the surface recharging her batteries after running the gauntlet of enemy warships when the battleship *Lützow* was sighted, returning to Germany at high sped. Forbes fired a salvo of torpedoes at her and one struck her right aft, wrecking her propellers and rudder and leaving her helpless. Unaware that the battleship had no anti-submarine escort, and with his batteries still not replenished, Forbes broke off the attack, leaving the *Lützow* wallowing in the water. She summoned help and was towed to Kiel in a near-sinking condition, and it was to be a year before she was ready for sea again – a year in which she might otherwise have been free to prey on Britain's convoys.

Also on 11 April, Admiral Forbes authorised a sortie towards Trondheim with the battleships *Rodney*, *Valiant* and *Warspite*, the carrier *Furious* and the heavy cruisers *Berwick*, *Devonshire* and *York*. The carrier launched a strike of eighteen Fairey Swordfish of Nos 816 and 818 Squadrons against the *Hipper*, reported to be at Trondheim, but the German cruiser had departed for Germany with the destroyer *Friedrich Eckoldt*. Three other destroyers, the *Paul Jacobi*, *Theodor Riedel* and *Bruno Heinemann* were still at Trondheim awaiting the arrival of their tanker and these were attacked, but the water was too shallow for the air-dropped torpedoes to function properly and they exploded harmlessly on the bottom.

The Admiralty, meanwhile, was anxious to finish the job begun by Captain Warburton-Lee's destroyers at Narvik on 10 April. On the 13th, the destroyers *Bedouin*, *Cossack*, *Eskimo*, *Forester*, *Foxhound*, *Hero*, *Icarus*, *Kimberley* and *Punjabi*, covered by the *Warspite*, were sent to comb the surrounding fjords for the eight surviving German vessels. The *Warspite*'s Swordfish floatplane, spotting for her 15-inch guns, sighted the submarine U-64 and sank her, while the destroyer force fell on the enemy ships which were starved of fuel and ammunition. The Germans fought bravely to the end, but they were no match for the British destroyers and the battleship's guns, and all were destroyed or scuttled. Three British destroyers were damaged, two seriously. Swordfish from the *Furious* also took part in this Second Battle of Narvik, but scored no successes and lost two of their number. After this, the carrier remained at Tromsø for several days to provide air reconnaissance facilities after the fleet returned to Scapa for replenishment, suffering damage from a near miss during an air attack. In all, she was in action for fourteen days, during which she lost nine Swordfish, with three aircrew killed and nine wounded. All the remaining aircraft of her air group were damaged to some extent.

Between 14 April and 2 May 11,000 Allied troops were landed at Åndalsnes and Molde (Sickle Force) and Namsos (Maurice Force), air support being provided by a squadron (No. 263) of Gloster Gladiator fighters, flown off H.M.S. *Glorious*. Both ports of disembarkation, however, were soon rendered unusable by the *Luftwaffe*, whose bombers were operating in the main from Stavanger airfield. In an ill-conceived scheme to deny the use of this base to the Germans, the 8-inch cruiser H.M.S. *Suffolk* (Captain J. Durnford) was dispatched to bombard it on 17 April. Predictably, she was dive-bombed, and damaged so severely that she only just managed to limp home with her quarterdeck awash.

Before the end of April it became clear that the position of the Allied forces facing Trondheim was untenable, and on the 28th, Admiral Forbes was ordered to re-embark the troops with all possible speed. This was sucessfully achieved by 3 May, nearly all the men being lifted off by eight cruisers, seven destroyers, one sloop and two troop transports. The King of Norway and the Crown Prince were also evacuated to Tromsø by the cruiser *Glasgow*. The British destroyer *Afridi*, the French destroyer *Bison* and the sloop *Bittern* were sunk by air attack during these operations.

Other naval forces, meanwhile, had been operating in support of landings further north, the objective being to capture Narvik. The naval side of these operations was under the command of Admiral of the Fleet Lord Cork and Orrery, who was later placed in command of the whole expedition. Air support was again provided by the Gladiators of No. 263 Squadron, joined this time by the Hurricanes of No. 46, flown off the carriers *Furious* and *Glorious* and operating from airstrips at Bardufoss and Skaanland. During the landing operations on 21 May, the cruiser *Effingham* grounded on a shoal off Bodø while taking avoiding action during an air attack and capsized.

On 26 May, the anti-aircraft cruiser H.M.S. *Curlew*, intended to be the flagship of Lord Cork, was bombed and sunk by Ju 88s of K.G. 30 off Skaanland. Cork transferred his flag to the A.A. cruiser *Cairo*, and on the night of 27/28 May this ship, together with the cruisers *Coventry* and *Southampton*, five destroyers and a sloop, gave fire support to French Foreign Legion and Polish troops advancing on Narvik, which was captured on the 28th.

Once again, it was too late. By this time, the focus of Allied operations had switched to France and the Low Countries, invaded by the Germans a fortnight earlier. The need for every available man to stem the enemy invasion left the Allies with no alternative but to evacuate Narvik as soon as its port facilities had been destroyed, and orders were issued for the evacuation of the 25,000-strong Allied force almost as soon as the town was captured. This task was accomplished by fifteen large troopships, with air cover provided by the few surviving fighters on shore and by aircraft from the *Ark Royal* and *Glorious*, and naval escort by the cruisers *Southampton* and *Coventry*, plus five destroyers (Lord Cork's flagship, H.M.S. *Cairo* having been damaged in an air attack).

Two major warships proceeded independently on 7 June. One was the cruiser *Devonshire*, sailing for Scapa Flow with King Haakon of Norway and members of his government; the other was the carrier *Glorious*, homeward bound at reduced speed because she was short of fuel. She carried the surviving Gladiators and Hurricanes, together with the personnel of the two fighter squadrons, and was escorted only by the destroyers *Ardent* and *Acasta*.

In the afternoon of 8 June, *Glorious* and her escorts were intercepted by the *Scharnhorst* and *Gneisenau*, out on a sortie against the Allied troop transports west of Harstad. The carrier was caught completely unawares; for reasons that were never explained, none of her reconnaissance Swordfish were airborne. Desperate attempts were made to arm and launch them as the enemy battlecruisers came in sight, but she was overwhelmed and sunk before this could be accomplished. Her escorting destroyers were also sunk, but not before the *Acasta*, already doomed, had hit the *Scharnhorst* with a torpedo. The warship limped into Trondheim, and on 13 June the *Ark Royal* flew off a strike of fifteen Skuas of Nos 800 and 803 Squadrons against her. One 500 lb bomb hit the battlecruiser and failed to explode; eight Skuas failed to return.

On 21 June, a reconnaissance Sunderland reported that the *Scharnhorst* had left Trondheim and was steaming slowly south escorted by eight destroyers and torpedo-boats. Attacks by R.A.F. Beaufort torpedo-bombers and by Fleet Air Arm

Swordfish were beaten off, the attackers suffering heavy losses, and the *Scharnhorst* reached Kiel on 23 June without further damage. The important fact, though, was that H.M.S. *Acasta*'s torpedo hit had almost certainly averted the destruction of the Allied convoys which were the German warships' main objectives. Just before making the attack, the *Acasta*'s captain addressed his crew with these words: 'You may think we are running away from the enemy. We are not. Our chummy ship (*Ardent*) has sunk, the *Glorious* is sinking; the least we can do is make a show.'

Make a show he and his crew did. And as the destroyer went down, her survivors saw Commodore Charles Glasfurd standing alone on her shattered bridge, smoking a cigarette, waving to them and wishing them good luck. He was never seen again.

CHAPTER THREE

Dunkirk

On 10 May 1940, German forces invaded France and the Low Countries, and within ten days were menacing the Channel ports of Calais and Boulogne. Despite gallant resistance by French troops and British reinforcements, the Allied position quickly became untenable and orders were issued for evacuation. This was carried out in the main by eight British and three French destroyers, H.M.S. *Wessex* being lost to air attack during the Calais evacuation on 24 May.

Meanwhile, by 19 May, the prospect of massive evacuation as the only means of saving the British Expeditionary Force had already become reality. On that day, the task of operational planning for such an eventuality was assigned to Admiral Sir Bertram Ramsay, the Flag Officer Commanding Dover. Together with Admiral Sir Reginald Drax, the C.-in-C. Nore, Ramsay had hitherto been responsible for the naval units – mainly destroyers detached from Scapa Flow – which had been providing a shuttle service for naval and military personnel to IJmuiden, the Hook of Holland, Flushing and Antwerp. With the Dutch collapse, these craft had been involved in evacuating servicemen and V.I.P.s, including the Dutch Royal Family, in clearing useful shipping from the harbours and in transferring the substantial Dutch reserves of gold and diamonds to England. Attention was then switched to the Belgian ports, and naval parties successfully removed large numbers of merchantmen, barges and tugs from Antwerp. The relatively small destroyer force worked tirelessly, embarking and landing troops, bringing out Allied missions and foreign nationals, and bombarding shore targets as well as providing additional anti-aircraft capability against the *Luftwaffe*'s increasingly furious attacks.

When Admiral Ramsay took inventory on 19 May, the picture that presented itself was depressing enough. Apart from the destroyers,

which were fully committed, he had only 36 personnel craft of various types and tonnage at his disposal, based either at Southampton or Dover; hardly sufficient to evacuate from Calais, Boulogne and Dunkirk at the rate of 10,000 men from each port every 24 hours, as was envisaged during a meeting of the War Cabinet on the morning of 20 May. During this meeting Winston Churchill advised that, 'as a precautionary measure, the Admiralty should assemble a large number of small vessels in readiness to proceed to ports and inlets on the French coast', the registration of such craft having begun several days earlier. In the meantime, Ramsay's force was increased by the addition of 30 passenger ferries, twelve naval drifters and six small coasters, while on 22 May the Admiralty ordered forty Dutch *schuits* which had come to Britain on Holland's collapse to be requisitioned and manned by naval crews.

Even at a time when Boulogne and Calais were still in Allied hands, it was clear that any major evacuation would have to be from Dunkirk; and Ramsay, who knew those waters intimately from service in the 1914–18 war, was well aware of the difficulties likely to be caused by the geography of the port and its surrounding terrain, quite apart from any interference by the enemy. The beaches east of Dunkirk, stretching for 16 miles beyond Nieuport to the mouth of the river Yser, formed the longest continuous stretch of sand in the whole of Europe. They were remarkable for their uniformity, sloping down gradually into the sea along their entire length; some three-quarters of a mile from low-water mark there was the deep-water channel of the Rade de Dunkerque, about half a mile wide and between 40 and 50 feet deep, with waves of sandbanks to seaward.

The depth of the beaches was also a notable factor. The sands proper were bounded on the landward side by brick sea-walls, beyond which lay a broad expanse of dunes dotted with clusters of rough sea-grass and interlaced with drainage channels; here and there poplars and windmills stood out starkly against the skyline. Taking the area of the dunes into account, the overall width of the beaches was, on average, one mile. It was small wonder that in the days of peace the area had been immensely popular with holidaymakers. The main holiday resort had been Malo-les-Bains to the east of Dunkirk; farther to the east was a small resort, Bray Dunes, and farther still along the beach lay the village of La Panne. None of these places had a pier or jetty, or indeed any facility that might assist embarkation.

Although that vast expanse of dunes would prove ideal for the assembly of large numbers of troops, the nature of the beaches themselves would make evacuation a slow and arduous task; yet, as Ramsay was well aware, it was from the beaches that the biggest lift would have to be made. Because of strong tidal currents sweeping past the entrance, Dunkirk was never an easy harbour to enter at the best of times; the flotsam of war would now make the task doubly difficult, especially since most pickup operations would have to be carried out at night to avoid the worst of the enemy air attacks and the naval crews would have no peacetime navigation beacons to guide them.

To make matters worse, there was no possibility of using the main harbour, with its seven dock basins; this had already been blocked by air attack on 20 May, and if it had not been for the action of Admiral Jean Abrial, C.-in-C. French Naval Forces (North), who had ordered several merchantmen and French naval craft out to sea as soon as the attacks began, the blockage would certainly have been much worse. As it was, only two main embarkation points were left in Dunkirk itself; a jetty to the west of the harbour and the Jetée de l'Est, or East Mole, a strong wooden structure thrusting out north-north-west into the sea from the Promenade de la Digue, a 900-yard stone causeway bounding the canal mouth on the north side. Although 1,400 yards long, the mole itself was very narrow, only five feet across for most of its length.

It was clear that the operation was going to be a job for small craft – boats capable of running a ferry service from the beaches to ships offshore, and ships with a shallow enough draught to enable them to negotiate the obstacle-ridden waters in and around Dunkirk harbour. Destroyers were vital to Ramsay's plans; although far from ideal as troopships, they could take their quota of men, and their speed and manoeuvrability would make them difficult targets to hit. Moreover, their firepower would prove an invaluable asset, particularly in the anti-aircraft role. The problem was that in May 1940 destroyers were fast becoming worth more than their weight in gold; of the 220 on the Royal Navy's inventory at that time, the majority were in the Mediterranean or the Far East, and many of those serving with the Home Fleet were heavily committed to the Norwegian campaign. The withdrawal of destroyers and, to a lesser extent, cruisers from the Home Fleet for service with the Nore and Dover Commands was a serious step, at a time when the protection of the Atlantic shipping routes was becoming vital to the survival of Britain, but it was a risk that had to be taken. Fortunately, although the British did not know it at the time, the losses suffered by the German Navy off Norway had been extensive enough to prevent any forays into the Atlantic for some time to come.

After conferring with Admiral Sir Charles Forbes, Ramsay took stock. He could count on the use of some forty destroyers, although it would be a week before some of them could be released from their stations. Meanwhile, those that were available were placed on readiness, although their captains were not yet briefed on the task that lay ahead of them. The task of requisitioning merchant ships went ahead smoothly; by nightfall on 26 May Ramsay would have 130 at his disposal, from steam packets and cross-Channel ferries to Dutch *schuits*, the flat-bottomed barges whose shallow draught would make them invaluable for close-in work.

Around him, the dapper 57-year-old Ramsay gathered a first-rate staff. There was Captain William Tennant, who would have command of the operation on shore at Dunkirk with twelve naval officers and 150 ratings under him; Commander Archibald Day, who as hydrographer had the job of working out the cross-Channel routes to be followed by the evacuation fleet; Commander James Stopford, Ramsay's flag officer, who would be at the hub of all communications; and others, all of them specialists in their own fields; all of them working as a team to control both ends of the lifeline that stretched across the English Channel.

Estimates on how many troops could be lifted from the beaches varied, although it was generally thought that between 30,000 and 40,000 could be brought away in the two days or so that would be available before the enemy closed the net. Speed was the essential factor, and for this reason it was planned to use the shortest sea crossing between Dunkirk and Dover, the 39-mile passage designated Route Z. Ramsay's hydrographer had also set up two alternative crossings: Route Y, an 87-mile dogleg that ran from Dover to the Kwinte Buoy off Ostend before veering to approach Dunkirk from the east, and the 57-mile Route X, which crossed the Ruytingen Bank and joined the deep-water channel halfway between Dunkirk and Gravelines. It was as well that these two alternates were available, for by 26 May the Germans had reached Gravelines and had seized the French coastal gun batteries there, menacing all shipping on the short Route Z.

As 26 May drew to a close, the Admiralty dared wait no longer. Every hour's delay from now on would mean the sacrifice of men as the jaws of the German vice tightened. At 18.57 hours on that day, the signal went out: 'Operation *Dynamo* is to commence.' It was a singularly appropriate codename, thought up by someone on Ramsay's staff because the operations room at Dover Castle had once housed electrical plant. The room was now a powerhouse of a different kind, and in the days to come it would be taxed to the utmost of its capacity.

The ships that were to spearhead *Dynamo* – the elderly Isle of Man steam packets *Mona's Isle* and *King Orry* – were already at sea. They berthed at Dunkirk shortly after dark and at once began taking on troops. The *Mona's Isle* was the first to leave, at dawn on the 27th, carrying 1,420 sol-diers. As she retraced her path along Route Z she was straddled by enemy shellfire, and a few minutes later low-flying Messerschmitts raked her decks. By the time she reached Dover, twenty-three of her passengers were dead and sixty wounded.

Meanwhile, five more transports had made an abortive attempt to reach Dunkirk early that morning. They ran into heavy fire from the Gravelines batteries. The motor vessel *Sequacity* was hit and sank within minutes; the remainder, unable to break through the fearsome curtain of water hurled up by the shells, turned away and came back to Dover empty.

It was clearly only a matter of time before Route Z would have to be closed, which meant using the longer routes – and then, with the armada of ships exposed for hours on the long haul, it would be the *Luftwaffe*'s turn. For the bulk of the B.E.F., still fighting its way back to the perimeter, the chances of survival now seemed slender indeed.

In the afternoon of 27 May, Captain William Tennant and his small command of naval officers and ratings reached Dunkirk on the destroyer *Wolfhound*, the ship having survived determined *Stuka* attacks en route, and set about organising the departure of the troops. About 3,300 British troops had already been evacuated from Dunkirk and its neighbouring beaches, together with 4,000 French soldiers and 1,250 wounded, but these were all so-called 'useless mouths', non-combatants who could play no part in the defence of the port area, and the fighting troops had yet to arrive.

The lifting of troops had been a desperately slow prcess, and Tennant knew that unless immediate steps were taken to augment the lift the chaos during the next 24 hours would become insupportable. He accordingly signalled Admiral Ramsay that every available craft must immediately be sent to the beaches east of Dunkirk, otherwise evacuation on the 28th might become impossible.

The naval forces committed to *Dynamo* by Ramsay on this, the first major day of the evacuation, consisted of one anti-aircraft cruiser (H.M.S. *Calcutta*), nine destroyers and four

36

The 'Sands Patrol': a Lockheed Hudson of R.A.F. Coastal Command with Dunkirk's oil storage tanks ablaze in the background.

minesweepers, all of which had been ordered to close the beaches and use their small boats to supplement the lifts being carried out by the cross-Channel steamers and drifters. But at low tide the destroyers could approach no closer than a mile offshore, which meant that the crews of their whalers faced a 20-minute pull to the beaches, at the end of which they could take on a maximum of 25 men. By this method, loading a destroyer to its maximum capacity of 1,000 men could take six hours or more, and there was also the weather factor to be considered. The approaches to the beaches were tricky in ideal conditions and if the wind, at present blowing from the east, veered to the north small-boat operations in the shallows would become extremely hazardous.

The only other alternative was to use the East Mole, although it was by no means certain that ships would be able to berth safely alongside it.

The gunboat H.M.S. Locust *had a proud record at Dunkirk; she survived the war*

Nevertheless, it was a risk that had to be taken. At 22.30 on the 27th, Tennant ordered the personnel vessel _Queen of the Channel_ (Captain W. J. Odell) to come alongside the mole; the ship berthed successfully, which gave Tennant a glimmer of hope. Where one ship had gone, others could follow, and the mole was long enough to accommodate sixteen vessels at a time.

During the early hours of 28 May, five destroyers – the _Wakeful_, _Mackay_, _Harvester_, _Codrington_ and _Sabre_ – bore the brunt of the evacuation. Dispatched hurriedly from Dover and other ports along England's south coast, their captains had not had time to receive any briefing other than that they were to proceed to Dunkirk to pick up troops.

Meanwhile, at Dover, Ramsay and his staff were making desperate attempts to assemble the small craft so badly needed by Tennant. So far, they had about a 100 at their disposal; forty craft which had so far been registered as a result of the Admiralty's appeal of 14 May, and another fifty or so boats based in and around Dover.

But many, many more were needed if even a fraction of the B.E.F. was to be snatched from the beaches, and early on the 28 May, for the first time, the Royal Navy's M.T.B.s took a hand. They were drawn from the 3rd, 4th and 10th Flotillas based at Felixstowe, and they had already been employed in evacuating servicemen and civilians from Holland. The sight of the M.T.B.s, and of other small craft which began to arrive off the beaches during the afternoon of the 28th, heartened the troops considerably, even though towards the end of the day a growing swell meant that the burden of the evacuation had to fall on Dunkirk's East Mole, towards which the columns of fatigued men now tramped. Despite all the difficulties, 17,804 men were landed in England before midnight on the 28th – double the previous day's total, thanks to the use of the mole and to prevailing low cloud and drizzle which kept the _Luftwaffe_ at bay.

But it was not the German Air Force that struck the first serious blow against the Royal Navy during _Dynamo_. In the early hours of 29 May, the destroyer _Wakeful_, homeward bound with 640 troops along Route Y, was torpedoed and sunk by

Homeward bound: the relief is evident on the faces of these British soldiers as they leave Dunkirk on the destroyer H.M.S. Mackay

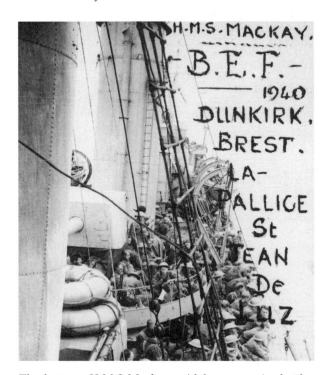

The destroyer H.M.S. Mackay, _with her evacuation battle honours inscribed on the photograph_

the German M.T.B. S30, one of three *Schnellboote* that had sailed from Wilhelmshaven the previous afternoon and entered the operational area after dark. Torn in two, *Wakeful* went down in less than a minute, taking over 700 men with her. Some time later, the destroyer *Grafton*, searching for *Wakeful*'s survivors, was torpedoed by the German submarine U-62 and disabled. Her guns, and those of the minesweeper *Lydd*, opened fire on what looked like the silhouette of a torpedo-boat, which was then rammed and sunk by the *Lydd*; but the 'enemy intruder' was in fact the drifter *Comfort*, laden with men from the *Wakeful*. There were only five survivors, among them the *Wakeful*'s captain, Commander Ralph Fisher. As for the stricken *Grafton*, she was sunk by the destroyer *Ivanhoe* after her survivors had been taken off.

The troops at Dunkirk made jetties from abandoned vehicles to reach the vessels offshore. This **Luftwaffe** *photograph of the beach at La Panne was taken on 5 June 1940 after the evacuation was over*

Casualty of the Dunkirk evacuation: the French luxury liner Champlain *sunk by a mine*

It was only the beginning of a terrible toll that was to be exacted from the British ships on 29 May. In the afternoon, Dunkirk came under attack by 180 *Stuka*s, and the destroyer *Grenade*, taking on troops at the East Mole, was an early casualty. Hit by three bombs, ablaze from stem to stern, she was towed clear by a trawler minutes before she exploded. Next to suffer was the destroyer *Jaguar*, which had just got underway when she took a direct hit and had to be abandoned, although she miraculously remained afloat and was rescued later. Another destroyer, H.M.S. *Verity*, succeeded in getting clear, with near misses exploding all around, only to run aground beyond the harbour mouth and suffer damage. The armed boarding vessel *King Orry*, the trawler *Calvi*, the paddle-minesweeper *Gracie Fields* and the personnel ship *Fenella* were also sunk in the *Stuka* attack, the *King Orry* after being hit colliding with the mole and putting it temporarily out of action.

After the *Stuka*s came the horizontal bombers, the Heinkels and Dorniers, together with more dive-bombers, this time twin-engined Junkers 88s. The latter attacked the biggest merchant vessel used in the Dunkirk evacuation, the 6,900-ton Glasgow freighter *Clan MacAlister*, setting her on fire and killing a third of her crew as well as many of the soldiers who had recently boarded her. Her survivors were taken off by the minesweeper *Pangbourne*, which was already laden with those from the *Gracie Fields*.

Six miles west of Dunkirk, Heinkels caught the Southern Railway ship *Normannia* in the open sea off Mardyck and sent her to the bottom. Her sister ship, the *Lorina*, suffered a similar fate minutes later, while the minesweeper *Waverley*, with 800 troops on board, went down in that same cauldron. Hard by the beaches, the old Thames river paddle-steamer *Crested Eagle*, filled to capacity with troops and the survivors of the *Fenella*, was hit by a single bomb and burst into flames. A red-hot furnace, with burning men leaping overboard into the oily water, she slowly approached the beach under the direction of her skipper, Lt-Cdr Booth. At last she grounded and the survivors were able to struggle ashore through the shallows.

Such was the awful toll of 29 May; and, in addition to the ships sunk, many others had been seriously damaged. They included the sloop *Bideford*, her stern a mass of tangled wreckage; the crippled destroyer *Jaguar*, which somehow refused to sink; and the destroyers *Gallant*, *Greyhound* and *Intrepid*, among the Royal Navy's most modern warships of their kind. Yet, despite all the destruction, despite the chaos and loss of life, the embarkations had continued even through the worst of the air raids, the vessels' captains taking incredible risks to get the men away – like Lt Edwin Davies, commanding the paddle-minesweeper *Oriole*, who deliberately grounded his ship to provide a kind of jetty over which 2,500 men scrambled to other waiting boats, then managed to free her and set course for home with 600 troops of his own on board.

As dusk fell on the 29th, the scene off the beaches at Dunkirk was one of utter carnage. Nevertheless, 47,310 men had been lifted off during the day, 33,558 of them from the East Mole before it was put out of action. But the day's losses had persuaded the First Sea Lord, Admiral Sir Dudley Pound, to withdraw the Navy's eight most modern destroyers from *Dynamo*. This meant that the burden of the evacuation would now fall on the fifteen elderly destroyers still at Ramsay's disposal, and these would be capable of lifting not more than 17,000 men in the next 24 hours.

On the morning of 30 May, fog descended on the beaches, enabling the small craft to go about their evacuation task without interference from the *Luftwaffe*. And as the fog persisted, the evacuation received an unexpected boost when the First Sea Lord decided to lift his restriction on the use of the modern G, H, I and J class destroyers. The lifting of the ban was supposed to be temporary, but in the event the demands of Operation *Dynamo* were to become so pressing over the next 24 hours that the destroyers remained committed to the end.

The activities of the rescue ships were now coordinated by Rear-Admiral Frederick Wake-Walker, controlling a staff of 80 officers and ratings. His primary concern was to get the East Mole operational once more, and by 20.30 on 30 May, following hasty repairs, he judged that it was once again fit for use by destroyers and minesweepers (the latter being particularly hard-worked during the evacuation) and sent a signal to that effect to Admiral Ramsay in Dover. With ships once again working from the mole, the number of troops lifted off increased substantially and by midnight the day's total had reached 53,823, of whom some 30,000 had been taken from the beaches.

On Friday 31 May, the task of the evacuation personnel doubled, for now the decision had been taken to lift off French troops in equal numbers – and the evacuation fleet had already suffered badly, from collisions, groundings and mechanical troubles as much as from enemy action. Moreover, navigation on the approaches to Dunkirk was becoming extremely hazardous because of sunken wrecks; and to make matters worse, the wind had risen to Force 3, seriously complicating the task of the small craft in the shallows. Many small boats, laden to the gunwales with troops, set course for home – a move which Wake-Walker tried hard to stop, for every small craft would be needed that night to ferry men to the ships waiting offshore. For a time, towards noon, boat work off the beaches became virtually impossible, and enemy bombing and artillery fire had become so intense that larger ships could not use the port. The crisis seemed grave; and then, in the afternoon, both enemy activity and the swell decreased, and by the time the day ended, no fewer than 68,104 men had been taken off – the highest daily total of the whole operation.

The morning of 1 June dawned bright and clear, and the _Luftwaffe_ was over the beaches from first light. It was a terrible day. It began with the destruction of the fleet minesweeper H.M.S. _Skipjack_. She was lying at anchor, still taking on troops, when she took a full delivery from a dive-bomber and exploded. She sank like a stone with 275 men on board; there were few survivors.

The bombers now turned their attention to the big fleet destroyer H.M.S. _Keith_, to which Admiral Wake-Walker had recently transferred his flag. The _Keith_'s gunners were down to their last 30 rounds of ammunition and there was little the warship's captain could do except take violent evasive action. The first attack on her came as she

was turning under full port helm and no fewer than nine bombs exploded in a pattern close to her starboard side, throwing her over on her beam ends and causing severe damage to her hull as well as jamming her rudder. As she circled helplessly, a heavy bomb went down her aft funnel and exploded in her boiler room, while near misses caused further damage. She lost way rapidly, enveloped in clouds of steam, and wallowed to a stop with a twenty-degree list to port. Wake-Walker was taken off by an M.T.B. and transferred his flag to another vessel; shortly afterwards the _Keith_ was hit yet again and the warship turned turtle and sank.

Meanwhile, the destroyer _Basilisk_ had also been hit and damaged. She survived another attack and began the long struggle back to Dover, but she later had to be abandoned and was sunk by a torpedo from the destroyer H.M.S. _Whitehall_.

The massacre went on unchecked. Some vessels, in the act of taking on troops, were powerless to take evasive action; other captains, like Lt-Cdr Kirkpatrick of the minesweeper H.M.S. _Dundalk_, suspended operations and kept their ships on the move, zigzagging along the coast amid a hail of bombs. One of the _Dundalk_'s crew, Bill Elmslie, remembers an unforgettable sight: the fleet destroyer H.M.S. _Havant_ forging out into the Channel with so many troops on board that her entire superstructure seemed to be covered in khaki. The next instant a full salvo of bombs hit her, killing all her engine-room staff. Immediately, two minesweepers closed alongside her and the troops poured from the stricken ship on to their decks. The _Havant_ had taken two bombs through her engine-room and a third exploded as she passed over it. The minesweeper H.M.S. _Saltash_ tried to take her in tow, but it was hopeless. At 10.15, after further air attacks, she sank with the loss of 34 hands.

Other ships were more fortunate. The destroyer _Ivanhoe_ had a bomb rip through her forward funnel and explode in the boiler room; terror-stricken soldiers scrambled from her lower decks and on to the minesweeper H.M.S. _Speedwell_, which came alongside. Despite her damage, the destroyer remained afloat and was taken in tow by the tug _Persia_.

The air attacks continued throughout the day, and claimed other victims. The French destroyer *Foudroyant* took three direct hits and went down in minutes, her survivors defiantly singing *La Marseillaise* as they drifted with the tide amid islands of debris and pools of oil. And not only the warships suffered, although they were the bombers' primary targets. The old *Brighton Queen*, a paddle-boat converted for minesweeping, had just set out for Dover with 700 French troops on board when the *Stuka*s pounced and hit her afterdeck with a 550 lb bomb, causing fearful casualties. The survivors were taken off by the minesweeper *Saltash* before the *Brighton Queen* sank. There were casualties, too, on the personnel vessel *Prague*, which was steaming away from Dunkirk with 3,000 French troops on board when she was hit and damaged; another merchant ship, the *Scotia*, was also hit while carrying 2,000 French troops, many of whom were drowned when they panicked and rushed the boats. The destroyer H.M.S. *Esk* took off most of the survivors. The *Scotia*, of 3,454 tons, was the largest ship to be lost that day.

On some ships that managed to limp back to Dover the casualty toll was frightening. The old destroyer H.M.S. *Worcester* was relentlessly attacked for 30 minutes by dive-bombers, sustaining damage that reduced her speed to a mere 10 knots; yet she limped across the Channel with her pitiful cargo of 350 dead and 400 wounded.

In all, the evacuation fleet lost 31 vessels sunk and eleven damaged on 1 June, a day in which the seaborne units nevertheless managed to lift off 64,429 British and French troops. Since the last stretches of beach still in Allied hands, and the ships offshore, were now being heavily shelled, Admiral Ramsay planned to lift as many men as possible in a single operation on the night of 1/2 June, concentrating all available ships after dark in the Dunkirk and Malo areas. For this purpose, he had at his disposal some 60 ships, together with the many small craft still involved in the operation; the French could provide ten ships and about 120 fishing craft.

The port of La Pallice burning after a German air attack, June 1940

By midnight on 2 June, a further 26,256 soldiers had been evacuated, the last British troops to leave being the 1st King's Shropshire Light Infantry, which had covered the withdrawal of 1st Division the previous evening. There remained the French; some 30,000 of them, who continued to defend the Dunkirk perimeter throughout 3 June. The last great effort of Ramsay's evacuation fleet therefore had to be made during the night of 3/4 June, and the resources available to accomplish the task were seriously depleted. Of the 41 destroyers originally allocated to *Dynamo* only nine remained, and only five of the 45 personnel vessels. Nevertheless, they performed a magnificent task on this last night, and when the last ship – the elderly destroyer *Shikari* – left the East Mole just before dawn on 4 June, her load brought the total for the night to 26,209, all but seven of them French troops. At 09.00, the Dunkirk garrison capitulated.

The Royal Navy still faced a massive evacuation task after Dunkirk. These photographs show H.M.S. Mackay *at Brest*

Later that day, at 14.23 to be precise, the Admiralty announced the completion of Operation *Dynamo*. In nine days of incredible achievement, 198,284 British troops had been brought away; counting the 26,042 'useless mouths' taken off before the start of the evacuation proper, this made a grand total of 224,686

The port of La Rochelle, with H.M.S. Mackay's *twin Lewis A.A. guns in the foreground*

St-Jean-de-Luz, the last French port to be evacuated during Operation Aerial

men of the British Expeditionary Force, of whom 13,053 were wounded. The number of Allied troops evacuated eventually rose to 141,445, making a combined total of of 366,131.

It should not be forgotten that the Royal Navy participated in other evacuation operations after Dunkirk. Between 4 and 25 June 1940, British ships carried out a whole series of evacuations beginning at Le Havre, moving west to the Gulf of St-Malo, the Channel Islands and Cherbourg, round Ushant to Brest, along the French Biscay coast to St-Nazaire and La Pallice, and finally from Bayonne and St-Jean-de-Luz near the Spanish frontier. These operations, collectively known by the code-name of *Aerial*, resulted in the rescue of an additional 191,870 fighting troops and 35,000 civilians. The biggest loss incurred during this phase occurred at St-Nazaire, when the troopship *Lancastria* was sunk with 9,000 on board; 5,000 men were killed or reported missing.

The cost of Operation *Dynamo* had been terribly high for the seaborne forces engaged. Of the 693 British ships committed, 226 had been sunk, 56 of them destroyers, minesweepers and personnel vessels. For the small ships of the Royal Navy, Dunkirk was a chapter of gallantry and achievement that was not to be surpassed in the grim years to come.

A troop-laden warship about to leave Brest harbour during Operation Aerial

CHAPTER FOUR
Defence of Home Waters, June–December 1940

While the British Army strove to make good the attrition it had suffered in France, and to fortify England's coastal defences against an expected invasion, the Royal Navy also strove to organise a strong defence force of four destroyer flotillas – thirty-two ships in all – based on Harwich, Dover, Portsmouth and Plymouth. It was a desperately difficult task, for most of the destroyers that had survived the Dunkirk evacuation had been dispersed for repairs and others were still engaged in evacuating British personnel from the Biscay ports and the Channel Islands.

Fortunately, because of the attrition suffered in the Norwegian campaign, the German Navy was as yet in no position to offer a serious challenge. In June 1940, the Germans had only one flotilla of large destroyers, two flotillas of smaller destroyers and many fast motor torpedo craft, the S-boats (referred to erroneously as E-boats by the British). It was these *Schnellboote* that would prove to be the biggest thorn in the Royal Navy's side, especially now that they were able to operate from newly captured French harbours. On 19 June, they struck their first blow against mercantile traffic in the Channel when S19 and S26 sank the freighter *Roseburn* off Dungeness, and on the night of 24/25 June S36 and S19 sank the tanker *Albuera* and the coaster *Kingfisher* in the same area. By this time, a flotilla of five British M.T.B.s was operating from Dover with the task of countering the S-boat threat, but it was to be some time before these craft became available in sufficient numbers to make any impression on the enemy. In any case, the S-boats were faster, bigger and better armed than the British craft, and it needed skill and judgement, which would only come with operational experience, to get the better of them.

Early in July, the *Luftwaffe* began a series of intensive air attacks on British east coast convoys, and in the course of the month these operations accounted for forty Allied merchant ships totalling 75,698 tons, together with the destroyers *Brazen* (20 July), *Codrington* (27 July), *Delight* (29 July) and *Wren* (27 July). Mines, too, remained a constant threat; in mid-July, enemy aircraft laid mines in the Thames Estuary and off Harwich, while surface craft sowed two new mine barrages in the English Channel. Two more barrages were laid in August, in the south-west part of the North Sea. Also in August, German minelaying aircraft extended their activities to the harbour entrances of Belfast, Falmouth, Liverpool, Penzance, Plymouth and Southampton. On 31 August, a German minefield off Texel brought about the loss of the destroyers *Esk* and *Ivanhoe*, a third destroyer, H.M.S. *Express*, being severely damaged. Minesweeping operations assumed high priority; the Royal Navy now had some 700 minesweepers at its disposal, the majority being auxiliary craft such as converted trawlers and drifters. Quite apart from the dangers inherent in their task, they were constantly attacked from the air and by enemy surface craft and U-boats. Their losses were not light. Theirs is an often forgotten page of quiet heroism in the story of Britain's fight for survival.

While the fighter pilots of the Royal Air Force fought their own grim battle in British skies, the Royal Navy took every available opportunity to strike at shipping movements off the enemy coast, even though operating conditions in the Channel had become very difficult because of air attack. On 8 September 1940, for example, three motor torpedo-boats, M.T.B. 14, M.T.B. 15 and

M.T.B. 17, set out from Dover to attack a German convoy of about 30 small vessels approaching Ostend. Two of the boats, M.T.B.s 15 and 17, entered Ostend harbour under cover of darkness and a R.A.F. air raid and launched their torpedoes, hitting two unidentified vessels. It was the first successful British M.T.B. torpedo attack of the war.

On the night of 10/11 September, a strikng force comprising the destroyers *Malcolm, Veteran* and *Wild Swan* set out to patrol the Channel off Ostend, which was again under air attack, when radar contact was made with an enemy convoy by *Malcolm*, the destroyer leader. Soon afterwards, the destroyers made visual contact with the enemy, aided by the light of flares dropped by R.A.F. aircraft, and opened fire, sinking an escort vessel, two trawlers that were towing barges, and a large barge. Offensive sweeps of this kind were a regular feature during September 1940, when the threat of invasion was at its height, the naval forces usually operating from Harwich or Portsmouth; the Dover destroyer flotilla had been dispersed, having suffered severely in air attacks. At the same time, aircraft of the Fleet Air Arm, operating from shore bases, joined the R.A.F. in attacks on enemy-held Channel ports where an invasion fleet of barges was being assembled.

The biggest guns the Navy could bring to bear on enemy coastal targets were mounted in two warships of First World War vintage, the battleship *Revenge* and the monitor *Erebus*. Both mounted 15-inch guns, the *Erebus* being fitted with a twin turret bearing her main armament and also with four twin 4-inch and two single 3-inch A.A. guns. She carried a crew of 300. On 20 September, she set out from Sheerness to bombard the German gun battery at Cap Gris-Nez, but the sortie had to be abandoned because of bad weather. On 30 September, however, she fired seventeen rounds into a concentration of invasion craft in the Calais docks area, the fire being directed by a Swordfish spotter aircraft. On the following day, the German battery at Wissant fired precisely the same number of rounds at Dover by way of retaliation.

On 10 October it was the turn of H.M.S. *Revenge*, the old battleship sailing from Plymouth with a screen of 5th Flotilla destroyers: the *Jackal, Kipling, Jupiter, Jaguar, Kashmir* and *Kelvin*. The cruisers *Newcastle* and *Emerald* were also at sea, protecting the western flank, while a flotilla of six M.T.B.s sailed from Portland to provide a screen against S-boats. *Revenge*'s target was Cherbourg, and for 18 minutes, beginning at 03.33 on 11 October, she laid a barrage of 120 15-inch shells across the crowded harbour, to which was added a total of 801 4.7-inch shells from the seven escorting destroyers. The resulting conflagration could be seen 40 miles out to sea. The British force reached Spithead at 08.00 without damage, despite being shelled for almost 10 miles by a German heavy battery.

On 16 October, H.M.S. *Erebus*, escorted by the destroyers *Garth* and *Walpole*, again bombarded the French coast in the vicinity of Calais with the aid of spotter aircraft. Forty-five salvoes were fired, beginning at 01.00, before the British force withdrew. Neither the *Erebus* nor the *Revenge* made any further sorties of this kind, even though the British heavy gun defences on the Channel coast in October were still pitifully weak. The pre-war heavy gun strength on the Straits of Dover, comprising two 9.2-inch and six 6-inch guns, had been reinforced during the summer by one 14-inch, two 6-inch and two 4-inch guns, all naval weapons, together with a pair of 9.2-inch guns on railway mountings; in October, these were further reinforced by two 13.5-inch guns from the old depot ship *Iron Duke*, also on railway mountings, and a battery of four 5.5-inch guns from H.M.S. *Hood*. Further heavy gun batteries, at Fan Bay, South Foreland and Wanstone, would not become operational until a much later date, by which time the invasion threat had passed.

While the British strove to disrupt German invasion plans, German destroyers were extremely active in the Channel area during September and October 1940, laying more minefields to protect the flanks of their projected cross-Channel invasion routes and also making hit-and-run sorties against British shipping. One particularly successful sortie was undertaken on the night of 11/12 October by the German 5th Flotilla from Cherbourg, comprising the destroyers *Greif, Kondor, Falke, Seeadler* and *Wolf*. They sank the armed trawlers *Listrac* and *Warwick Deeping* with gunfire and torpedoes, and shortly afterwards destroyed the Free French submarine chasers CH6 and CH7, manned by mixed French and Polish crews. The German ships withdrew safely; although they were engaged by the British destroyers *Jackal*, *Jaguar*, *Jupiter*, *Kelvin* and *Kipling*, the latter achieved nothing more spectacular than several near misses. Another inconclusive action was fought between British destroyers of the 5th Flotilla, supported by the light cruisers *Newcastle* and *Emerald*, and the enemy destroyers *Karl Galster*, *Hans Lody*, *Friedrich Ihn* and *Erich Steinbrinck* off Brest on 17 October, with no damage suffered by either side.

The destroyers of the British 5th Flotilla were again in action on the night of 27/28 November 1940, when they intercepted the four German warships named above as they made a sortie towards Plymouth. In the ensuing engagement H.M.S. *Javelin* was hit by two torpedoes, which blew off her bow and stern and detonated the ammunition in her magazine, destroying her superstructure as well as killing three officers and 43 ratings. Remarkably, she remained afloat and was towed into harbour, to spend 13 months in dock being virtually rebuilt. She eventually returned to operations and went on to survive the war.

Notwithstanding actions such as these, it was enemy mines that accounted for the highest proportion of British shipping losses in the closing months of 1940. Of the 42 Royal Navy vessels lost in the Channel area between 1 September and the end of the year, 28 were sunk by mines.

By the end of October 1940, the threat of invasion had receded, and Hitler's eyes were already turning east. But the question must be asked whether the planned invasion might have succeeded, had it gone ahead. In the opinion of Captain Stephen Roskill, the official Royal Navy historian, it would have failed. He wrote:

We who lived through those anxious days may reasonably regret that the expedition never sailed; for, had it done so, it is virtually certain that it would have resulted in a British victory comparable for its decisiveness to Barfleur or Quiberon Bay; and it can hardly be doubted that such a victory would have altered the entire course of the war. It is indeed plain today that, of all the factors which have contributed to the failure of Hitler's grandiose invasion plans, none was greater than the lack of adequate instruments of sea power and of a proper understanding of their use on the German side.

Fine words, and it has to be admitted that the Germans never properly understood how to put their available sea power to its best use. But the principal factor that contributed to the frustration of Germany's invasion plan was the gallantry and determination of a dwindling band of R.A.F. fighter pilots; and the Royal Navy, despite its foretaste off Norway and Dunkirk, had yet to assimilate fully the lesson of what enemy air power could achieve against warships stripped of their own air cover.

CHAPTER FIVE
The Mediterranean Theatre, 1940

When Italy entered the war on 10 June 1940, she had at her disposal six battleships (only two of which were ready for operations), seven heavy cruisers, 12 cruisers, 59 destroyers, 67 torpedo boats and 116 submarines. Against this, the British in the eastern Mediterranean had four battleships, nine light cruisers, 21 destroyers and six submarines, to which could be added one French battleship, three heavy cruisers, one light cruiser, a destroyer and six submarines. Six more British submarines and a destroyer were at Malta. In the western Mediterranean, the combined Anglo-French naval assets were five battleships (four of them French) one aircraft carrier, four heavy cruisers, seven light cruisers (six of them French) 46 destroyers (37 French) and thirty-six submarines (all French).

By 10 June, the Italian Navy had laid extensive mine barrages on the Italian Mediterranean coasts and also in the Adriatic. In addition, 54 submarines were deployed to their war stations. On 12 June, one of these, the *Bagnolini*, achieved an early success by sinking the British light cruiser *Calypso*. The British also lost three submarines in quick succession, *Odin* being sunk by the destroyer *Strale* in the Gulf of Taranto on 13 June, *Grampus* by torpedo-boats off Syracuse three days later, and *Orpheus* by the destroyer *Turbine* off Tobruk.

Shortly before Italy's declaration of war, Admiral Sir Andrew Cunningham, Commander-

---

The Italian submarine Brin *operated in the Mediterranean from June 1940 until Italy's surrender in 1943, and afterwards served with the Allies in the Indian Ocean*

upon to carry out one of the most tragic and melancholy operations in the history of the Royal Navy; the attempted destruction of the French Fleet at Oran and Mers-el-Kebir (Operation _Catapult_). Admiral Somerville was ordered to sail with his squadron to Oran and to offer an unpleasant ultimatum to the French commander, Admiral Gensoul. If the latter refused to join forces with the British, to sail to the French West Indies with reduced crews or to scuttle his ships, then Somerville had orders to destroy them. On 3 July, Captain C. S. Holland, in command of the _Ark Royal_, was sent to Oran to parley with Gensoul, but the French admiral refused even to consider any of the alternatives.

Shortly before 18.00 the _Valiant, Resolution_ and _Hood_ opened fire, their guns directed by Swordfish spotter aircraft from the _Ark Royal_, while another flight of Swordfish laid mines in the entrance of the nearby port of Mers-el-Kebir. The heavy shells hit the magazine of the battleship _Bretagne_ and she blew up; the _Dunkerque_ and _Provence_ were badly damaged, and two destroyers were sunk.

As the sun went down, the battleship _Strasbourg_ and five destroyers made a dash for safety. They were attacked by the _Ark Royal_'s Swordfish, but in the face of heavy anti-aircraft fire and the gathering darkness the pilots' aim was poor and the French warships got away to Toulon. The following morning, the _Ark Royal_ launched another strike of torpedo-carrying Swordfish of No. 820 Squadron to finish off Gensoul's flagship, the _Dunkerque_, which was aground in Oran harbour. The Swordfish were escorted by Skuas of No. 803 Squadron, two of which were shot down by Curtiss Hawk 75A fighters of _Groupe de Chasse_ I/10 that came up to intercept. Four torpedoes hit the the auxiliary vessel _Terre Neuve_, which was lying alongside _Dunkerque_ with a cargo of depth-charges; these exploded and ripped open the battleship's side, putting her out of action.

Another French squadron, comprising the battleship _Lorraine_, four cruisers and a number of smaller warships, was at Alexandria, where it had been operating under Admiral Cunningham, commanding the British Eastern Mediterranean Fleet, before France's collapse. Here Cunningham managed to arrive at a peaceful settlement with his French opposite number, Admiral Godfroy, and the French warships were deactivated. That still left the new battleships _Jean Bart_ and _Richelieu_ – which had escaped from Brest before the port was captured by the Germans – in the West African ports of Casablanca and Dakar, and on 8 July a fast motor-boat from the carrier _Hermes_ entered the harbour of Dakar and dropped depth-charges under the _Richelieu_'s stern in an attempt to put her rudder and propellers out of action. But the depth-charges failed to explode, and although the battleship was later attacked by Swordfish of 814 Squadron from the _Hermes_ their torpedoes only inflicted light damage. She was attacked again two months later, this time by the _Ark Royal_'s aircraft, during an abortive British landing in Senegal; but once again the air strikes proved ineffective, and this time nine Swordfish and Skuas were shot down.

The controversy over this unfortunate affair, which cost the French Navy 1,297 dead, has raged ever since. The three senior British naval officers involved – Admiral Sir Dudley North at Gibraltar, Admiral Cunningham and Admiral Somerville – were all opposed to it, believing that a solution without the use of force would have been reached in time. But time, in the summer of 1940, was something Britain did not have. The British Government did not know which way the wind that was steering Marshal Petain's post-armistice regime would blow; the only certainty was that if the French warships ceased to be neutral, their power would tilt the balance in the Mediterranean towards the enemy. Under the circumstances, the British Government's decision was the only one possible; and it showed the world that Britain, alone now, was prepared to act ruthlessly if the occasion demanded.

On 7 July, Admiral Cunningham, having dealt with the French squadron in Alexandria, sailed from that port with the twofold intention of providing protection for two convoys carrying supplies from Malta to Alexandria, and of throwing down a challenge to the Italian Navy by operating within sight of the southern coast of Italy. Cunningham's force was split into three; the leading unit (Force A) consisted of five cruisers, the centre (Force B) of the battleship *Warspite* and her destroyer screen, and bringing up the rear was Force C, comprising the aircraft carrier *Eagle*, accompanied by ten destroyers and the veteran battleships *Malaya* and *Royal Sovereign*. The British Fleet's air cover consisted of 15 Swordfish of Nos. 813 and 824 Squadrons and three Sea Gladiators of a fighter flight, forming *Eagle*'s air group. Two days earlier, the Swordfish had scored a resounding success when, operating from a R.A.F. airfield in Egypt, they had sunk the Italian destroyer *Zeffiro* and the 4,000-ton freighter *Manzoni*, as well as badly damaging the destroyer *Euro* and the 15,000-ton troopship *Liguria*, in a torpedo attack on Tobruk harbour.

Early on 8 July, a patrolling submarine reported that a strong enemy force, including two battleships, was steaming southwards between Taranto and Benghazi. Reconnaissance Swordfish were launched and they in turn reported that the enemy warships were following an easterly course, which led Cunningham to believe that they were covering a convoy en route to Benghazi. Postponing the departure of the British convoy from Malta, he altered course in order to position himself between the enemy and their base at Taranto.

In the afternoon of that same day, the British Fleet was subjected to a series of high-level attacks by 126 Italian bombers. The *Eagle* was singled out as a special target, but despite several near misses she emerged unscathed. Only one ship, the cruiser *Gloucester*, was hit and damaged. Even so, the Italian bombing was very accurate, and at the bombers' operating height of over 10,000 feet most of the British warships' anti-aircraft armament was ineffective.

The air attacks went on for five days, and several of the raids were intercepted by the *Eagle*'s Sea Gladiator flight. The three aircraft were flown by the Swordfish pilots of No. 813 Squadron, who destroyed five Savoia-Marchetti S.M.79 bombers without loss to themselves.

At dawn on 9 July, Cunningham was 60 miles off the south-west tip of Greece, with the enemy force – two battleships, sixteen cruisers and thirty-two destroyers – about 150 miles ahead of

him, in the Ionian Sea. By 11.45 only 90 miles separated the two forces, and the *Eagle* launched a strike force of nine Swordfish in an attempt to slow down the enemy. They failed to find the main force, which had altered course, but launched their torpedoes through a heavy barrage of fire at an Italian cruiser that was bringing up the rear, missed, and returned to the *Eagle* to refuel and rearm.

At 15.15 Cunningham's advance force of cruisers sighted the enemy, who immediately opened fire on them. Ten minutes later the *Warspite* arrived on the scene and engaged the Italian cruisers with her 15-inch guns until they were forced to withdraw under cover of a smoke screen. At 15.45 a second Swordfish strike was flown off, and three minutes after the aircraft had gone, the *Warspite* made contact with the Italian flagship *Giulio Cesare* and opened fire on her from a range of 26,000 yards, severely damaging her and reducing her speed to 18 knots. The Italian commander, Admiral Campioni, at once broke off the action and headed for the Italian coast, accompanied by the *Cesare*'s sister ship *Conte di Cavour*, at the same time ordering his destroyer flotillas to attack and lay down smoke.

At 16.15, the nine Swordfish, led by Lt-Cdr Debenham, arrived in the vicinity of the Italian warships, the pilots striving to identify targets in the dense pall of smoke that now hung over the sea. After a few minutes, Debenham spotted two large warships emerging from the smoke and led his aircraft in to the attack. In fact, the two ships were the 8-inch cruisers *Trento* and *Bolzano*; they immediately turned away into the smoke once more, throwing down a heavy barrage in the path of the attacking Swordfish as they did so. The torpedoes failed to find their mark, and all the aircraft returned safely to the carrier. They landed-on at 17.05 in the middle of yet another high-level attack by Italian bombers; fortunately none of the British warships was hit, although both *Eagle* and *Warspite* were shaken by near misses.

At 17.30, Cunningham abandoned the chase and set course for Malta. Without adequate fighter cover, it would have been suicidal to sail any closer to the Italian coast. Late in the following day, however, *Eagle's* Swordfish flew off on one more strike, this time against a concentration of enemy cruisers and destroyers that had been reported in the Sicilian harbour of Augusta. The aircraft arrived over the harbour at dusk to find only one destroyer and an oil tanker still there; both were torpedoed, the destroyer – the *Leone Pancaldo* – capsizing and sinking within minutes.

Having refuelled and rearmed his force in Malta, Cunningham now turned to his main task of escorting the convoy to Alexandria. The ships were repeatedly attacked by the *Regia Aeronautica* during the next three days, but they reached Alexandria without loss on 14 July.

The Action off Calabria, as Cunningham's brush with the Italians came to be known, was the first fleet action in which carrier aircraft took part. Presumably due to lack of experience on the part of the Swordfish crews, the Fleet Air Arm had made little material contribution other than to help convince the enemy, perhaps, that in the face of repeated if ineffective torpedo attacks withdrawal was the best policy. If the Italians had possessed an aircraft carrier, even one as outdated as the *Eagle*, with a complement of fighter aircraft, the outcome might have been very different, and prohibitive losses inflicted on the Swordfish.

As far as the *Regia Aeronautica* was concerned, the precision and concentration of its high-level bombing had been little short of poetic, but totally ineffective against the elusive moving targets presented by the warships. The Italian Air Force's lack of success against Cunningham's force did, however, have one damaging effect. It bred a sense of complacency, a belief that bombing could not seriously interfere with the Royal Navy's freedom of movement in the Mediterranean. The belief was strengthened when, on 17 August – following a bombardment of Bardia and Fort Capuzzo in Cyrenaica by the battleships *Warspite*, *Malaya* and *Ramillies*, the heavy cruiser *Kent* and twelve destroyers – the British force was attacked by Italian aircraft and suffered no damage; moreover, twelve enemy bombers were destroyed by shore-based fighters of the *Eagle's* air group. The complacency, however, was to be shattered before many months had passed, with the arrival of the first German dive-bomber squadrons in Sicily

and Italy.

Towards the end of the month, the Royal Navy's striking force in the Mediterranean received a powerful new addition in the shape of the 23,000-ton armoured fleet carrier H.M.S. *Illustrious*. In addition to her two Swordfish squadrons, Nos 815 and 819, she carried No. 806 Squadron, the first to equip with the Fairey Fulmar monoplane fighter. Powered by a Rolls-Royce Merlin engine, the Fulmar was armed with eight Browning 0.303 machine-guns, and although its maximum speed of 270 m.p.h. – a limit partly imposed by the addition of a second crew member – made it a good deal slower than contemporary land-based fighters such as the Hurricane, it was a distinct improvement on the Sea Gladiator and Skua. Fourteen Fleet Air Arm squadrons were eventually equipped with it.

For the first time, thanks to the Fulmars, Admiral Cunningham now had an effective means of countering the Italian high-level bombers and the reconnaissance aircraft that shadowed his warships. After some two months of operations, the pilots of No. 806 Squadron had claimed the destruction of over 20 enemy aircraft. One of the most successful pilots was the C.O., Lt-Cdr C. L. G. Evans, who had shared in the destruction of the first enemy aircraft of the Second World War in September 1939.

During September, the Swordfish of Nos 813, 824, 815 and 819 Squadrons, operating from *Illustrious* and *Eagle*, made several night dive-bombing attacks on Italian airfields in the Dodecanese. On one occasion, during a raid on Maritza airfield on the Island of Rhodes, the Swordfish failed to get clear of enemy territory before sunrise and were attacked by Italian C.R.42 fighters. Four of the thirteen Swordfish, all from the *Eagle*, were shot down. The Fleet Air Arm had its revenge on the night of 17 September, however, when 15 Swordfish from the *Illustrious* sank two Italian destroyers and damaged several other vessels in Benghazi harbour.

The *Ark Royal's* Swordfish were also in action during this period, carrying out a series of bombing raids on airfields in Sicily to divert attention from the carriers *Furious* and *Argus*, which had just arrived from Britain with reinforcement Hurricanes for Malta. The island had been under attack by the *Regia Aeronautica* ever since Italy's entry into the war in June, and for nearly three weeks the sole air defence had been provided by three Sea Gladiators, a fourth being retained for spares.

The worst of Malta's ordeal was yet to come, but in the meantime events in the Mediterranean were moving towards the action that was to form the very basis of the Fleet Air Arm's tradition in the years to come: the attack on the Italian Fleet at Taranto.

Plans for an attack on Taranto by carrier-borne aircraft had been laid as long ago as 1935, when Italian forces invaded Abyssinia. There were actually two main Italian naval bases, one at Naples and the other at Taranto; and it was at the latter, in the autumn of 1940, that the Italians began to concentrate their heavy naval units to counter the threat from the British Mediterranean Fleet.

With only the old *Eagle* at Admiral Cunningham's disposal, an attack on the big Italian base had been regarded as impracticable, but the arrival of the *Illustrious* changed the picture completely. The plans were revised, and it was decided to mount a strike from the *Illustrious* and *Eagle* on the night of 21 October, the anniversary of the Battle of Trafalgar. Before that date, however, a serious fire swept through *Illustrious*'s hangar; some of her aircraft were totally destroyed and others put temporarily out of action, and the strike had to be postponed by three weeks.

Air reconnaissance had revealed that five of the six battleships of the Italian battle fleet were at Taranto, as well as a large force of cruisers and destroyers. The battleships and some of the cruisers were moored in the outer harbour, the Mar Grande, a horseshoe-shaped expanse of fairly shallow water, while the other cruisers and destroyers lay in the inner harbour, the Mar Piccolo. The ships in the outer harbour were protected by torpedo nets and lines of barage balloons. It was the balloons, perhaps even more than the anti-aircraft batteries, that would present the greatest hazard to the low-flying Swordfish.

The date of the attack (Operation *Judgment*) was fixed for the night of 11 November. Because of defects caused by the many near misses she had suffered, the *Eagle* had to be withdrawn from the operation at the last moment; five of her aircraft were transferred to the other carrier. The *Illustrious* and the fleet sailed from Alexandria on 6 November, and two days later the warships made rendezvous with several military convoys in the Ionian Sea, on their way from Malta to Alexandria and Greece. The concentration of ships was located and attacked by the *Regia Aeronautica* during the next two days, but the attacks were broken up by 806 Squadron's Fulmars, which claimed the destruction of ten enemy aircraft for no loss.

At 18.00 on the 11th, with the convoys safely on their way under escort, the *Illustrious*, with a screen of four cruisers and four destroyers, detached herself from the main force and headed for her flying-off position 170 miles from Taranto. Twenty-one aircraft were available for the strike: twelve from 815 Squadron, led by Lt-Cdr K. Williamson, and nine from No. 819 under Lt-Cdr J. W. Hale. Because of the restricted space available over the target, only six aircraft from each wave were to carry torpedoes; the others were to drop flares to the east of the Mar Grande, silhouetting the warships anchored there, or to dive-bomb the vessels in the Mar Piccolo.

The first wave of Swordfish began taking off at 20.40 and set course in clear weather, climbing to 8,000 feet and reaching the enemy coast at 22.20. The Swordfish formation now split in two, the torpedo-carriers turning away to make their approach from the west while the flare-droppers headed for a point east of the Mar Grande. At 23.00 the torpedo aircraft were in position and began their attack, diving in line astern with engines throttled well back. Williamson, descending to 30 feet, passed over the stern of the battleship *Diga di Tarantola* and released his torpedo at the destroyer *Fulmine*; it missed and ran on to explode against the side of a bigger target, the battleship *Conte di Cavour*. Then the Swordfish was hit by A.A. fire and had to ditch; Williamson and his observer, Lieutenant N. J. Scarlett, were taken prisoner. Two torpedoes from the remaining Swordfish hit the brand-new battleship _Littorio_; the aircraft all got clear of the target area and set course for the carrier. So did the other six Swordfish, whose bombs had damaged some oil tanks and started a big fire in the seaplane base beside the Mar Piccolo.

The second wave, which had taken off some 50 minutes after the first, had no difficulty in locating Taranto; the whole target area was lit up by searchlights and the glare of fires. There were only eight aircraft in this wave; the ninth had been forced to turn back to the carrier with mechanical trouble. This time, the five torpedo-carriers came in from the north. Two of their torpedoes hit the _Littorio_ and another the _Caio Duilio_;

a fourth narrowly missed the _Vittorio Veneto_. The fifth Swordfish (Lt·G. W. Bayley and Lt H. G. Slaughter) was hit and exploded, killing both crew members.

By 03.00 all the surviving Swordfish had been recovered safely, although some had substantial battle damage. Some of the crews who had bombed the vessels in the Mar Piccolo reported that some bombs had failed to explode; one had hit the cruiser _Trento_ amidships, only to bounce off into the water, and the same had happened with a hit on the destroyer _Libeccio_.

The following day, R.A.F. reconnaissance photographs told the full story of the damage inflicted on the Italian Fleet. The mighty _Littorio_, with great gaps torn in her side by three torpedoes, was badly down by the bow and leaking huge quantities of oil; it would take four months

The Italian naval base at Taranto after the Fleet Air Arm's attack in November 1940

to effect repairs. The *Caio Duilio* and the *Conte di Cavour* had taken one hit each; the former had been beached and the latter had sunk on the bottom. The *Duilio* was repaired and returned to service after six months; the *Cavour* was later salvaged and moved to Trieste, and she was still there when R.A.F. bombers sank her on 17 February 1945.

It was the first time that a formidable battle fleet had been crippled by carrier aircraft, and the effect on the morale of the Italian Navy was shattering. After Taranto, the Italian Fleet was permanently on the defensive, and the superiority of the Royal Navy in the Mediterranean was assured. The Italian warships would never again present a serious threat to the security of the British convoys that were passing through the Mediterranean in increasing numbers, *en route* to Malta, Port Said and Alexandria.

On the night of 24/25 November, three large British transports passed through the Straits of Gibraltar and headed eastwards, accompanied by

Gateway to the Mediterranean: a Coastal Command Catalina before the Rock of Gibraltar

A Catalina carries out a dummy depth-charge attack off Gibraltar

the warships of Admiral Somerville's Force H. Meanwhile, a detachment of the Eastern Mediterranean Fleet steamed westwards to meet the convoy south of Sardinia and escort it on to Malta and Alexandria. On the morning of the 27th, when Force H and the merchantmen were southwest of Sardinia, reconnaissance aircraft from the *Ark Royal* sighted a large force of enemy battleships and cruisers to the north. It included the *Vittorio Veneto* and the *Giulio Cesare*, the survivors of Admiral Campioni's once proud battle fleet, whose remnants had put out from Taranto in order to escape a possible second strike by the Fleet Air Arm.

Somerville immediately sent his five cruisers under Rear-Admiral L. E. Holland after the enemy, backed up by the *Renown* and *Ark Royal*. In the early afternoon, the British and Italian cruisers sighted each other and exchanged fire; no hits were registered and the enemy withdrew in the direction of the *Vittorio Veneto* and *Giulio Cesare*. At 13.00, the latter opened fire on Holland's cruisers and he turned away, but soon afterwards he saw the enemy battleships making off to the north-east and continued the chase.

By refusing action, Admiral Campioni was obeying strict orders from the *Supermarina*, the Italian Admiralty, which forbade him to risk his two remaining capital ships. Since both were faster than Somerville's warships, the British Admiral's only hope lay in a strike by the *Ark Royal*'s aircraft. Eleven torpedo-carrying Swordfish were launched and they quickly overhauled the Italian squadron. The two battleships were protected by a screen of seven destroyers, which threw up a heavy A.A. barrage as the Swordfish made their attack. All the aircraft came through and dropped their torpedoes, but the battleships took violent evasive action and no hits

were scored. The only damage was to the *Vittorio Veneto*'s bridge, sprayed with bullets by the gunners of three Swordfish that flew past almost within touching distance.

The enemy force was now in full retreat under cover of a dense smokescreen, and Admiral Somerville, realising that the engagement had brought him within easy striking distance of enemy bomber bases, decided to break off the chase and return to the vital task of guarding the convoy. However, as the British cruisers turned south, the *Ark Royal* launched a second strike against the fleeing Italian warships. Seven Skuas, carrying bombs, were to locate and attack an enemy cruiser that was reported to be damaged and stopped, while nine Swordfish were to make another attack on the battleships. But the Swordfish were too late; by this time the battleships were close to the southern tip of Sardinia, and had the benefit of fighter cover. The Swordfish leader accordingly decided to attack the Italian cruiser squadron that was bringing up the rear, but the cruisers took effective evasive action and there were no hits. All the Swordfish returned safely. A few minutes later, the Skuas of No. 803 Squadron also sighted the cruiser squadron and bombed it, but to no avail.

Not long after the Skuas had landed-on, the *Regia Aeronautica* appeared and subjected the *Ark Royal* to two hours of high-level bombing. Fulmars and Skuas of 800 and 803 Squadrons destroyed four enemy aircraft, and the attacks ceased at dusk. The three merchantmen, escorted now by the battleship *Ramillies*, three cruisers and a screen of destroyers from the Eastern Mediterranean Fleet, went on their way safely; while Force H, its job done, set its face towards the west and Gibraltar.

CHAPTER SIX

Convoy Protection, 1940–41

By the summer of 1940, the maritime convoys that were Britain's lifeblood faced a threat from several directions. Firstly there were the U-boats, covering the North Sea and the Atlantic approaches; then there were the surface raiders, ranging from pocket battleships and heavy cruisers to fast merchantmen converted to the armed raider role; and finally, with the capture by the Germans of air bases in the North Sea/English Channel area and on the French Atlantic coast, there was the *Luftwaffe*.

The East Coast convoys, which operated on a two-day cycle between the Thames and the Firth of Forth, could be assured of reasonable protection from enemy air attack by R.A.F. Fighter Command, although they were always vulnerable to hit-and-run attacks by S-boats, particularly at night, when air cover was not available.

The Channel convoys, on the other hand, were so hard hit from the air in July 1940 that the Admiralty stopped them altogether for a time, although as the crisis of the Battle of Britain passed in the autumn, the R.A.F. was able to provide more adequate fighter protection, enabling these convoys to resume under strong air and surface escort. For them, mines and S-boat attacks were the principal dangers from then on.

The Atlantic convoys fell into several categories. First there were the convoys from Halifax, Nova Scotia, proceeding at 9 or 10 knots, and the slower convoys sailing at 7½–8 knots from Sydney, Cape Breton Island, some distance to the

The underwater enemy: a U-boat sails from a Biscay port for the Atlantic convoy routes

6

north-west; then there were the even slower convoys, U.K.-bound from Freetown, Sierra Leone, and vice versa; and also the convoys sailing to and from Gibraltar.

With U-boats and anti-shipping aircraft now established on the French Atlantic coast, all these convoys had to be re-routed. The Admiralty considered the passage south-west of Ireland to be too dangerous, and diverted the bulk of shipping to the north-west approaches and the North Channel leading to the Irish Sea. Because of the need to concentrate warships in U.K. waters to meet the invasion threat, few escort vessels were available at this time, and the enemy submarines consequently enjoyed considerable success; in June 1940 they sank 58 ships amounting to nearly 300,000 tons, their biggest triumph so far. The U-boats were now operating in packs of four or more craft, making their attacks at night and on the surface – tactics that rendered useless the ASDIC submarine underwater detection equipment carried by the British escort vessels. The Germans had used similar tactics in the 1914–18 war, and during the interwar years had made no secret of the fact that they would use them again; the commander of the German U-boat arm,

Iceland was a focal point of the North Atlantic convoy routes. Photograph shows a Hudson and an Anson of Coastal Command in the Icelandic snow

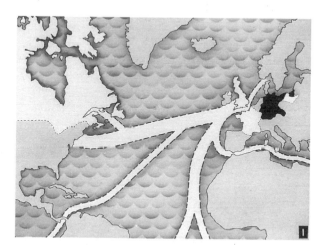

The Atlantic mercantile convoy routes to and from Britain

Admiral Karl Dönitz, had even described the surface night-attack method in a book published in 1939. Yet the Royal Navy's anti-submarine crews were trained only to deal with submerged submarines, and were consequently caught in a state of unpreparedness. The result was that for a period of some months, the German submariners enjoyed a complete tactical advantage and were able to inflict heavy losses on the North Atlantic convoys – and this with never more than 15 U-boats at sea at any one time.

Not every factor, however, was in the enemy's favour. At the beginning of September, an agreement was concluded between the British and American Governments whereby 50 surplus U.S. destroyers would be transferred to the Royal Navy in exchange for the lease of bases on British territory in the Western hemisphere. Old and ill-equipped those destroyers undoubtedly were, but for the hard-pressed British they were a godsend, and they were quickly brought into service on the Atlantic routes. In addition, new destroyers, sloops and corvettes were being commissioned in growing numbers, enabling the size of the escort groups to be increased; anti-submarine warfare training was gradually becoming more proficient; and cooperation between the Royal Navy and Royal Air Force Coastal

An Atlantic convoy setting out under the watchful eye of a Catalina

Command was steadily improving.

Despite its continuing successes, however, the German submarine service was hampered by a lack of operational U-boats throughout 1940; the low priority accorded to submarine construction in the early part of the war – partly because the German Naval planners had not expected going to war before 1944 – meant that the Germans did not have enough craft coming off the slipways to replace the 31 boats lost in the first 15 months of hostilities. There was also the German training system, which required a U-boat crew to undergo nine months of training in the Baltic and carry out 66 simulated attacks before it was considered operational. The overall result was that, by the end of 1940, their operational strength stood at only 22 submarines. It was fortunate for Britain that this was so, because even with the depleted U-boat resources at their disposal, the Germans came close to severing the Atlantic lifeline in the autumn of 1940. To give just one example, between 18 and 20 October convoys SC7 and HX71 lost 31 ships between them to U-boat attacks.

And German submarines were not the only ones with which the Royal Navy had to contend.

After some experimental forays through the Straits of Gibraltar in July and August 1940, the Italian Admiralty, the *Supermarina*, began to deploy submarines in considerable numbers to Bordeaux, from where they operated against the Atlantic convoys. By the end of October, 17 Italian boats were operating west of the Bay of Biscay – more submarines than the Germans had in the operational area at this particular time. Under the tactical command of the German Navy, they scored their first successes in the North Atlantic during November.

Although Germany's major warships were mostly inactive during the closing months of 1940, this was far from true of her armed raiders – fast merchantmen heavily armed with six to eight guns and torpedo tubes, and usually carrying a reconnaissance floatplane. The first of them, the *Atlantis*, put to sea on 31 March 1940, and in 622 days of operations she sank 22 ships amounting to 145,697 tons. By the end of 1940 six more were deployed: the *Orion, Widder, Thor, Pinguin, Komet* and *Kormoran*. Replenishing from supply ships at secret ocean rendezvous points, they were carefully disguised and preyed only on solitary unescorted vessels sailing the world's

A convoy in mid-Atlantic

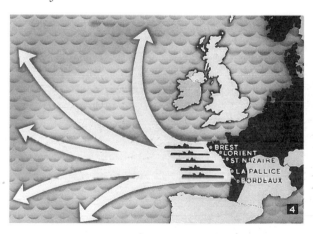

U-boat deployment in the Atlantic from the French bases

oceans. Some of their voyages were quite remarkable; the *Kormoran*, for example, left Bergen on 9 July 1940 and reached her operational area in the Pacific by way of the Siberian sea route, her passage assisted by Russian icebreakers.

The Admiralty's answer to these commerce raiders was to launch a major search for them using Armed Merchant Cruisers, 50 of which had been converted from fast liners. They were unarmoured and underarmed, and no match for their adversaries. A few actions were fought between these vessels towards the end of 1940; all resulted in the British ships suffering severe damage, while inflicting none on the enemy. They fared even worse when they encountered major German warships, as was demonstrated on 5 November 1940, when the *Admiral Scheer* – back at sea with the *Hipper* – attacked Convoy HX84, homeward bound from Halifax with 37 merchantmen and escorted only by the Armed Merchant Cruiser *Jervis Bay*. The latter's captain, E. S. F. Fegen, at once ordered the convoy to scatter under cover of a smoke screen and engaged the *Scheer*. The *Jervis Bay* was sunk with the loss of 191 crew, but Fegen's action (which earned him a posthumous Victoria Cross) had bought vital time for the convoy, which lost five ships to the *Scheer*'s guns. She also damaged three more, one of which was the tanker *San Demetrio*. Sixteen men of her crew, who had abandoned the

burning vessel, sighted her again 20 hours later and brought their lifeboat alongside; they boarded her, extinguished the fires after a struggle lasting two days, and brought her to harbour in Northern Ireland. Their exploit was made into a propaganda film.

However, there is a sad end to the *San Demetrio* story. On 17 March 1942, she was torpedoed by U-404 east of Chesapeake Bay, and this time she did not survive.

In the first half of 1941, German aircraft presented the main threat to Atlantic and North Sea traffic, causing the heaviest losses. In April alone they sank 116 ships totalling 323,000 tons, their highest figure of the whole war. The unit principally responsible for the losses was K.G. 40, whose four-engined Focke-Wulf Fw 200 *Kondor* aircraft, operating from Bordeaux and Stavanger, ranged far to the west of Ireland, seeking targets of opportunity and providing reconnaissance facilities for the U-boat packs. K.G. 40 had already enjoyed substantial success, claiming 363,000 tons of Allied shipping between August 1940 and February 1941. From 1 January 1941, K.G. 40 came under the direct control of the *Fliegerführer Atlantik*, a naval command. The Fw 200 threat

Scourge of the Atlantic convoys, in the early days, was the Focke-Wulf Fw 200 Kondor, *which in early 1941 sank more ships than the U-boats*

44

Coastal Command Beaufighters did much to combat the threat from German maritime aircraft. Here, a Blohm und Voss Bv 138 goes down in flames off western Ireland

began to diminish somewhat with the establishment of No. 252 Squadron at Aldergrove, in Northern Ireland, in the spring of 1941; equipped with long-range, heavily armed Bristol Beaufighters, the squadron and its successors formed a barrier of sorts between the German bombers and the convoys they were threatening, but their effectiveness was hampered in the early days by the reluctance of the R.A.F. to allow the convoy escorts to communicate directly with the aircraft, so that many interception chances were missed. It was not until the middle of 1941 that a form of fighter direction procedure was instituted.

Another solution to the problem of long-range enemy bombers, as envisaged by the Admiralty, was for the convoys to take their own defensive aircraft with them. For this purpose, and lacking proper escort carriers, a makeshift system was devised whereby merchant ships were fitted with catapults from which a single fighter – either a Fulmar or a Hurricane – could be launched with rocket assistance, the pilot either ditching or baling out after making his interception. Thirty-five merchant vessels were so equipped, each carrying an aircraft of the Speke-based Merchant

Rescuing survivors from a shot-down Fw 200 Kondor west of Ireland, 1943

Service Fighter Unit. The vessels were designated either Fighter Catapult (F.C.) ships, which were naval manned and flew the White Ensign, or Catapult Aircraft Merchantmen (C.A.M.) ships, which carried normal cargos and flew the Red Ensign. The ships were fitted with either R.A.F. Ground Controlled Interception (G.C.I.) or type 286P naval radar equipment to give warning of approaching aircraft. The first success was scored on 3 August 1941, when a Hurricane flown by Lt Everett, R.N. (No. 804 Sqn) from the Navy-manned *Maplin* – a converted banana boat – destroyed a Fw 200 400 miles from land. Only five *Kondors* were destroyed by the catapult fighters, but the knowledge that they were accompanying the convoys had an important effect on the morale of both sides.

In the winter of 1940–41, attacks by enemy *Schnellboote* on British coastal convoys were also presenting a serious threat to British coastal convoys, and in December 1940, as a counter-measure, the 6th Motor Gunboat (M.G.B.) Flotilla was formed. It consisted of three previously converted boats, each armed with four Lewis guns

Hurricanes and Fulmars of the Merchant Service Fighter Unit, though little more than a stop-gap measure, scored some successes against German maritime aircraft

and one Oerlikon; and five boats originally built for the French Navy armed with four Lewis guns and four 0.303 Browning machine-guns in a Boulton Paul power-operated turret. In March 1941, the 6th M.G.B. Flotilla deployed to Felixstowe and was soon in action against the enemy, joining the existing M.T.B. flotillas in patrolling lines from the Humber to the Hook of Holland and from Texel to the Thames. The Coastal Forces, as these light craft flotillas were collectively known, were to be greatly expanded before the end of 1941.

In May 1941, the Royal Navy faced the most serious threat so far to the vital convoy routes when the Germans initiated Operation *Rheinübung*, a sortie into the North Atlantic by the new battleship *Bismarck* and the heavy cruiser *Prinz Eugen*. The Germans had originally intended that a simultaneous sortie was to be made by the *Scharnhorst* and *Gneisenau*, but the latter had been badly damaged in a torpedo attack by a Beaufort of No. 22 Squadron R.A.F. Coastal Command at Brest on 6 April 1941. (The Beaufort was shot down in the attack and its pilot, Flying Officer Kenneth Campbell, awarded a posthumous V.C.)

Nevertheless, the battle group that sailed on 18 May from Gdynia in the eastern Baltic under the command of Admiral Lütjens, the Fleet Commander, was formidable enough. The *Bismarck* (*Kapitän* Lindemann) was at that time undoubtedly the most powerful warship afloat; displacing 42,500 tons and capable of 28 knots, she was armed with eight 15-inch and twelve 5.9-inch guns, while the 8-inch heavy cruiser *Prinz Eugen* (*Kapitän* Brinckmann) was also new, having been completed in 1940. The sortie was supported by a supply ship, six tankers, two patrol ships and three weather ships, deployed in the Arctic and Atlantic, while escort during the passage into the Norwegian Sea was provided by three destroyers and three minesweepers.

On 20 May the force was reported in the Kattegat by the Swedish cruiser *Gotland*, and intelligence of the enemy force's northward movement reached the British Admiralty early the next day. Admiral Sir John Tovey, who was now C.-in-C. Home Fleet, at once strengthened surveillance of the northern passages into the Atlantic, ordering the battleship *Prince of Wales*, the battlecruiser *Hood* and six destroyers to sail from Scapa Flow under Vice-Admiral L. E. Holland, flying his flag in the *Hood*, while reconnaissance aircraft were dispatched to search for the enemy warships. That same afternoon, the *Bismarck* and her consort were photographed by a P.R.U. Spitfire as they refuelled in Korsfjord, near Bergen. The Spitfire pilot, Flying Officer Michael Suckling, landed at Wick in north-east Scotland, where his film was developed; he then made a high-speed dash south with the precious prints, being forced to land at an airfield in the Midlands because of dense cloud. At 01.00 on 22 May, having completed his journey in a fast car, Suckling – unshaven and still wearing his flying kit – arrived at the Air Ministry in London, where he handed over the package of photographs to Air Chief Marshal Sir Frederick Bowhill, A.O.C.-in-C. Coastal Command.

Less than two hours after Suckling had walked into Bowhill's office, aircraft of Coastal Command were on their way to attack the German warships, but their operations were frustrated by bad weather. Then, shortly before nightfall on the 22nd, a Martin Maryland reconnaissance aircraft of No. 771 Naval Air Squadron from Hatston in the Orkneys penetrated Korsfjord. Its crew, Lt N. E. Goddard R.N.V.R. (pilot) and Cdr G. A. Rotherham (observer) returned with the news that the *Bismarck* and *Prinz Eugen* were gone.

At 22.45 Admiral Tovey left Scapa Flow with the main body of the Home Fleet, heading for Icelandic waters to reinforce the heavy cruisers *Norfolk* and *Suffolk* that were patrolling the Denmark Strait. Three more cruisers were guarding Lütjens's alternative breakout route, between Iceland and the Faeroes. First to arrive were the Home Fleet's two fastest ships, the *Prince of Wales* and the *Hood*, which had set out in advance of the main force; behind them came Tovey's Fleet Flagship, the new battleship *King George V*, the aircraft carrier *Victorious*, four cruisers and six destroyers. The carrier was not yet fully worked up, and her air group comprised only nine Swordfish and six Fulmars. She had been earmarked to escort Convoy WS8B, bound for the Middle East with troops, but had been released on Admiralty orders to take part in the hunt for the *Bismarck*. So had the battlecruiser *Repulse*, which also sailed north accompanied by three destroyers withdrawn from the Western Approaches.

At 19.22 on 23 May the *Bismarck* and *Prinz Eugen* were sighted by the cruiser *Suffolk* (Capt R. M. Ellis), emerging from a snow squall in the Denmark Strait. About an hour later, *Suffolk* was joined by *Norfolk* (Capt A. J. L. Phillips), flying the flag of Rear-Admiral W. F. Wake-Walker, commanding the 1st Cruiser Squadron. H.M.S. *Norfolk* came under enemy fire at a range of 13,000 yards and was straddled by three 15-inch salvoes before retiring under cover of smoke, miraculously undamaged, to radio her enemy sighting report to Admiral Tovey, whose main fleet was still some 600 miles to the south-west. The two cruisers continued to shadow Lütjens's ships at high speed throughout the night, *Suffolk* maintaining contact with her Type 284 radar. The *Prince of Wales* and *Hood*, meanwhile, were coming up quickly; Vice-Admiral Holland's ships had been about 220 miles away at the time of the first sighting report, and Holland was anticipating a night action. His plan was to concentrate the fire of his heavy ships on the *Bismarck*, leaving Wake-Walker's cruisers to deal with the *Prinz Eugen*. What he did not know was that the *Bismarck* was no longer in the lead; the blast from her guns had put her own forward radar out of action, so Lütjens had ordered the *Prinz Eugen* to change position.

As his heavy ships approached, Admiral Holland, conscious of the need for surprise, imposed strict radio and radar silence, relying on *Suffolk*'s reports to keep him informed of the enemy's position. Soon after midnight, however, *Suffolk* lost contact, and did not regain it until 02.47. In the meantime, Holland had turned his ships south to await full daylight, but when information once again began to come through from *Suffolk* he increased speed to 28 knots and turned on an interception course. It was now 03.40, and visibility was 12 miles.

At 05.37, the opposing forces sighted each other at a range of 17 miles, and opened fire at 05.53. Both German ships concentrated their fire on the *Hood* and, thanks to their stereoscopic rangefinders, straddled her immediately; the *Bismarck*'s second and third salvoes struck the battlecruiser amidships, and those from the *Prinz Eugen* started a fire among her ready-to-use A.A. ammunition.

At 06.00, as the British warships were altering course in order to bring all their guns to bear, the *Hood* was hit again by a salvo which pierced her lightly armoured decks and detonated in her after magazines. She blew up with a tremendous explosion and disappeared with a speed that stunned all who witnessed the event. Only three of her crew of 1,419 officers and ratings survived. As the *Prince of Wales* altered course sharply to avoid the wreckage she herself came under heavy fire. Within moments she sustained hits by four 15-inch and three 8-inch shells, one of which exploded on the bridge and killed or wounded almost everyone there except her captain, J. C. Leach, who ordered the battleship to turn away under cover of smoke. The *Prince of Wales* was so newly completed that she had not yet finished working-up; the contractors were still working on her 14-inch turrets when she sailed, and she was therefore not fully battle-worthy, a fact of which Captain Leach was obviously conscious. The additional damage had made her even more vulnerable, and Leach's intention now was to use his damaged ship to assist Wake-Walker's cruisers in maintaining contact with the enemy until Admiral Tovey's main force could reach the scene.

What Leach had no means of knowing was that his gunners had obtained three hits on the *Bismarck*, causing two of her fuel tanks to leak oil and contaminating others. Neither did he know that because of this Lütjens had decided to abandon the sortie and steer south-west for St-Nazaire, the only port on the Atlantic coast of France with a dry dock large enough to accommodate his flagship while repairs were carried out.

Tovey's ships were still 330 miles to the southeast and could not expect to make contact until 07.00 on 25 May at the earliest. However, other ships were also heading for the scene. Admiral Somerville's Force H had been ordered north from Gibraltar by the Admiralty to intercept the German squadron, and the battleships *Rodney*, *Revenge* and *Ramillies* and the cruiser *Edinburgh* were also released from escort duties to take part in the chase. The main concern now was to reduce the *Bismarck*'s speed, giving the hunters a chance to close in for the kill, and at 14.40 on 24 May Admiral Tovey ordered the carrier *Victorious* to race ahead to a flying-off point 100 miles from the enemy ships and launch a Swordfish strike against them.

At 22.10, the carrier flew off nine Swordfish of No. 825 Squadron, led by Lt-Cdr Eugene Esmonde. Flying through rain and sleet, they obtained radar contact with the enemy at 23.37 and briefly sighted the *Bismarck*, only to lose her again. Twenty minutes later the shadowing British cruisers redirected the Swordfish on to their target and they made their attack through heavy defensive fire. One torpedo hit the *Bismarck* amidships without causing significant damage; the other eight missed. All the attacking Swordfish recovered safely to the carrier, although two reconnaissance Fulmars out of nine dispatched failed to return. The returning crews reported no sign of the *Prinz Eugen*, which had in fact been detached by Admiral Lütjens to continue on her way alone.

At 03.00 on 25 May Lütjens altered course to the south-east, and at this critical juncture the shadowing cruisers, which had been following at extreme radar range, lost contact. The problems facing *Bismarck*'s pursuers were compounded by the receipt of some bearings transmitted by the Admiralty which, through a combination of errors, led Admiral Tovey to believe that the battleship was heading north-east, into the Atlantic. As a result, Tovey's flagship and many other pursuing vessels followed this false trail throughout most of the 25th, until, at about 18.00, deciding that the *Bismarck* was probably heading for Brest, they changed course accordingly. A signal received at 19.24 indicated that the Admiralty also thought that this was the case; in fact, the Admiralty, much earlier in the day, had already instructed Admiral Somerville's Force H

to position itself on a line from which its ships and aircraft could intercept the *Bismarck* should she head for the Bay of Biscay. It turned out to be a fortuitous move.

Although Tovey's warships had lost valuable ground during their false quest to the north-east, the net around *Bismarck* was gradually closing, and it was now that the experience and tactical awareness of one man came into play. Air Chief Marshal Bowhill, who had served in the Royal Navy as a young man, persuaded his colleagues in the Admiralty that Admiral Lütjens would not steer directly for Brest, but would instead make his landfall at Cape Finisterre. Coastal Command's search aircraft were accordingly instructed to patrol well to the south, and at 10.30 on the 26th *Bismarck* was sighted nearly 700 miles west of Brest by a Catalina of No. 209 Squadron from Castle Archdale (Lough Erne) in Northern Ireland. The aircraft's captain was Flying Officer Dennis Briggs, but the warship was actually sighted by his copilot, U.S. Navy Ensign Leonard B. Smith, one of several U.S. Navy pilots gaining operational experience with Coastal Command. As the United States was still neutral, Smith's presence on the aircraft was kept a strict secret.

Soon after the Catalina crew sighted the *Bismarck*, contact was also made by two Swordfish reconnaissance aircraft from the *Ark Royal*, Force H's aircraft carrier. Admiral Somerville sent the cruiser *Sheffield* to shadow the battleship with her Type 79Y radar and, when the opportunity arose, to direct a strike by the carrier's Swordfish torpedo-bombers. Fourteen of the latter were flown off at 14.50 in conditions of high winds, driving rain and rough seas, and some time later their radar revealed a target which their crews assumed was the *Bismarck*. In fact, it was the *Sheffield*, whose presence in the area had not been signalled to *Ark Royal*. The Swordfish came down through low cloud and attacked from different directions; several of them released their torpedoes before the mistake was recognised, but fortunately – thanks to a combination of effective evasive manoeuvring by the cruiser and faulty magnetic pistols fitted to the torpedoes – no damage was caused.

This first (and somewhat penitent) strike force

returned to the carrier, which at 19.10 launched a second wave of 15 Swordfish. The aircraft, led by Lt-Cdr T. P. Coode, were directed to the target by the *Sheffield*, but in the prevailing weather conditions, coupled with fading light and heavy defensive fire, they had little chance of making a coordinated attack. Nevertheless, two torpedoes found their mark; one struck the *Bismarck*'s armoured belt and did little damage, but the other struck her extreme stern, damaging her propellers and jamming her rudders fifteen degrees to port. At 21.40 Admiral Lütjens signalled Berlin: 'Ship no longer manoeuvrable. We fight to the last shell. Long live the *Führer*.'

Shortly afterwards, five destroyers, led by Captain Philip Vian in the *Cossack*, arrived on the scene, having been detached from convoy duty. They made contact with the *Bismarck* and shadowed her throughout the night, transmitting regular position reports and closing in to make a series of determined torpedo attacks, but these were disrupted by heavy and accurate radar-controlled gunfire. Whether any torpedoes hit their target or not is still a mystery; the destroyer crews maintained that they saw two explosions on the *Bismarck*, but the survivors of the battleship later stated that no hits were made. Whatever the truth, the *Bismarck* was seen to reduce speed, so driving a further nail into her own coffin.

During the night, the battleships *King George V* and *Rodney* came within striking distance of their crippled enemy, but Admiral Tovey, aware of the accuracy of her radar-directed gunnery, decided to wait until daylight before engaging her; she had no means of escaping him now.

Soon after dawn on 27 May he closed in from the north-west, his two battleships opening fire at about 08.45 from a range of 16,000 yards. By 10.20 the *Bismarck* had been reduced to a blazing wreck, with all her armament out of action, but she was still afloat despite the fact that the two British battleships had fired over 700 shells at her. Only a small proportion had found their target, prompting Admiral Tovey to tell his fleet gunnery officer that he would stand a better chance of hitting her if he threw his binoculars at her. In the end the battleships, undamaged but seriously short of fuel, were compelled to break off the action, and

it was left to the cruisers *Norfolk* and *Dorsetshire* to close in and finish off the *Bismarck* with torpedoes. She sank at 10.36, her colours still flying, in position 48° 10' N, 16° 12' W, taking all but 119 of her crew of over 2,000 officers and men with her. Her wreck was to lie undisturbed on the ocean floor for nearly half a century, when it was located and photographed by an underwater archaeology expedition, the swastika painted on the warship's bow still clearly visible.

The destruction of the *Bismarck* brought massive relief to the British Government. 'Had she escaped,' Winston Churchill wrote later

'the moral effects of her continuing existence as much as the material damage she might have inflicted on our shipping would have been calamitous. Many misgivings would have arisen regarding our capacity to control the oceans, and these would have been trumpeted around the world to our great detriment and discomfort.'

The *Prinz Eugen*, meanwhile, had headed south to refuel in mid Atlantic after parting company with the *Bismarck* on 24 May, but continuing engine defects persuaded *Kapitän* Brinckmann to abort his sortie and make for Brest. Although she was sighted by a Coastal Command patrol, she reached harbour unmolested on 1 June, aided by the fact that many British warships were in port refuelling and rearming after the pursuit of the *Bismarck*. For the rest of the year, the *Prinz Eugen*, together with the battlecruisers *Scharnhorst* and *Gneisenau*, were immobilised in the Biscay ports, where they were subjected to heavy and costly attacks by R.A.F. Bomber Command in which all three suffered damage. As a further insurance against future sorties by the enemy surface raiders, the Royal Navy began a systematic hunt for their tankers and supply ships following the sinking of the *Bismarck*; in June 1941 five tankers and three supply ships, plus a couple of weather-observation vessels, were destroyed or scuttled after being intercepted.

On 12 June, the German heavy cruiser *Lützow* (*Kapitän* Kreisch) attempted to break out into the North Atlantic, escorted by five destroyers, to attack merchant shipping. She was sighted by a R.A.F. reconnaissance aircraft off Lindesnes shortly before midnight, and fourteen Beaufort torpedo-bombers of Nos 22 and 42 Squadrons were dispatched to search for her. She was located by Flt Sgt R. H. Loveitt of No. 42 Squadron, who secured a torpedo hit amidships. The *Lützow* struggled back to Kiel with partially disabled engines and a heavy list, reaching harbour in the afternon of 14 June. She was to remain in dock for six months, and Loveitt was awarded a well-deserved D.F.M. It was the last attempt by a surface raider to interfere with the Atlantic convoys; when the German Navy's heavy warships once more joined battle in 1942, their focus of operations, dictated by the German invasion of Russia, would be the Arctic.

In the Atlantic, with the RAF's long-range fighters making life difficult for the Focke-Wulf *Kondors*, there remained the threat posed by the German and Italian submarines. In the summer of 1941 there was a welcome decrease in the tonnage of shipping sunk by these boats, and several factors contributed to it. From late May, for example, continuous escort was provided for U.K.-bound North Atlantic convoys by groups of Canadian and British warships, something that had not previously been possible because of a shortage of escort vessels; and May saw the genesis of the Atlantic 'support groups', whereby the escorts of other convoys could be diverted to strengthen the defences of one under threat. This system was first tested from 23–28 June 1941, when Convoy HX133 was attacked by ten U-boats south of Greenland. For five days and nights a fierce battle raged between the U-boats and thirteen escort vessels; five merchantmen were lost, but the escorts sank U-556 and U-651. The convoys in passage to and from West Africa did not as yet enjoy the benefit of this system, and it was in this area that the Italian submarines enjoyed their limited successes.

The real key to what seemed to be a growing Allied success, however, was intelligence. The story of *Ultra* and the code-breaking operation at Bletchley Park is now well known, although it was kept a closely guarded secret for more than 30 years after the war; and without the efforts of this dedicated band of experts, the outcome of the Battle of the Atlantic might have been very different.

CHAPTER SEVEN
Ultra and the Intelligence War

On 8 May 1941, the experts at Bletchley Park had a real windfall when the destroyer *Bulldog*, escorting Convoy OB318, drove a German submarine to the surface. She was the U-110 (*Kapitänleutnant* Julius Lemp). The Germans set explosive charges and abandoned ship; but the detonators failed, and a party from *Bulldog* went aboard the U-boat at no small risk to themselves and removed her code-books and *Enigma* code-machine. In the words of the official history, these captures yielded the short-range code books, which enabled GC&CS (Government Code and Cypher School) to read from May onwards the *Kurzsignale*, the short signals in which the U-boats transmitted their sighting reports and weather information. Captures enabled GC&CS to read all the traffic for June and July, including 'officer-only' signals, currently. By the beginning of August it had finally established its mastery over the Home Waters settings [the code used by the German naval *Enigma* machine] a mastery which enabled it to read the whole of the traffic for the rest of the war except for occasional days in the second half of 1941 with little delay. The maximum delay was 72 hours and the normal delay was much less, often only a few hours.

The Home Waters setting of the *Enigma* cypher, which was changed daily, carried 95 per cent of the German Navy's radio message traffic. Its yield, and that of other enemy high-grade cyphers, became known as *Ultra*. The breakthrough of May 1941 moved the whole war against the U-boats into a new dimension. The code-breakers and the Admiralty Submarine Tracking Room staff now had an insight into the whole operational cycle of a U-boat, and although many months were to pass before the Tracking Room could claim to know more about the U-boats' deployment than Admiral Dönitz's own staff, the summer of 1941 was the point at which Bletchley moved the process out of the realms of guesswork. It was this knowledge of U-boat movements and positions, derived from *Ultra*, that enabled the Admiralty to re-route convoys to avoid the U-boat packs, and it was this knowledge which enabled it to reinforce the escort of HX133, with results we have seen.

The decryption of enemy naval signals traffic was by no means new; the monitoring and decryption of enemy radio signals dated from the earliest days of August 1914, and in the anti-submarine war of 1914–18 it was perhaps the most significant contribution to British and Allied victory. During the latter half of 1941, by a very cautious estimate, the Admiralty Submarine Tracking Room, using *Ultra* decrypts, re-routed the convoys so cleverly around the German wolf-packs that as many as 300 ships may have been saved from destruction – surely a decisive factor in the outcome of the Battle of the Atlantic.

Admiral Dönitz's U-boat offensive in the spring of 1941 had been launched in the expectation that the previously high rate of merchant ship sinkings could not only be maintained but decisively increased as more submarines were deployed. In this way the German Naval Command hoped to neutralise Britain before help arrived from the United States in significant proportions, avoiding a two-front war and leaving the German armies free to deal with Russia. In Whitehall, as the offensive got under way, the outlook was bleak. At the beginning of 1941 food stocks in Britain were dangerously low: there was enough wheat for fifteen weeks; meat (rationed to one shilling's-worth per person per week) for only two weeks; butter for eight weeks on ration; margarine for three weeks on ration; and bacon for 27 weeks on ration. There were no longer any stocks of imported fruit. All this added up to the grim fact that, unless merchant ship sinkings could be reduced, Britain would starve before new merchant vessels could be built fast enough to maintain imports at the level needed for her survival.

At this point, mercifully, came the *Ultra* breakthrough. The intelligence it yielded came in two categories, the first and most important being that for immediate operational use. The wolf-pack tactics employed by the U-boats called for the transmission of sighting reports and homing signals between boats so that they could concentrate and attack on the surface at night in areas out of range of shore-based aircraft. Convoys were, at this time, virtually defenceless against these tactics, but their success depended on tightly centralised control by U-boat Command and the transmission of a stream of tactical orders, patrol instructions, situation reports and so on. This made them vulnerable to *Ultra* and to high-frequency direction finding (H.F./D.F.). Secondly, *Ultra* provided huge quantities of valuable background information that included such details as the exit and approach routes from and to the U-boat bases, frequency of patrols and the rate of commissioning of new boats. It also revealed operational characteristics such as the speed, diving depths, endurance, armament, signals and radar equipment of the various types of U-boat, and the current operational state of boats at sea.

Despite *Ultra*, merchant ship sinkings remained high in June 1941, partly because of difficulties in interpreting the disguised grid references for U-boat positions in the decrypts, and partly because of an increase in enemy submarine operations in West African waters, where the defences were ill-prepared and many ships were still sailing independently. The submarines involved in these operations had to return to their bases at the end of June as they had no refuelling facilities at sea, the tankers sent out to supply them (and the *Bismarck*) all having been sunk. When they resumed operations in this area in September they achieved comparatively little, since the convoy and escort group system was now established and the Allied ships could be routed clear of danger, thanks to *Ultra*.

The North Atlantic saw an even more important, if not dramatic, decline in sinkings from the end of June. This was partly because steps had been taken to reduce the number of ships sailing independently, but mainly because *Ultra*-directed evasive routeing – in other words, steering convoys clear of known U-boat patrol lines, the grid reference difficulties having been solved for the time being – could now be practised on a large scale. By the summer of 1941 Coastal Command had driven the U-boats westward, beyond the range of air patrols, which gave more scope for evasive routeing and at once brought about a sharp fall in the number of convoy attacks. Sinkings dropped from 300,000 tons in May and June to 100,000 in July and August. Mystified, Dönitz switched his boats back and forth in a mostly vain effort to find the elusive convoys. Although the German authorities knew that the British were obtaining valuable intelligence information, they never suspected that their naval codes had been compromised. Although they knew that the British had captured an *Enigma* machine, they did not know that their enemies had access to the daily settings, without which the machine was useless; the information, therefore, must be coming from leaks in other communications. Dönitz was so enraged by the fact that the British frequently transmitted accurate plots of U-boats (information ironically gained from German decrypts of British codes, broken before the war) that he took drastic steps to stem the leaks, even to the extent of having himself investigated as a possible source.

The great mistake made by the Germans, however, was to place the investigation in the hands of their cryptanalysts. Because these men and women had such unshakeable faith in *Enigma*, and considered its code to be unbreakable in a timescale that would produce useful intelligence, they wasted their time in following one false trail after another. They were also unaware of the importance of H.F./D.F. in determining U-boat dispositions, and of the fact that knowledge of their weather codes also assisted the British analysts.

In September 1941 sinkings rose again, mainly because of renewed grid reference difficulties, but by October these had been overcome. Evasive routeing could be practiced once more and sinkings again declined, despite the fact that the number of U-boats known to be at sea – now 80 – was double that at the start of the offensive. In November sinkings dropped to 62,000 tons, the lowest for 18 months. At this point many boats were diverted to the Arctic and Mediterranean while the rest were mostly concentrated off Gibraltar, to which area Coastal Command's patrols were at once directed. For the time being, the offensive against the trans-Atlantic routes was virtually abandoned.

Some weeks earlier, in August, the British intelligence effort against the U-boats had been assisted by the capture of one intact. She was the U-570, one of a group operating south-west of Iceland against Convoy HX145, which had been located by the German B Signals Intelligence Service (B-Dienst). The submarine was attacked in bad weather by a Hudson of No. 269 Squadron flown by Sqn Ldr J. H. Thompson and damaged; her commander, Lt Hans Rahmlow, raised the flag of surrender and the Hudson continued to circle the boat until relieved by a Catalina of No. 209 Squadron. The first of a succession of armed trawlers reached the scene on 27 August; the submarine's crew was taken off and she was towed to Iceland, where she was beached. Although her crew had destroyed most of the secret material on board, the capture of an intact U-boat was an important achievement. After Royal Navy service as H.M.S. *Graph*, she was decommissioned and used in depth-charge trials, yielding important information on the effects of explosions on her pressure hull.

Despite the carnage that was to come, some German historians see the end of 1941 as the turning point in the Battle of the Atlantic, the 300 ships calculated as having been saved by evasive routeing not only defeating Dönitz's offensive but also providing a cushion against future heavy losses. The second half of 1941 also provided something of a breathing space in which the Allies could forge ahead with the development of anti-submarine weapons and tactics, and lay the foundations for the later surge in merchant ship building which was to ensure victory.

The triumph of 1941 was *Ultra*'s, and it was a triumph that also extended to the Royal Navy's operations in the calmer waters of the Mediterranean.

CHAPTER EIGHT
The Mediterranean Theatre, 1941

On 9 January 1941, a convoy of four big supply ships, escorted by H.M.S. *Ark Royal* and the other warships of Force H, entered the narrows between Sicily and Tunis on its way to Malta and Piraeus. The passage of the ships through the troubled waters of the central Mediterranean – known as Operation *Excess* – at first followed the pattern of earlier convoys. In the afternoon of the 9th the usual formation of Savoia-Marchetti S.M.79s appeared and bombed from high altitude without scoring any hits; two of the S.M.79s were intercepted by *Ark Royal*'s Fulmars and shot down.

As darkness fell, Force H turned back towards Gibraltar, leaving the cruiser *Bonaventure* and the destroyers *Jaguar*, *Hereward*, *Hasty* and *Hero* to shepherd the convoy through the narrows under cover of night. At dawn on the 10th, the transports were met by the ships of the Eastern Mediterranean Fleet (Force A), comprising the carrier *Illustrious*, the battleships *Warspite* and *Valiant* and seven destroyers 60 miles west of Malta. Admiral Cunningham's ships had already suffered; shortly before first light, the destroyer *Gallant* had been badly damaged by a mine and had to be taken in tow by H.M.S. *Mohawk*.

Torpedo attacks by ten S.M.79s were beaten off in the course of the morning, and the Italian M.T.B. *Vega* was sunk by the *Bonaventure*. Then *Illustrious*'s radar detected another incoming formation of enemy aircraft, which soon afterwards was sighted approaching the warships at 12,000 feet. Sailors who had fought in the waters off Norway and Dunkirk recognised the enemy aircraft at once; they were Junkers Ju 87 dive-bombers.

The *Stuka*s were the aircraft of St.G. 1 and St.G. 2, led by *Hauptmann* Werner Hozzel and *Major* Walter Enneccerus. They formed the mainstay of the *Luftwaffe*'s special anti-shipping formation, *Fliegerkorps* X, and they had arrived at Trapani in Sicily less than a week earlier. Their presence should not have come as a surprise; Air Ministry Intelligence, thanks to *Ultra* intercepts, had been aware since 4 January of *Fliegerkorps* X's move south from Norway, and it was also aware of the unit's specialised role. The threat to the Mediterranean Fleet was clear; unfortunately, at this point there appears to have been a breakdown in communication between the Air Ministry and the Admiralty, and the *Stuka*s came as an unpleasant shock.

Now, as they began their attack dive, it was clear that they had singled out *Illustrious* as their principal target. The first bomb tore through S1 pom-pom on the carrier's port side, reducing the weapon to twisted wreckage and killing two of its crew before passing through the platform and exploding in the sea. Another bomb exploded on S2 pom-pom and obliterated it, together with its crew. A third hit the after-lift well, on its way to the flight deck with a Fulmar on it; debris and burning fuel poured into the hangar below, which quickly became an inferno of blazing aircraft and exploding fuel tanks. Splinters struck the eight 4.5-inch gun turrets aft, putting them all out of action. A fourth bomb crashed through the flight deck and ripped through the ship's side, exploding in the water; splinters punched holes through the hull and the shock of the detonation caused more damage in the hangar. The fifth bomb punched through the flight deck and hangar deck and exploded in the wardroom flat, killing everyone there and sending a storm of fire raging through the neighbouring passages. A sixth plunged down the after-lift well and exploded in the compartment below, putting the steering-gear out of action.

Illustrious was terribly hurt, but her heavy armour had saved her. Slowly the crew gained a measure of control and she turned towards Malta, shrouded in a pall of smoke from the fires that still raged, steering on her main engines as the stokers worked in dense, choking fumes and temperatures reaching 140°F as they strove to maintain steam. Two hours later, the *Stukas* attacked again and the carrier was hit by yet another bomb; she was now listing badly, but she remained afloat. As darkness fell, she limped into Valletta's Grand Harbour and stopped alongside the dockyard wall.

During the weeks that followed, *Illustrious* sustained several more bomb hits as she underwent repairs, but she escaped crippling damage and by 23 January she had been made seaworthy enough to sail for Alexandria. From there she later sailed for the U.S. Navy shipyards at Norfolk, Virginia, where she underwent more permanent repairs before returning to active service.

With the *Illustrious* out of action, Admiral Cunningham was forced to restrict the operations of the Eastern Mediterranean Fleet for several weeks because of the lack of air cover. Until

The Fairey Fulmar equipped fourteen F.A.A. fighter squadrons, and performed sterling service in defending the Mediterranean convoys in 1941–2

March, with the arrival of *Illustrious*'s sister carrier *Formidable*, the full burden of naval air operations in the Mediterranean rested on the *Ark Royal*. The carrier had recently taken on two new Fulmar squadrons, Nos 807 and 808. With the air defence of Force H assured by these aircraft, Admiral Somerville now made plans to use his Swordfish in a more offensive role, by striking at targets on the Italian mainland and in Sardinia. Accordingly, on 2 February, eight Swordfish took off from the *Ark Royal* and set course for Sardinia. Their target was the dam on the Tirso, the river that fed Lake Omodeo, the site of the island's only major hydroelectric plant. The mission was ill-starred from the beginning; the Swordfish pilots had a hard time flying down the twisting Tirso Valley, blinded by rain, and when they reached the lake they were met by heavy fire from fully alerted A.A. defences. Only four Swordfish managed to make a torpedo run, but the dam was unscathed and one aircraft was shot down. While this abortive attack was in progress, other Swordfish bombed an oil refinery at Livorno (Leghorn).

Between 6 and 11 February, Somerville's Force H executed a carefully planned attack on Genoa, where the damaged battleship *Caio Duilio* lay in

The aircraft-carrier H.M.S. Formidable

dock. Somerville split his force into three groups, Group One comprising the *Ark Royal*, the battleship *Malaya*, the battlecruiser *Renown* and the light cruiser *Sheffield*, and the other two groups consisting of six and four destroyers respectively. On 6 February, Groups One and Two sailed from Gibraltar on a westerly heading, ostensibly to escort the U.K.-bound convoy HG53, but during the night they reversed course and slipped back through the straits to join Group Three, which had been carrying out a submarine search to the east of the Rock. On 8 February, the Italian *Supermarina*, having received reports of British naval aircraft operating to the south of the Balearics, dispatched a strong naval force under Admiral Iachino and comprising the battleships *Vittorio Veneto*, *Andrea Doria* and *Giulio Cesare*, with ten destroyers and three heavy cruisers, to rendezvous south-west of Sardinia in order to intercept what was believed to be a Malta convoy.

It was exactly what Somerville wanted the Italians to think. Meanwhile, Force H sailed north-eastwards, approached the Italian coast and fired 273 15-inch, 782 6-inch and 400 4.5-inch shells into Genoa, sinking four freighters and damaging 18 more, as well as causing severe damage to the city. Belatedly, Iachino's force headed north to intercept the British but, without the benefit of radar, failed to make contact in thick mist. By 11 February, Force H was back in Gibraltar.

On 9 March, the carrier gap was filled when H.M.S. *Formidable* joined the Mediterranean Fleet. She carried only four Swordfish; the rest of her aircraft complement was made up of ten Fairey Albacores – biplanes, like the Swordfish, but bigger and faster, with longer range and enclosed cockpit – of No. 826 Squadron, and the 13 Fulmars of No. 803 Squadron, transferred from the *Ark Royal*. The fighter complement would be brought up to full strength in the following month, when No. 806 Squadron joined the carrier from Malta. Before that, however, *Formidable* and her aircraft were to play a decisive part in another large-scale action against the Italian Fleet.

At dawn on 28 March, while the Mediterranean Fleet was engaged in covering the passage of convoys of British Commonwealth troops from Alexandria to Greece to counter an imminent German invasion of that country, a reconnaissance Albacore from the *Formidable* reported a force of enemy cruisers and destroyers to the south of Crete. This force, which actually comprised the battleship *Vittorio Veneto* (Admiral Iachino's flagship), six heavy cruisers, two light cruisers and 13 destroyers, had put to sea from Taranto, Naples, Brindisi and Messina and had made rendezvous south of the Straits of Messina on 27 March with the object of intercepting the British troop convoys. Iachino had agreed to the operation only when the *Luftwaffe* promised him extensive fighter cover and reconnaissance facilities, and after the crews of two He 111 torpedo-bombers had erroneously reported hits on two large warships – 'possibly battleships' – during an armed reconnaissance flight 30 nautical miles west of Crete on 16 March. It was a mistake that was to have serious consequences for the Italian admiral.

At 08.15 on 28 March, the Mediterranean Fleet's cruisers, which were about 100 miles ahead of the main force, came under fire from the Italian warships and were in danger of being cut off by the enemy, who was steaming in a large pincer formation. With no hope of Admiral Cunningham's heavy brigade arriving in time to ease the situation, it was apparent that only a torpedo strike by *Formidable*'s aircraft could ease the pressure on the outgunned British cruisers, and at 10.00 six Albacores – the only ones available, as the other four were earmarked for reconnaissance duties – took off with an escort of two Fulmars and headed for the Italian squadrons. Their orders were to attack the enemy cruisers, but the first ship they sighted was the *Vittorio Veneto*, whose 15-inch guns were pounding the British cruiser squadron. The Fleet Air Arm pilots attacked in two waves at 11.25, but the Italian battleship took evasive action and all the torpedoes missed. The two Fulmars, meanwhile, had engaged two Ju 88s high overhead and destroyed one of them, driving off the other.

Admiral Iachino, seeing his air cover melt away, now turned away and headed west at speed, reducing Cunningham's hopes of bringing him to action. The British commander ordered a second air strike, this time with the object of slowing down the *Vittorio Veneto*. The *Formidable* accordingly flew off three Albacores and two Swordfish, again escorted by a pair of Fulmars. An hour later they sighted their target – which meanwhile had been unsuccessfully attacked by R.A.F. Blenheim bombers from bases in Greece. This time, mainly because they were on the alert for more R.A.F. aircraft approaching from a differ-

ent direction, the Italian gunners failed to see the Fleet Air Arm aircraft until the latter began their attack. The Albacores came in first, led by Lt-Cdr Dalyell-Stead; he released his torpedo seconds before his aircraft was hit and blew up. The torpedo ran true and exploded on the battleship's stern, jamming her steering-gear and flooding the compartment with 4,000 tons of water. No further torpedo hits were registered, but the *Vittorio Veneto* was forced to slow down and stop while her engineers made temporary repairs, spurred by the knowledge that Cunningham's battleships were now only three hours' steaming time away. They succeeded in repairing the propeller shaft and gradually the battleship's speed was worked up until she was able to proceed at 15–18 knots, with the cruisers and destroyers forming a tight screen around her.

The *Formidable*'s third and last attack was launched at dusk. Led by Lt-Cdr W. H. G. Saunt, six Albacores and four Swordfish, two of the latter from Máleme airfield on Crete, caught up with the damaged battleship and her escort and attacked through heavy A.A. fire. The *Vittorio Veneto* escaped further harm, but one torpedo heading for the battleship was blocked by the cruiser *Pola*, which was badly damaged. Admiral Iachino detached the cruisers *Zara* and *Fiume* and four destroyers to escort her, while the rest of the Italian force accompanied the *Vittorio Veneto* to safety.

At 22.10, the three cruisers and the destroyers were detected by radar on board the battleship H.M.S. *Valiant* and the cruiser *Orion*. Fifteen minutes later the Italian ships were engaged by *Valiant* and *Warspite*, and the *Zara* and *Fiume* were quickly reduced to blazing hulks; two destroyers were sent in to finish them off with torpedoes. The crippled *Pola* was also sunk before morning, as well as two of the Italian destroyers. The enemy warships, which were not equipped with radar, had no idea that they were steaming across the bows of the British force until the battleships opened fire on them.

The Italians had lost five warships and nearly 2,500 officers and men; the British had lost just one Albacore. So ended the action that was to become known as the Battle of Cape Matapan. It represented an overwhelming victory for the British Mediterranean Fleet, and it had been made possible by two factors: the priceless gift of *Ultra*, which had alerted the Admiralty to the movements and dispositions of Iachino's fleet; and naval air power.

The jubilation, however, was destined to be short-lived. On 6 April German forces attacked Yugoslavia and Greece. Two days later the Yugoslav armies crumbled and the *Wehrmacht* smashed its way into Greek territory through the thinly defended Aliakhmon Line, forcing an Allied withdrawal. The German Army, with powerful air support, poured southwards through Greece and the Greek forces rapidly disintegrated before its onslaught, leaving the burden of defence on the New Zealand Division, the 6th Australian Division, the 1st Armoured Brigade and a handful of depleted R.A.F. squadrons. By 2 May the position in Greece was untenable and 43,000 Allied troops were evacuated from Greek soil, 11,000 being withdrawn to Crete.

On 20 May, in the wake of a massive air bombardment, German airborne forces landed on Crete (Operation *Merkur*) and the next morning the *Luftwaffe* launched the first of a series of heavy attacks on British warships in the area, sinking the destroyer *Juno* and damaging the cruiser *Ajax*. During the night of 21/22 May the Germans attempted to send in reinforcements by sea, but the convoy, comprising 20 motor sailing vessels, was attacked by the British Force D under Rear-Admiral Glennie (the cruisers *Ajax*, *Dido* and *Orion*, supported by four destroyers) 18 nautical miles north of Caneá and scattered. Ten enemy vessels were sunk, and 297 of the 2,331 troops on board lost their lives. The toll would almost certainly have been greater had it not been for a determined defence put up by an escorting Italian torpedo-boat, the *Lupo* (Cdr Mimbelli), whose sister craft, the *Sagittario* (Cdr Cigala) also fought a gallant action after daybreak while escorting a second troop convoy. This convoy was attacked by Rear-Admiral King's Force C (the cruisers *Naiad*, *Perth*, *Calcutta* and *Carlisle*, with three destroyers) but the British warships came under constant air attack by the Ju 88s of L.G. 1 and K.G. 30 and the Do 17s of K.G. 2 and suc-

ceeded in destroying only two transports. The *Carlisle* and *Naiad* were both damaged by bomb hits.

The Royal Navy suffered heavily in the afternoon, when the fleet came under heavy attack by Ju 87s, Ju 88s, Me 109 fighter-bombers and also, to a lesser extent, by Italian high-level bombers. The battleship *Warspite* was hit several times, the cruiser *Gloucester* and the destroyer *Greyhound* sunk – the former with the loss of 45 officers and 648 ratings – and the cruiser *Fiji* so badly hit that she had to be abandoned. The *Carlisle* and *Naiad* suffered further damage, and the battleship *Valiant* was also damaged to a lesser extent. On 23 May the destroyers *Kashmir* and *Kelly* were both sunk by air attack, while attacks on Suda Bay by Me 109 fighter-bombers destroyed five M.T.B.s of the 10th M.T.B. Flotilla.

On 25 May, Vice-Admiral H. D. Pridham-Wippell put to sea from Alexandria with the battleships *Barham* and *Queen Elizabeth*, the aircraft-carrier *Formidable* and nine destroyers to attack St.G. 2's airfield at Scarpanto. Returning from this sortie on the 26th, the *Formidable* and the destroyer *Nubian* were both badly damaged by Ju 87s, and the next day the *Barham* was also damaged by Ju 88s.

By this time it was clear that the situation on Crete was untenable. Suda Bay was being so heavily bombed that it was no longer possible to run in supplies and reinforcements. Without air cover, Admiral Cunningham's forces were certain to suffer unacceptable losses in their efforts to prevent seaborne landings on the island, a task that in any case could not be guaranteed. In the afternoon of 27 May, therefore, the War Cabinet decided to evacuate the garrison of some 32,000 troops, and on the night of 28/29 May, 4,700 were embarked at Heráklion and Sfakia. During this operation the destroyer *Imperial*, part of the evacuation force, was damaged by enemy aircraft and had to be abandoned and sunk by the *Hotspur* off Maléa Bay. Another 6,000 troops were evacuated on the next night, but during the day *Stukas* sank the destroyer *Hereward* and damaged the cruisers *Ajax*, *Dido* and *Orion*, as well as the destroyer *Decoy*. *Orion* suffered fearsome casualties among the troops she was carrying; of the

1,100 soldiers on board, 260 were killed and 280 wounded.

On the night of 31 May/1 June Rear-Admiral King sent in the destroyers *Abdiel, Hotspur, Jackal* and *Kimberley* in a last attempt to evacuate at least some of the 6,000 troops assembled at Sfakia. By herculean efforts the destroyers lifted off 4,000 men before the onset of dawn brought an end to the operation; the destroyers then headed for Alexandria, and the A.A. cruisers *Calcutta* and *Coventry* were dispatched to meet them. These two warships, however, were located about 100 nautical miles north of Alexandria by two Ju 88s, which dive-bombed and sank the *Calcutta*; 255 survivors were rescued by the other cruiser.

The Royal Navy had succeeded in evacuating 17,000 troops from Crete, but 15,743 had been killed or captured. In addition, the Navy had lost 2,011 personnel. German casualties had not been light, either; the enemy had suffered 6,580 dead, wounded or missing.

The battle for Crete had cost the Royal Navy three cruisers and six destroyers; in addition, two battleships, an aircraft carrier, six cruisers and seven destroyers had sustained varying degrees of damage. It was exactly a year since the Royal Navy had suffered terrible losses at Dunkirk, and yet again the Royal Air Force came in for much criticism from both Navy and Army for its failure to provide fighter cover. At Dunkirk R.A.F. Fighter Command had done its best, but in the case of Crete there was simply nothing the R.A.F. fighters could have done. The handful of British aircraft – both R.A.F. and Fleet Air Arm – on the island at the start of the invasion were quickly destroyed, and it must be said that of six Hurricanes sent out from Egypt to provide cover for the evacuation, two were shot down by friendly naval fire. Once the Cretan airfields had been captured, the R.A.F. was powerless to intervene. Not only was it stretched to the utmost in North Africa, but Crete was beyond the combat radius of its existing single-engined fighters. If blame is to be apportioned for the Balkans fiasco – and its postscript, Crete – one must seek it in the realms of the political decisions of the time, a theme that is outside the scope of this book.

Hard on the heels of the evacuation of Crete came more crises, this time in the Middle East. An insurrection in Iraq, begun in April, was put down after several weeks by troops ferried from India, supported by warships of Vice-Admiral G. S. Arbuthnot's East Indies Squadron, deployed to Basra, and by the R.A.F., which assisted loyal Iraqis in containing the rebellion until the ground forces arrived. From 7 June to 14 July, Vice-Admiral King's 15th Cruiser Squadron was in action in the Eastern Mediterranean in support of the occupation of Vichy French Syria by Commonwealth and Free French forces. Several British warships sustained damage during this short but bitterly contested campaign, either by air attack or in engagements with Vichy French destroyers. The British blockade was effective, and Vichy supply vessels were prevented from landing at Beirut. One of them, the 2,778-ton *St Didier*, was sunk by Albacores of No. 829 Squadron off the coast of Anatolia. These operations – followed by others aimed at preventing a seizure of power by pro-Axis factions in Iran during August – secured the passage of Allied shipping through the Red Sea and also forestalled a potentially dangerous threat to Britain's oil supplies.

As we shall see in a later chapter, the Admiralty's main preoccupation in the Mediterranean theatre in 1941 was to sustain the island of Malta, which was entirely dependent on supplies brought in by sea. So, too, was the besieged garrison of Tobruk, isolated by the British retreat from Libya in April 1941. Night after night, when conditions were favourable, pairs of destroyers and other fast vessels made the dangerous 'Tobruk run', and by the time the siege was lifted on 8 December 1941 the Royal Navy had brought in 72 tanks, 92 guns, 34,000 tons of stores and 34,113 reinforcement troops. But the cost to the Navy was twenty-five warships, together with five merchant vessels. (*See* Appendix 1).

During the closing months of 1940, the British submarine offensive in the Mediterranean had been sustained mainly by the large P class and R class boats of the 1st Submarine Flotilla, based on Alexandria, but in January 1941 the 10th Submarine Flotilla was formed, based on Malta and equipped with small 630-ton U class boats which were better suited to operations in the shallow waters of the central basin. They began to make their mark in the summer, and between June and September 1941 they sank 49 troop transports and supply ships totalling 150,000 tons. One particularly successful sortie was carried out by H.M.S. _Upholder_ (Lt-Cdr M. D. Wanklyn), which on 18 September sank the Italian troop-carrying liners _Neptunia_ and _Oceania_, both of 19,500 tons.

It was the Axis powers, though, that had the last word in the Mediterranean battles of 1941. On 25 November, the battleship _Barham_, part of Admiral Cunningham's main fleet which had put to sea from Alexandria to search for an Italian convoy, was torpedoed by the U-331 and blew up with the loss of 861 men; there were 450 survivors. Then, on the night of 14/15 December, the U-557 sank the cruiser _Galatea_ off Alexandria, and four days later the cruiser _Neptune_ and the destroyer _Kandahar_ were sunk by mines, the former with the loss of all but one of her 550 crew.

To cap it all, as the British warships returned to Alexandria, three Italian human torpedo teams penetrated the harbour through the open boom. Launched from the submarine _Scire_ (Cdr Prince Borghese) the teams were Lt-Cdr Durand de la Penne and S.M. Bianchi; Capt. Marceglia and L/Cpl Schergat; and Capt. Martellotta with S.M. Marino. They succeeded in placing explosive charges under the battleships _Queen Elizabeth_ and _Valiant_ and the Norwegian tanker _Sagona_, all of which came to rest on the bottom, badly damaged. The destroyer _Jervis_, lying alongside the tanker, was also damaged. It was a most gallant action, and, with the loss of the _Barham_, it deprived Admiral Cunningham of the battle squadron which had kept the Italian fleet at bay for so long.

Worse still, this Axis triumph came hard on the heels of a succession of Allied naval disasters in the Far East, beginning with the Japanese attack on Pearl Harbor, base of the United States Pacific Fleet, on 7 December 1941; an event followed by a tragedy that had few parallels in the history of the Royal Navy.

CHAPTER NINE

Defeat in the Far East, 1942

Britain's decision to build a strong naval base in the Far East was taken in the early 1920s in the hope of ensuring that an increasingly powerful Japan would be deterred from threatening important British political and economic interests in South-East Asia, Australasia and India. The choice of Singapore was based on the backward-looking assumption that naval power would be the key; in other words, that a battle fleet based on Singapore would be sufficient to deter and if necessary repel attack.

In the two decades that followed, several strategic factors came to be appreciated. Firstly, it was unlikely that a large naval force could, in reality, be spared from elsewhere and get there in time; secondly, an attack was more likely to come overland from the north than a seaborne assault, which meant that the key to Singapore's defence lay in the defence of the Malayan approaches; and thirdly, any successful defence of Malaya and Singapore would be impossible without the presence of a substantial air force. All three factors were appreciated as early as 1937 by the military authorities on the spot, who were convinced that the best way for the Japanese to attack would be to use Indo-China as the base for landings in south Siam and north-east Malaya and then advance south.

The Admiralty's plan to reinforce the Indian Ocean theatre with warships drawn from the Mediterranean Fleet, leaving the French Navy to concentrate on the Mediterranean, was dislocated by the collapse of France in 1940. In August 1941, another Admiralty plan envisaged reinforcing the Far East with six capital ships, a modern aircraft carrier and supporting light forces by the spring of 1942; in the meantime, the best that could be done was to send out the new battleship *Prince of Wales*, supported by the old battlecruiser *Repulse* (she had been launched in 1916) and the aircraft carrier *Indomitable*, which was to provide the essential air component. Even this plan was disrupted when the *Indomitable* ran aground off Jamaica while she was working up there; it was another fortnight before she was ready to sail.

The *Prince of Wales*, meanwhile, flagship of Rear-Admiral Sir Tom Phillips, had sailed from the Clyde on 25 October accompanied by the destroyers *Electra* and *Express*, under orders to proceed to Singapore via Freetown, Simonstown and Ceylon, where they were joined on 28 November by the *Repulse* from the Atlantic and the destroyers *Encounter* and *Jupiter* from the Mediterranean. The force reached Singapore on 2 December.

The Admiralty had always been reluctant to concentrate its warships on Singapore, preferring to base them further back on Ceylon; the fact that they were there at all was at the insistence of Winston Churchill, whose view – supported by the Foreign Office – was that their presence would be enough to deter the Japanese from taking aggressive action. There were justifiable fears, in view of the *Indomitable*'s absence, of the force's vulnerability to enemy air attack. The RAF's air defences on Singapore and the Malay peninsula were woefully weak: about 80 American-built Brewster Buffalo fighters equipped four squadrons, two R.A.A.F., one R.A.F. and one R.N.Z.A.F. All four squadrons had been formed within the last eight months, many of their pilots were inexperienced, and their aircraft – heavy, underpowered and underarmed – were wholly outclassed by the Japanese fighters they would soon encounter.

Not long before Admiral Phillips took up his new command (he had been Vice-Chief of Naval Staff), a friend made a cautionary remark to him: 'Tom, you've never believed in air. Never get out from under the air umbrella; if you do, you'll be for it.' They were prophetic words, and the man who made them was Air Marshal Sir Arthur Harris, soon to be appointed A.O.C.-in-C. Bomber Command.

Anxiety over the exposed position of Phillips's ships led the Admiralty to urge him to take them away from Singapore, and on 5 December 1941 the *Repulse* (Capt. Tennant) sailed for Port Darwin in North Australia. The next day, however, a Japanese convoy was reported off Indo-China, and Tennant was ordered back to Singapore to rejoin the flagship. Only hours later came the news of the Japanese attack on the U.S. Pacific Fleet at Pearl Harbor, with simultaneous amphibious assaults elsewhere, including Malaya and Siam. On the evening of 8 December Admiral Phillips took the *Prince of Wales*, *Repulse* and four destroyers, collectively known as Force Z, to attack Japanese amphibious forces which had landed at Singora on the north-east coast of Malaya. Early the next morning, Singapore advised him that no fighter cover would be available and that strong Japanese bomber forces were reported to be assembling in Siam, and this, together with the knowledge that his warships had been sighted by enemy reconnaissance aircraft, persuaded Phillips to abandon his sortie at 20.15 on 9 December, reversing course for Singapore. (In fact Force Z had also been sighted by the submarine I-65, but the position it transmitted was inaccurate, and other enemy submarines failed to detect the ships at this time.)

Just before midnight, Phillips received a signal that the Japanese were landing at Kuantan and he turned towards the coast, intending to intercept this new invasion force. The report was false, but in the early hours of 10 December Force Z was sighted by the submarine I-58 (Lt-Cdr Kitamura). He made an unsuccessful torpedo attack, then shadowed the British ships for five and a half hours, sending regular position reports that enabled reconnaissance aircraft of the 22nd Naval Air Flotilla to sight them and maintain contact. Already airborne from airfields in Indo-China were 27 bombers and 61 torpedo aircraft, the flotilla's attack element, flying steadily south. They passed to the east of Force Z and flew on for a considerable distance before turning, and at about 11.00 they sighted the ships.

The air attacks were executed with great skill and coordination, the high-level bombers – Mitsubishi G4M1 *Bettys* – running in at 12,000 feet to distract the attention of the warships' A.A. gunners while the torpedo-bombers, G3M2 *Nells*, initiated their torpedo runs from different directions. Two torpedo hits were quickly registered on the *Prince of Wales*, severely damaging her propellers and steering-gear and putting many of her A.A. guns out of action. For some time the *Repulse*, by skilful evasive action, managed to avoid the attackers; but there were too many aircraft, and eventually she was hit by four torpedoes. At 12.33, she rolled over and sank, and 50 minutes later the same fate overtook the flagship which had meanwhile sustained two more torpedo hits. The accompanying destroyers picked up 2,081 officers and men; 840 were lost, among them Admiral Phillips and Captain Leach of the *Prince of Wales*. Captain Tennant of the *Repulse* survived, having been literally pushed off the bridge by his officers at the last moment.

A mystery still hangs over the loss of the two ships: it is the failure of Admiral Phillips to break radio silence and call for help even when he knew his vessels had been sighted by the enemy. It was only an hour and a half later, when the ships had been under air attack for three-quarters of an hour, that a signal was sent to inform Singapore what was happening, and even then it was Captain Tennant, not Phillips, who sent it. Eleven Buffaloes of No. 453 Squadron R.A.A.F. were immediately dispatched and arrived in the area 90 minutes later, long after the Japanese had departed. Had a signal been sent when the ships were first spotted the squadron would have been there by the time the first torpedo attack was developing; as the bombers were heavily laden and unescorted, the Buffaloes could certainly have caused them serious problems, but their combat time would have been very limited and it is too optimistic to think that they might have averted the disaster – although their disruption of the air attacks might have reduced the number of torpedo hits and prevented one or both of the ships from going down. But that is conjecture, as indeed is speculation on what might have happened if the carrier *Indomitable* had accompanied Force Z. One can only surmise that her thirty-odd fighters might have forced a very different outcome of that tragic day. But *Indomitable* had only got as far as Cape Town when the Japanese struck their crippling blow; she was afterwards dispatched to Aden, to pick up Hurricanes destined for the defence of Singapore. (In the event, the collapse in Malaya occurred so rapidly that the aircraft were diverted to Java).

After the naval disaster off Malaya, with its incalculable consequences for the morale of the defenders of the peninsula and Singapore, came the news on Christmas Day that Hong Kong had also fallen, with the loss to the Royal Navy of the destroyer *Thracian*, a minelayer, four gunboats and eight M.T.B.s. Meanwhile, command of the British Eastern Fleet had been assumed by Admiral Sir Geoffrey Layton – or rather reassumed, for he had just handed it over to the unfortunate Admiral Phillips. It was a command with precious few ships, and a new Allied naval command, A.B.D.A. (American, British, Dutch, Australian) set up on Java in January 1942 under Admiral T. C. Hart, U.S.N., was scarcely in better shape. For five weeks in January and early February, Hart's motley collection of warships – mostly British and Dutch – were employed in escorting troop convoys to Singapore, but by the end of January the Singapore naval base was so badly damaged that it could barely function. What had become the barest trickle of reinforcements was finally stopped after the Japanese gained a foothold on Singapore island on 9 February 1942, and on the 12th, three days before the Singapore garrison surrendered, there was a mass exodus of every seaworthy vessel from the base, laden with civilian and military personnel.

On 13 February a Japanese invasion force was reported to be heading for Sumatra and the A.B.D.A. Command dispatched a naval force of five cruisers and ten destroyers (including the British cruiser *Exeter*) to intercept it. However, the Allied ships were heavily attacked from the air, and although none was lost to air attack the force commander, the Dutch Admiral Karel Doorman, decided to call off the operation and withdraw.

The enemy blows now fell thick and fast. On 18 February Japanese forces landed on the island of Bali, isolating Java from the east, and on the following day aircraft of their main striking force, the 1st Carrier Air Fleet, launched a devastating attack on Port Darwin, sinking eleven transports and supply ships and causing severe damage to the port installations. As Darwin was the only base in north Australia from which Java could be reinforced and supplied, this attack effectively sealed the fate of the defenders.

On 27 February, Admiral Doorman, who had meanwhile been in action against the Japanese in the Bandoeng Strait with a mixed force of Dutch and American warships, sailed from Soerabaya with five cruisers (including the *Exeter*) and nine destroyers (including the *Electra*, *Encounter* and *Jupiter*) to intercept Japanese invasion forces in the Java Sea. The Japanese force was escorted by four cruisers and 14 destroyers, and at 16.00 the opposing cruisers began an exchange of gunfire. Shortly afterwards the *Exeter* was hit by a heavy shell and compelled to withdraw to Soerabaya escorted by the Dutch destroyer *Witte de With*; another Dutch destroyer, the *Kortenaer*, was sunk by a torpedo. Of the 120 torpedoes launched by enemy destroyers during this phase of the battle, it was the only one that found a target. To cover the *Exeter's* withdrawal the three British destroyers became engaged in a short-range action with eight enemy destroyers accompanying the cruiser *Naka*, and in a confused battle in poor visibility, caused by dense smoke screens, the *Electra* was sunk.

Admiral Doorman then reformed his force with four cruisers and six destroyers and made a sortie to the north-west, where his ships fought a brief action in the dark with the cruisers *Haguro* and *Nachi*. Soon after this, the British destroyer *Jupiter* blew up – either as the result of striking a Dutch mine, or because she was torpedoed in error by the American submarine S38. The Allied force suffered further losses during the night when the Dutch cruisers *Java* and *De Ruyter* were sunk by torpedoes; the two remaining cruisers, the U.S.S. *Houston* and H.M.A.S. *Perth*, headed for Batavia in a bid to escape from the trap that was rapidly closing on them. The four American destroyers, meanwhile, had returned to

Soerabaya to rearm and refuel, while the sole remaining British destroyer, the *Encounter*, had been despatched to pick up survivors from the *Kortenaer*.

Early in the morning of 28 February, the four U.S. destroyers passed through the Bali Strait bound for Australia, which they reached after a short and indecisive engagement with three Japanese warships. In the afternoon, the cruisers *Houston* and *Perth*, followed by the Dutch destroyer *Evertsen*, sailed from Batavia and headed into the Sunda Straits, making for Tjilatjap. During the night the two cruisers encountered another enemy invasion force and attacked it, braving formidable odds. Both cruisers were sunk by the covering force, but not before they had destroyed two transports and damaged three destroyers and a minesweeper. The *Evertsen*, coming up behind, was shelled and set on fire; her crew managed to beach her.

H.M.S. *Exeter*, meanwhile, had sailed from Soerabaya at dusk, also heading for the Sunda Strait, accompanied by the destroyers H.M.S. *Encounter* and U.S.S. *Pope*. On the morning of 1 March, trapped between two enemy forces, *Exeter* and *Encounter* were sunk by a combination of gunfire and torpedoes; the *Pope* was disabled by dive-bombers from the Japanese carrier *Ryujo* and subsequently sunk by shellfire. Some 800 survivors from the three ships were picked up by the Japanese, many to die miserably in captivity.

So ended the Battle of the Java Sea, and with it any hope of contesting the Japanese invasion of South-East Asia. The Royal Navy's assets in the theatre were effectively reduced to the old light cruisers *Danae* and *Dragon* and the destroyers *Scout* and *Tenedos*, which, accompanied by the Australian cruiser H.M.A.S. *Hobart*, had set out from the Sunda Strait for Colombo on 28 February, picking up refugees *en route*. Another British destroyer, H.M.S. *Stronghold*, was sunk by enemy warships on 2 March during the withdrawal from Java, together with H.M.A.S. *Yarra*.

In the spring of 1942, while the victorious Japanese consolidated their lightning conquests in South-East Asia and the Pacific, the British Admiralty focused its attention on constructing a new Eastern Fleet to operate from Ceylon, the base the Admiralty had recommended in the first place. By the end of March the new Eastern Fleet comprised: two large aircraft carriers, the *Indomitable* and *Formidable*, the latter operational once more after a ten-month break following the damage she had sustained off Crete in May 1941, and a small one, the *Hermes*; five battleships, the *Ramillies*, *Resolution*, *Revenge*, *Royal Sovereign* and *Warspite*, all of First World War vintage; seven cruisers, sixteen destroyers and seven submarines. The Fleet was commanded, from 27 March, by Admiral Sir James Somerville, the able and experienced former commander of Gibraltar's Force H.

Somerville faced an immediate crisis. On 4 April, a Catalina flying boat sighted a Japanese task force approaching Ceylon from the south and radioed its position minutes before it was shot down. The enemy force was Admiral Nagumo's 1st Carrier Striking Force, comprising the aircraft carriers *Akagi*, *Hiryu*, *Shokaku*, *Soryu* and *Zuikaku* – the ships whose aircraft had wrought such havoc on Pearl Harbor and Port Darwin – accompanied by four battleships, three cruisers and nine destroyers. Between them, the five carriers mustered some 300 strike aircraft and fighters; Admiral Somerville's air assets consisted of 57 strike aircraft and 40 fighters on his carriers, with the Fulmars of Nos. 803 and 806 Squadrons based ashore at Ratmalana. There were also 50-odd R.A.F. Hurricanes delivered by *Indomitable* on a second ferry run to the Indian Ocean.

The Japanese intention was clearly to destroy the Eastern Fleet. For the British this was a most dangerous move; for all they knew, the Japanese might try to seize the island, from where not only India but also the ocean supply routes to the Middle East could be threatened. This was at a time when all supplies had to be routed around the Cape; Rommel was driving the Eighth Army back towards Egypt, and a new German offensive was building in Russia. The possibility of a Germany–Japan link-up in the Middle East seems far-fetched with hindsight, but it was of very real concern to Churchill and his colleagues. Later, he was to call it the most dangerous moment of the war.

As soon as the news of the approaching

Japanese task force was received, Admiral Layton ordered every ship that could do so to sail from Colombo harbour. The cruisers *Cornwall* and *Dorsetshire*, which had been detached earlier on Somerville's instructions, were also ordered to rejoin Force A, the fast group of the Eastern Fleet which included the aircraft carriers and the *Warspite*.

Early on 5 April – Easter Sunday – the Japanese fleet was sighted by a second Catalina. Soon afterwards, the Japanese launched a strike of 53 Nakajima B5N *Kate* high-level bombers and 38 Aichi D3A *Val* dive-bombers, escorted by 36 Zero fighters, to attack Colombo. Fierce air battles developed over the city and harbour as the raiding force was intercepted by 42 Hurricanes and Fulmars; seven Japanese aircraft were destroyed, but 19 British fighters were shot down. The Zeros also pounced on a luckless formation of six 814 Squadron Swordfish, on their way from Trincomalee to Minneriya, and shot them all out of the sky. The attack caused heavy damage to built-up areas; the damage to shipping and the port installations was relatively light, although the auxiliary cruiser *Hector* and the destroyer *Tenedos* were sunk.

R.N.A.S. Katakarunda, Ceylon, was an important base for Fleet Air Arm operations in the Indian Ocean

Airfield defence: Royal Marines manning an anti-aircraft gun in Ceylon

Fairey Swordfish of No. 756 Squadron, Katakarunda, Ceylon

Fairey Albacores running up at R.N.A.S. Katakarunda, Ceylon

At about noon, the cruisers _Cornwall_ and _Dorsetshire_ were sighted by a reconnaissance aircraft from the heavy cruiser _Tone_ and 53 _Val_ dive-bombers were immediately sent out to attack them. The bombing was devastatingly accurate and both ships were sunk, 1,112 men (of a total of 1,546) being rescued later by the cruiser H.M.S. _Enterprise_ and two destroyers. Albacores from the _Indomitable_ later made a night radar search for the enemy force, but it had withdrawn to the southeast to refuel before heading back north to strike at Trincomalee naval base. At this time Admiral Somerville's Force A was steaming towards Ceylon from Addu Atoll, with his slow division (Force B) a long way behind; his ships were at times only 200 nautical miles from Nagumo's task force, but neither side made contact with the other. Addu Atoll had been set up as the Eastern Fleet's secret base, and Somerville, unable to locate the enemy, turned back towards it to safeguard it against a possible surprise attack.

On 8 April a Catalina once again established contact with the Japanese carrier force 400 nautical miles to the east of Ceylon and the ships at Trincomalee were ordered to put to sea. All units – including the light carrier _Hermes_ – were able to get clear before the expected attack by 91 high-level bombers and dive-bombers, escorted by 38 fighters, developed early on the 9th. Of the 23 Hurricane and Fulmar fighters sent up to defend the harbour, nine were shot down, as were five out of a formation of nine Blenheim bombers sent out to try to locate the enemy force.

Only light damage was inflicted on the target, but on the way back to their ships the Japanese aircrews sighted several ships, including the

Hermes, the Australian destroyer *Vampire*, the corvette *Hollyhock* and two tankers. Three hours later, 80 dive bombers arrived on the scene and sank all three warships and the tankers about 65 miles from Trincomalee. The *Hermes*, which had no aircraft on board, radioed desperately for help, but the surviving fighters at Trincomalee were in no position to offer it.

Meanwhile, part of Nagumo's force – a light carrier and six cruisers under Admiral Ozawa – had been detached to operate against shipping in the Bay of Bengal. In a five-day spree beginning on 7 April Ozawa destroyed 23 merchant ships totalling 112,312 tons, to which Japanese submarines operating off the west coast of India added a further 32,400 tons.

Fortunately perhaps for the Eastern Fleet (whose Force A deployed to Bombay immediately after the attacks on Ceylon, Force B deploying to East Africa to protect the convoy route) a Japanese task force never again made an appearance in the Indian Ocean.

Instead, Admiral Nagumo withdrew to the Pacific in readiness for the next big venture: the occupation of Midway Island. In the event it proved to be a costly exercise, for during the

Battle of Midway on 4–7 June 1942 the carriers *Akagi*, *Kaga*, *Hiryu* and *Soryu* were all sunk by U.S. naval aircraft.

Meanwhile, in May, H.M.S. *Indomitable* had been detached from the Eastern Fleet to join *Illustrious* in attacks on the Vichy French held island of Madagascar, leaving the *Formidable* as the only carrier under Somerville's command. The following August, however, *Formidable* also had to be redeployed to replace the *Indomitable* after the latter was badly damaged in the Mediterranean, which left *Illustrious* as the only carrier in the Indian Ocean. As well as providing air cover for the campaign in Madagascar (Operation *Ironclad*, which was also supported by the battleship *Ramillies*, the cruiser *Hermione* and a number of destroyers and submarines) she also made a few anti-submarine sweeps in the Indian Ocean from her base at Mombasa before rejoining the Home Fleet in January 1943.

By that time, events in the Mediterranean and North Africa had become the focus of attention, and had taken a dramatic turn in the Allies' favour.

British warships at Aden, 1943

CHAPTER TEN

The Battle of Malta's Lifelines, 1941–42

The key to British control of the Mediterranean, and therefore the Middle East, was the strategically placed island of Malta. On 10 June 1940, the day Italy declared war on the Allies, the island's air defences comprised only five Fairey Swordfish of the Fleet Air Arm, used mainly for anti-aircraft cooperation, and three Gloster Sea Gladiators, hastily assembled from crated components, with a fourth held in reserve.

The Italians carried out seven major air raids on Malta in the first ten days of the war and the Sea Gladiators (immortalised in the popular Press by the names *Faith*, *Hope* and *Charity*) scored their first success on 22 June, when Sqn Ldr G. Burges shot down a lone S.M.79 reconnaissance aircraft. The Gladiators destroyed two more enemy aircraft in the following week, and on 28 June, by which time only two of the biplanes were still airworthy, four Hurricanes were flown in from North Africa. Twelve more reinforcement Hurricanes were flown to the island from the carrier H.M.S. *Argus* on 4 August under cover of diversionary operations by Force H, and a complete Hurricane squadron, No. 261, was soon operational. In addition, a small striking force gradually built up on the Maltese airfields; this consisted of the Swordfish of No. 830 Squadron, F.A.A., detachments of Wellington bombers from R.A.F. squadrons in the Canal Zone, and detachments of two Sunderland squadrons, Nos 228 and 230. A similar operation by the *Argus* in mid-November, however, was less successful; twelve Hurricanes and two Skuas were flown off, but they encountered strong unforecast head winds and only four Hurricanes and one Skua reached Malta.

Although Malta was kept supplied in late 1940 by convoys from Alexandria, heavily escorted by the Mediterranean Fleet, providing adequate fighter reinforcements presented an ongoing

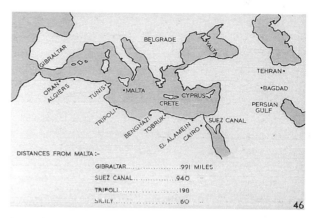

Map showing distances to Malta from key points in the Mediterranean

problem, as these had to make the long and dangerous passage from Gibraltar. On 10 January 1941, as we have already seen, the newly arrived *Luftwaffe* dive-bombers based on Sicily joined with the *Regia Aeronautica* to inflict substantial damage on a Malta-bound convoy, including the aircraft carrier *Illustrious*. After that, no further supplies reached the island – which was under almost continual air attack – until the last week in March, when a small convoy of four ships was sent through from Alexandria. Even then, two of the ships and their precious stores were damaged by bombs while unloading.

The situation was critical, and was only saved by the transfer of *Luftwaffe* units from Sicily to support the German invasion of Russia in June 1941, leaving the Italians to conduct the Malta air offensive alone. On 2 April, in an operation codenamed *Winch*, the carrier *Ark Royal*, with a strong Force H escort, set out from Gibraltar carrying twelve Hurricanes and three Skuas; these were flown off at a distance of 400 nautical miles from Malta, and all arrived safely. On 28 April twenty more Hurricanes, ferried from the U.K. by the *Argus* and transferred to the *Ark Royal* at Gibraltar, were also flown off to Malta, together with three Fulmars (Operation *Dunlop*).

The scene now briefly shifted to Egypt, where the Eighth Army, under heavy pressure from General Erwin Rommel's *Deutsches Afrika Korps*, was in urgent need of reinforcements, with particular regard to tanks and fighter aircraft. Between 5 May and 12 May 1941, therefore, Force H and the Mediterranean Fleet mounted a joint operation, code-named *Tiger*, to push a convoy of five fast merchantmen carrying the necessary equipment through the Mediterranean from Gibraltar to Alexandria. At the same time, the battleship *Queen Elizabeth* and two light cruisers from U.K. waters were being sent out to join Admiral Cunningham's fleet. The convoy passed Gibraltar on 6 May and was escorted by Force H to a point south of Malta, where it was covered by destroyers and cruisers from the island base until it could be met by a strong force sent out from Alexandra. Several German and Italian air attacks *en route* were broken up by Fulmars from the *Ark Royal* and *Formidable* and the ships suffered no loss from this quarter, although one of the transports, the *Empire Song*, was sunk by

---

H.M.S. Furious, *the carrier that took part in several operations to fly desperately needed Spitfires to Malta. A converted light battlecruiser of 1916 vintage, she served in the Home Fleet until 1944, when she passed to the Reserve*

mines on 9 May. The remainder reached Alexandria, carrying the surviving 238 tanks and 43 Hurricanes.

Admiral Somerville's Force H had scarcely returned to Gibraltar when, on 21 May, it was required to undertake Operation *Splice*, involving the flying-off of 48 more Malta-bound Hurricanes from the carriers *Ark Royal* and *Furious*. All these aircraft arrived safely, providing a much-needed boost for the island's air defences. This was followed, on 6 June, by Operation *Rocket*, in which the same two carriers flew off another 35 Hurricanes, led by Blenheim bombers from Gibraltar, and on 14 June by Operation *Tracer*, in which *Ark Royal* and *Victorious* launched 47 more Hurricanes from a point south of the Balearics, led on this occasion by four Hudsons. Four of this latter batch failed to reach Malta. Finally, on 26 June, came the week-long Operation *Railway*, in which *Ark Royal* flew off another 22 Hurricanes and returned to the flying-off position three days later to launch 26 more. The carrier *Furious* also took part in this operation, intending to fly off nine Hurricanes, but because of a take-off accident she only launched one. Some of the Hurricanes involved in these operations stayed only a short time on Malta before going on to the Middle East, but enough remained on the island to keep three squadrons (Nos 126, 185 and 261) up to reasonable strength.

Because the British naval forces in the eastern Mediterranean were heavily committed to opera-

tions in the Levant in June and July 1941, the Admiralty decided to take a considerable risk and run a convoy of six supply ships and one troop transport through to Malta from the west, covered by Force H and supported by warships detached from the Home Fleet. The operation was named *Substance*. The convoy left the Clyde on 11 July and reached Gibraltar safely, but when the eastward movement started on the 21st the troopship *Leinster* – carrying replacement R.A.F. ground crews for Malta – went aground and had to be left behind. On 23 July the ships were attacked by Italian aircraft, which secured hits on the cruiser *Manchester* and the destroyer *Fearless*, which had to be abandoned. The destroyer *Firedrake* also received a bomb hit and had to return to Gibraltar. Further losses were averted by the spirited action of *Ark Royal*'s Fulmars. The convoy reached Malta on the following day to discharge its precious supplies, the merchantmen making their way back independently to Gibraltar. One of them, the *Hoegh Hood*, was hit by a torpedo south of Sardinia, but survived. The R.A.F. personnel, and troops which had been on the *Leinster* – some 1,800 men in all – were later ferried to the island by fast warships.

On the night of 25/26 July, the Italian 10th M.T.B. Flotilla made a gallant attempt to penetrate Grand Harbour and attack the merchantmen while they were still unloading. The frigate *Diana*, with eight explosive boats and two M.T.B.s carrying human torpedo teams, reached Malta, but their approach had been detected by radar and the defences were alerted. One human torpedo team and two explosive boats wrecked the harbour boom but this was to the defenders' advantage, because the explosion caused the St Elmo bridge to collapse and barred the way to the other six explosive boats, which were then destroyed by shore batteries. The two M.T.B.s were also sunk the next morning by fighter-bombers.

Between 8 September and 14 September the *Ark Royal* and *Furious* flew off a further 55 Hurricanes to Malta (Operation *Status*), and on the 24th the Admiralty mounted a large resupply operation code-named *Halberd*. This involved the passage to Malta of nine large merchantmen,

laden with the most urgently needed supplies and escorted by Force H, heavily reinforced by warships of the Home Fleet, while Admiral Cunningham staged a diversion in the eastern Mediterranean. The Italian main battle fleet put to sea, together with a strong force of submarines, but air reconnaissance had greatly under-estimated the strength of the British force and the Italian surface vessels made no attempt to attack. On the evening of 27 September, when the convoy reached the narrows between Sicily and Tunisia, Force H turned back and the convoy sailed on to Malta escorted by five cruisers and nine destroyers, losing one transport to an aerial torpedo attack. The remainder reached the island safely, bringing the total of merchantmen getting through to Malta since the beginning of the year to 39. The Royal Navy suffered one casualty in this operation; the battleship *Nelson* was torpedoed by an Italian aircraft south of Sardinia, but reached Gibraltar without further incident.

With the *Luftwaffe* still occupied in Russia, the naval war in the Mediterranean, despite strong opposition by the *Regia Aeronautica*, seemed to have turned firmly in Britain's favour, and the Admiralty decided to exploit the situation by basing a small force of cruisers and destroyers (Force K) on Malta. They arrived on 21 October and were soon in action; on 9 November, in a brilliantly executed night attack, they sank all seven merchant ships in a heavily defended Italian convoy, and later in the month they sent two Africa-bound tankers to the bottom. Malta's striking force had been further augmented in October with the arrival of eleven Albacore and two Swordfish torpedo-bombers, so that Axis convoy losses began to climb steadily.

On 13 November, however, Force H suffered a major setback. Three days earlier, the carriers *Ark Royal* and *Argus* had set out from Gibraltar to a flying-off point 450 miles from Malta, and on the 12th they launched 37 Hurricanes, of which 34 reached the island together with seven Blenheim bombers. As the carriers made their homeward run, the *Ark Royal* was hit by a torpedo, one of a salvo of four fired by the German submarine U-81, near her starboard boiler room. Only one crew member lost his life in the attack and valiant efforts were made to save the carrier, but she sank under tow only 25 miles from Gibraltar.

By late November 1941, the supply situation of the Axis forces in North Africa, thanks to the attacks on their convoys by the Malta-based warships, submarines and strike aircraft, was fast becoming critical. In an attempt to redress matters, the Germans heavily reinforced their U-boat fleet in the Mediterranean. At the same time, they also ordered the *Luftwaffe* back to Sicily: not *Fliegerkorps* X this time (it had been deployed to Norway for operations against the Arctic convoys), but *Fliegerkorps* II, mostly equipped with Ju 88s and with substantial fighter support, the latter including Z.G. 26 (Me 110s) and J.G. 53 (Me 109s), both highly experienced units.

Malta resupply operations during the early weeks of 1942 were carried out from Alexandria using fast merchant vessels under heavy naval escort and also large minelaying submarines. By this time, Admiral Cunningham's forces were so overstretched because of the losses of 1941 he could not hope to fulfil all his commitments in the Mediterranean, and the Italian Navy was once again in a position to push through supply convoys to the Axis forces in North Africa, enabling Rommel to take the offensive. And what lay in store for the British convoys bound for Malta was demonstrated in mid-February, when German bombers attacked three transports heading for the island from Alexandria, sinking two and damaging the other so badly that she had to put into Tobruk, with the result that Malta obtained no relief at all.

Another attempt to run a supply convoy – this time of four transports – through to Malta was made on 20 March, when the ships left Alexandria protected by four light cruisers and sixteen destroyers under the command of Rear-Admiral Vian. The convoy's passage was detected by two Italian submarines and a strong Italian surface force, comprising the battleship *Littorio*, three cruisers and ten destroyers, sailed from Taranto and Messina on the 22nd to intercept it. The Italian warships were sighted at 14.27 by the cruiser *Euryalus* and Vian ordered his ships to deploy in six divisions according to a pre-arranged plan, some to attack the enemy with tor-pedoes, others to lay a smokescreen to windward of the convoy, and others to protect the merchantmen from air attack. *Euryalus*, together with Vian's flagship, the *Cleopatra*, engaged in a long-range gun duel with the Italian cruisers, which turned away. Vian's ships now rejoined the convoy, which by this time was coming under heavy air attack. Soon afterwards the *Littorio* put in an appearance, accompanied by the cruisers, but they were kept at bay by four destroyers, which made a series of gallant torpedo attacks until the *Cleopatra* and *Euryalus* came up to their assistance. In the confused, high-speed action that followed in heavy seas, the destroyers *Havock* and *Kingston* were badly damaged, but the convoy remained unharmed thanks to Vian's skilful use of smoke and resumed its course for Malta. The Italians broke off their attacks at about 19.00 as darkness began to fall, the weather now being stormy; on their passage home almost all the ships, British and Italian alike, suffered varying degrees of storm damage and two Italian destroyers, the *Lanciere* and *Scirocco*, foundered during the night.

So ended the action that became known as the Second Battle of Sirte. There is a sad postscript to it. Because of the combined effects of the battle and the storm, the convoy did not reach Malta until after daybreak on 23 March. The bombers of *Fliegerkorps* II pounced. The transport *Clan Campbell* was sunk with 20 miles to run; the *Breconshire*, heroine of previous Malta runs, was so badly damaged that she had to be beached, a total loss; and the two merchantmen that did reach harbour, the *Pampas* and *Talabot*, were both sunk on 26 March. Of the 29,500 tons of cargo carried by the four vessels, only 5,000 tons were brought ashore.

At this time, the attentions of *Fliegerkorps* II were concentrated on Malta's airfields, of which only Luqa remained serviceable, and the fighter defences themselves were suffering severely from attrition. On 7 March, by which time they had been reduced to 30 Hurricanes, they received a welcome boost with the arrival of 15 Spitfires, the first of their kind to reach the island, flown off the carriers *Eagle* and *Argus* south of the Balearics (Operation *Spotter*). On 21 March and 29 March, in Operations *Picket I* and *Picket II*, the *Eagle* flew off nine and seven more Spitfires respectively, all of which arrived safely.

The loss of the *Ark Royal*, with her greater capacity, was keenly felt, but on 20 April it was temporarily made good by the arrival in the Mediterranean of the American carrier U.S.S. *Wasp*, which launched 47 Spitfires to Malta. All but one arrived safely, but most were destroyed or made unserviceable by air attacks within the next 48 hours. This operation, named *Calendar*, was followed on 9 May by *Bowery*, in which the *Wasp* and *Eagle* between them flew off another 64 Spitfires, sixty of which reached Malta.

In May, June and July, following the *Wasp's* departure, it was the *Eagle* that bore the brunt of Malta's air reinforcement. Except for one occasion on 18 May, when she and *Argus* flew off 17 Spitfires in Operation *L.B.*, she single-handedly launched 125 Spitfires to Malta in Operations *Style* (3 June), *Salient* (9 June), *Pinpoint* (16 July) and *Insect* (21 July). Of these, 118 arrived.

The fighter reinforcements flown to Malta in June brought the island's air defences up to numerical strength, but the supply situation was desperate. In the middle of the month, therefore, two convoys sailed to Malta's relief: one from Alexandria, Port Said and Haifa, code-named *Vigorous* and consisting of eleven transports, escorted by units of the Mediterranean Fleet; and *Harpoon* from Gibraltar, shepherded as usual by Force H, again strengthened by warships of the Home Fleet. Air cover for *Harpoon* was provided by the *Eagle* and *Argus*, the former with 16 Sea Hurricanes of No. 801 Squadron and the latter with half a dozen Fulmars. The *Vigorous* convoy, on the other hand, had no carrier and consequently no air support.

Harpoon entered the Mediterranean on 12 June and was detected by enemy reconnaissance aircraft south of the Balearics later that day, but it was not until the 14th that it was located by Italian S.M.79 torpedo-bombers. They sank one transport, the *Tanimbar*, and scored a hit on the cruiser *Liverpool*, which had to be towed back to Gibraltar. Further air attacks were unsuccessful; the Sea Hurricanes and Fulmars put up an effective defence and claimed the destruction of six

The Sea Hurricane, one of which is seen here after coming to grief on a slippery carrier deck, peformed valuable serice on the Malta convoys of 1942

Italian aircraft during the day. On 15 June the western convoy was attacked by cruisers and destroyers of the Italian 7th Naval Division from Palermo, which sank the destroyer *Bedouin* and badly damaged the *Partridge*. The Italians were beaten off by the convoy's remaining seven escorting destroyers, but more heavy air attacks developed while these were engaged. The freighters *Burdwan* and *Chant* and the tanker *Kentucky* were so badly damaged that they had to be abandoned. The two surviving freighters reached Malta, but the escort suffered more casualties when it ran into a minefield, losing one destroyer (the Polish *Kujawiak*), with three more damaged.

The *Vigorous* convoy from Port Said and Haifa, which was the main one and was designated Convoy MW11, had also sailed on 12 June, to be joined by its escort and covering force of eight cruisers, 26 destroyers, four corvettes and two minesweepers under Admiral Vian. Thirteen British submarines were also stationed off Taranto and south of the Straits of Messina. The convoy was detected almost immediately by air reconnaissance and attacked south of Crete by the Ju 87s of I/K.G. 54; the transport *City of Calcutta* was damaged and had to put into Tobruk. Another freighter, the *Aagterkerk*, also had to divert to Tobruk on 14 June because of engine trouble, but was sunk a few miles short of the harbour by enemy bombers; the escorting corvette *Primula* was damaged. In the afternoon, Ju 88s of L.G. 1 from Crete attacked the main eastern convoy, sinking the freighter *Bhutan* and damaging another, the *Potaro*, and in attacks by the German 3rd S-boat Flotilla from Derna that evening the cruiser *Newcastle* was torpedoed by the S56 and the destroyer *Hasty* sunk by the S55.

Soon afterwards, Rear-Admiral Vian learned that the main Italian Fleet had put to sea in strength from Taranto and was steaming south, its forces including the battleships *Littorio* and *Vittorio Veneto*, two heavy cruisers, two light cruisers and twelve destroyers. The fleet was attacked during the night by torpedo bombers from Malta; a Beaufort of No. 217 Squadron torpedoed the cruiser *Trento*, which was later sunk by the submarine *Umbra*. After daybreak on 15 June, B-24 Liberator bombers of No. 160 Squadron, based at Aqir in Palestine, also took part in the attacks and one scored a bomb hit on the *Littorio*, but did her little damage.

In the afternoon of 15 June the eastern convoy was heavily attacked by the Ju 87s of St.G. 3, which sank the cruiser *Birmingham* and the destroyer *Airdale* and damaged another destroyer, the *Nestor*, so badly that she sank the next day. Faced with these losses, and with the Italian Fleet apparently still steering a course to intercept, Admiral Vian decided to abandon the operation and make for Alexandria. The Italian Fleet also turned away, and as it was heading for Taranto a Wellington of No. 38 Squadron from Malta (Plt Off. O. L. Hawes) got a torpedo hit on the *Littorio*, again without inflicting serious damage.

The two merchantmen of the western convoy that had got through to Malta carried enough supplies to bring the island a breathing space, but it was short-lived. By the beginning of August the situation on Malta was once again critical. On the 10th, the Admiralty mounted Operation *Pedestal* which was virtually a desperate, do-or-die attempt to relieve the island. On that day, thirteen freighters and the tanker *Ohio* passed into the Mediterranean *en route* for Malta. To support the convoy, every available warship had been assem-

bled; the escort and covering force included the carriers *Victorious*, *Indomitable* and *Eagle*, the battleships *Nelson* and *Rodney*, seven cruisers (three anti-aircraft) and 25 destroyers. The convoy also included the old carrier *Furious*, which was to accompany the main body to a point 150 miles west of Malta and fly off 38 badly needed Spitfires (Operation *Bellows*).

The convoy was sailing into the teeth of formidable odds. On airfields in Sardinia and Italy, the Germans and Italians had massed nearly 800 aircraft. Across the convoy's route, between Gibraltar and the Narrows, nineteen enemy submarines were lying in wait. In the Sicilian Channel, a force of cruisers, destroyers and M.T.B.s was lurking, ready to attack under cover of darkness after the main escort had turned away.

The first day passed fairly quietly. On the carriers, the fighter pilots remained at readiness and the crews of the torpedo aircraft helped to man the ships' guns. Early on 11 August, however, the first Ju 88 reconnaissance aircraft appeared and circled the convoy at a respectful distance. The *Indomitable* sent up two flights of Sea Hurricanes of Nos 800 and 880 Squadrons to try to intercept the shadowers, but the Ju 88s easily outpaced their pursuers. Then, at 13.16, a series of explosions reverberated through the convoy. For a few moments nobody knew quite what had happened; then the *Eagle* was seen to be listing and shrouded in smoke. She had been hit by four torpedoes from the submarine U-73 (*Kapitänleutnant* Rosenbaum). The other ships of the escort immediately increased speed and began to take evasive action, depth-charging at random. Just eight minutes later the *Eagle* had gone, taking 160 of her crew to the bottom with her; 759 were rescued, and four Sea Hurricanes of No. 801 Squadron which had been on patrol landed on the fleet carriers.

The loss of the old carrier was a bitter blow; during her time in the Mediterranean she had dispatched 185 fighters to Malta, quietly and without the publicity that had attended some of the other carrier reinforcement operations. She had become synonymous with the island's survival.

Minutes after the *Eagle* had sunk, the white track of a torpedo crossed the bow of the *Victorious*. As the convoy continued to take evasive action, a submarine was sighted and the escorts raced off to unload their depth-charges on it, but without any visible result. In all, six submarine sightings were reported in the hours that followed.

Shortly before sunset the *Furious* flew off her Spitfires and turned back towards Gibraltar, her mission completed, escorted by five reserve destroyers. The Italian submarine *Dagabur* attempted to attack her, but was rammed and sunk by the destroyer *Wolverine*. Another submarine, the *Giada*, was bombed and damaged by a Gibraltar-based Sunderland. The *Furious* was to undertake two more fighter reinforcement missions before Malta was relieved: *Baritone* on 17 August (32 aircraft) and *Train* on 24 October (31 aircraft).

Soon after *Furious* had flown off her aircraft, as dusk was beginning to spread over the sea, the convoy was subjected to its first air attack; 36 Ju 88s and He 111s dropped their bombs and escaped before the defending fighters could engage them – except for three which were shot down by A.A. fire. None of the ships was hit, but one of the Hurricanes from *Indomitable* caused something of a drama when, out of fuel, its pilot tried to land on the *Victorious* while the carrier was still turning and out of wind. The fighter collided with another on deck and burst into flames. Luckily, the crash crew was able to put out the fire and clear the wreckage in six minutes flat, permitting more fighters to land on. Six of the *Victorious*'s own aircraft were missing, but they turned up on the *Indomitable*.

First light on the 12th revealed a pair of S.M.79s shadowing the convoy; both were shot down by 809 Squadron's Fulmars. It was a good start to the day, but everyone knew that the real test was still to come. The convoy was now coming well within range of enemy airfields, and the bombers that came that day would undoubtedly have fighter escorts. The first raid materialised at 09.00, when a formation of 20 Ju 88s appeared at 8,000 feet. They were intercepted by the *Indomitable*'s Hurricanes, which shot down two on their first

pass and forced several others to jettison their bombs. More Hurricanes and Fulmars from the *Victorious* arrived a couple of minutes later and joined the fray, destroying four more bombers and driving away the others.

After two more small and unsuccessful attacks that morning, a really big raid appeared at noon. Nearly a 100 aircraft – 37 Ju 88s, 33 S.M. 79s, twenty S.M. 84s, and eight Cant 1007s, with a strong fighter escort – were hotly engaged by every available Fleet Air Arm fighter as they approached the convoy. Harried by the fighters, the enemy formations became dislocated while still some distance from the target. The only real damage was caused by a formation of Ju 88s that broke through the fighter screen and dive-bombed the freighter *Deucalion*; badly damaged, the vessel began to lag behind the rest of the convoy and had to be left, escorted by the destroyer *Bramham*. She was attacked and sunk before dusk by two torpedo-bombers.

The *Victorious* had a narrow escape when a pair of Italian Reggiane Re. 2000 fighter-bombers came down in a very fast dive on the carrier's port quarter. Levelling out just above the sea they pulled up over the flight deck, releasing two bombs. One was a dud; the other bounced off the armoured deck and exploded in the water.

That afternoon, the convoy ran into a submarine ambush laid by the Italian Navy. One submarine, the *Cobalto*, was brought to the surface by depth-charges and rammed by the destroyer *Ithuriel*, which was herself badly damaged. None of the torpedoes launched by the submarines scored hits. The convoy was under continual air attack throughout the afternoon, but emerged relatively unharmed. By 17.00, however, the ships were within range of *Fliegerkorps* II's dive-bombers in Sicily, and from now on the attacks were pressed home with great determination. For two hours the bombers came over without pause, allowing the exhausted Navy pilots no respite. Part of a formation of 29 Ju 87s of St.G. 3, harried by Fulmars and Martlets (nine of which were operated by *Indomitable*'s No. 806 Squadron) broke through and dropped three bombs on the carrier; they failed to penetrate her flight deck, but for the time being she could not operate her aircraft, and those of her fighters still airborne had to land on the *Victorious*. An attack was also made by 14 S.M.79s, which torpedoed the destroyer *Foresight*; she had to be abandoned and sunk later.

By 19.30 the last of the raiders had disappeared; the convoy was still more or less intact and was now only 130 miles from Malta, within range of the island's Beaufighters. The first of these arrived overhead as dusk was falling, and the two fleet carriers, their job done, now turned away towards the sunset. They had lost 13 of their aircraft, but their pilots had claimed 39 enemy aircraft definitely destroyed during the three days of air fighting, plus a further nine probables. It had been a classic demonstration of the value of carrier-borne fighters; the Navy pilots had ably proved their ability to break up even the most determined enemy attacks, and the fact that the convoy had come this far without suffering serious harm was due in large measure to them.

Now, however, the carriers had turned for home, leaving the convoy to steam on through the night with only the scant air cover that could be provided by the R.A.F. on Malta. And the story of 13 August was to be tragically different from that of the three preceding days.

During the night, the convoy was repeatedly attacked by enemy M.T.B.s and submarines, followed by a savage air onslaught that lasted until the surviving ships reached Malta. Only four of the merchantmen – including the vital tanker *Ohio* – got through, and the escort suffered the loss of the cruisers *Cairo* and *Manchester*. Nevertheless, the supplies that did get through enabled the island to keep going until November, when relief reached the defenders following the Allied landings in North Africa that month and the Eighth Army's decisive victory over Rommel at El Alamein in October.

CHAPTER ELEVEN

Disaster and Daring in Home Waters, 1942

At the beginning of 1942, against the depressing backdrop of Allied reverses in the Far East and North Africa, Admiral Sir John Tovey, the Commander-in-Chief Home Fleet, had two main anxieties. The first concerned the German Brest Squadron – the *Scharnhorst, Gneisenau* and *Prinz Eugen* – now believed to be seaworthy again following repairs. The second arose through the movement of the new and very powerful battleship *Tirpitz* to join the Trondheim Squadron in mid-January, clearly to form the nucleus of a powerful battle group for operations against the Allied Arctic and North Atlantic convoys.

On 12 January, following a further attack on the warships at Brest by R.A.F. Bomber Command, Adolf Hitler decided that the vessels must be moved if they were to avoid further damage. Since there was little likelihood that they might break out into the Atlantic unscathed, only two options remained open. The first was to return them to Germany by means of a high-speed dash through the English Channel; the second was to decommission them.

Faced with such a choice, *Vizeadmiral* Ciliax, commanding the Brest Squadron, produced an outline plan for a breakout operation, which was allocated the code-name *Cerberus*. (In Greek mythology, Cerberus was the three-headed dog that guarded the gates of hell.) The ships would leave Brest at night to avoid detection for as long as possible, and they would pass through the Straits of Dover in daylight, placing them in a better position to fight off torpedo attacks by surface vessels and aircraft. Also, they would have full advantage of the strong air umbrella that could be provided by the *Luftwaffe*.

The British maintained their surveillance of Brest throughout January, and on the 25th air reconnaissance showed that all three ships had left their berths and were in the main harbour.

The photographs also showed an increasing number of supporting craft at Brest and concentrations of S-boats at various Channel ports. German naval activity in the Channel increased. On 25 January, the destroyer *Bruno Heinemann* was sunk by one of the thousand or so mines laid by the fast minelayers *Welshman* and *Manxman* off the French coast between Ushant and Boulogne.

On 2 February, the Admiralty distributed to all authorities a study of the various alternatives open to the Germans, in which it was concluded that their most probable course of action was a dash through the Channel to their home bases. The main burden of countering this move would fall not on the Home Fleet, but on the naval commands at Plymouth, Portsmouth and Dover – especially on the latter, whose forces would be most favourably placed for interception. As a preliminary step the Admiralty ordered certain redeployments of destroyers, submarines, minelayers and M.T.B.s. To supplement these forces, six Swordfish of No. 825 Squadron, Fleet Air Arm, were deployed to Manston in Kent on 4 February; every available aircraft of Bomber Command was bombed-up and placed on two hours' readiness, No. 19 Group of Coastal Command stepped up its surveillance of the south-western approaches, and Fighter Command stood ready to provide air cover. After a week, however, the state of readiness was downgraded and squadrons released for other operations, with the proviso that they would immediately be switched to anti-shipping operations if need be.

On 8 February, British intelligence received a warning from the French Resistance that the warships were making ready to sail, and subsequent air reconnaissance showed the *Scharnhorst* and *Prinz Eugen* in the harbour and the *Gneisenau* just outside. Armed with this knowledge, and with information to the effect that weather conditions would be favourable for a breakout within 48 hours, the Admiralty and Air Ministry concluded that the Germans would make their attempt during the week beginning 10 February. On the 11th, air reconnaissance revealed that the three warships were once again in the main harbour, with six destroyers and a concentration of smaller craft. Bomber Command carried out a small-scale attack during the night, but its only result was to delay the start of the breakout by an hour.

The ships eventually formed up in the roads outside Brest at 22.45, and now began an unfortunate chain of circumstances that was to deprive the British of vital intelligence of their movements. A French Resistance agent saw them sail, but was unable to reach his transmitter because of a strong security cordon around the harbour. A Coastal Command Hudson patrol aircraft had to return early with radar failure, and its replacement detected nothing at all, even though the enemy ships were well within range of its A.S.V. radar. No replacement arrived to cover the gap left by this aircraft, and the fact that this stretch of the coastline was no longer being watched was not reported to the Admiralty. In fact, the third patrol Hudson had been recalled because of fog; had it reached its station, patrolling an area off the Sussex coast, it would almost certainly have detected the ships at first light.

By that time the Brest Squadron was steaming at full speed off Barfleur, following a channel swept by eight minesweeping flotillas in the preceding weeks and escorted by the destroyers *Z25*, *Z29*, *Friedrich Ihn*, *Hermann Schoemann*, *Paul Jacobi* and *Richard Beitzen*. At the narrowest stretch of the Channel, between Le Havre and Dunkirk, the force would be strengthened by fourteen vessels of the 2nd, 3rd and 5th Torpedo-boat Flotillas, while the 2nd and 6th S-boat Flotillas would join the escort in the North Sea. *Luftflotte* 3 had allocated 176 bombers and fighters (mainly the Me 109s and Fw 190s of J.G. 2 and J.G. 26) to the operation, covering the force with relays of at least 16 aircraft at all times.

For almost 13 hours the Brest Squadron continued its passage up the Channel unmolested, even though it had been sighted by the pilots of two sections of patrolling Spitfires, at least one of whom broke radio silence to report the warships' position. The subsequent slowness of the British reaction can only be explained by a communications breakdown somewhere along the line. It must be said, however, that the German ships were greatly helped by the weather conditions, which effectively ruled out air attack at this time. The Royal Navy's surface units were also poorly placed for an attack; the destroyers were exercising in the North Sea, and the small force of M.T.B.s at Ramsgate had suffered in an engagement during the night.

At 11.20 the German force reduced speed to 10 knots to allow sweepers to clear a path through the minefield laid by British destroyers. The passage took 20 minutes and the ships once again went ahead at full speed; a golden opportunity to attack them during the interval had been lost. At 12.18 the gun batteries at Dover – the first units to try to engage the enemy – opened fire on the warships, but their shells fell short. At the same time, five M.T.B.s from Dover under Lt-Cdr Pumphrey began their attack run, heading for the outer screen of torpedo-boats and the destroyers beyond, the latter laying a smokescreen. The battlecruisers were visible beyond the smoke and Pumphrey signalled their position, speed and course, information that was relayed to the M.T.B.s at Ramsgate and the Fleet Air Arm detachment at Manston. Bereft of any support from fighter-bombers or M.G.B.s, both of which had been promised, Pumphrey's small force tried to slip through the escort screen. Intense fire from the escort vessels and from enemy aircraft forced the M.T.B.s to split up and make individual attacks; most of their torpedoes were launched at a range of two miles or more, and no hits were observed.

Meanwhile, alerted by the M.T.B.s' signals, the six Swordfish of No. 825 Squadron had taken off from Manston, led by Lieutenant-Commander Eugene Esmonde, at 12.25. Esmonde had been promised an escort of five Spitfire squadrons, but a combination of bad weather and a timing error resulted in only ten Spitfires turning up three minutes after the Swordfish had set course. Within ten minutes the Spitfires were engaged in a fierce low-level battle with enemy fighters, in the course of which they lost contact with the Swordfish. The latter, flying in two sections of three, pressed on unescorted towards the warships, harassed by fighters all the way. The pilots of the first three Swordfish selected the *Scharnhorst* as they broke through the outer screen and launched their torpedoes, despite the fact that all three pilots were badly wounded. Esmonde went down into the sea immediately afterwards and the other two Swordfish were forced down within a minute or so, five of their six crew members later being picked up alive by the M.T.B.s. The second flight of Swordfish was seen passing over the torpedo-boat screen, then the three aircraft vanished in the smoke and the geysers of water flung up by the cruisers' armament. All three were shot down and their crews killed. Of the 18 crew involved in the operation, therefore, only five survived. Lieutenant-Commander Esmonde, who had not expected to return, was posthumously awarded the Victoria Cross.

It was now 13.00 and the warships, still unscathed, were passing Ramsgate, from where three M.T.B.s under Lt-Cdr Long set out to attack them. Like their colleagues at Dover, they found the enemy's defensive screen too strong to penetrate and they were soon left behind, returning to harbour in rapidly deteriorating weather and rising seas. But trouble for the Brest Squadron was not far over the horizon: at 14.21, while passing at reduced speed through another dangerous bottleneck – the Ruytingen Narrows – the *Scharnhorst* struck a mine. Her engines were temporarily stopped and it was half an hour before she could get underway – half an hour during which not a single British aircraft was sighted. Admiral Ciliax and his staff were transferred to the leading destroyer by cutter, only to be transferred again when the warship was damaged by the premature explosion of one of its own shells.

At about 14.45 aircraft of Bomber Command arrived overhead. Before nightfall, the Command had flown 242 sorties against the ships, although only one in six managed to bomb them. They succeeded in sinking the patrol ship V1302 and in

damaging the torpedo boats T13 and *Jaguar*. Attacks by Beaufort torpedo-bombers were fragmented and produced no result. In all, the R.A.F. lost forty-one aircraft, including seventeen fighters; the *Luftwaffe*'s losses amounted to seventeen aircraft.

The assault by the first wave of bombers coincided with an attempted attack by six destroyers from Harwich, the *Campbell*, *Mackay*, *Vivacious*, *Worcester*, *Whitshed* and *Walpole*, led by Captains C. T. M. Pizey and J. P. Wright. The *Walpole* developed mechanical trouble and returned to Harwich, leaving the other five to execute the attack. It was a hazardous operation; not only did the destroyer crews have to contend with enemy fire, but they also had to thread their way through a British minefield – which luckily was clearly marked on their charts – and run the gauntlet of British bombs. The ships reached the outer screen at about 15.30 and initiated individual attacks on the *Gneisenau* and other vessels, but intense fire from the battlecruisers' heavy armament kept the destroyers at arm's length and they were forced to launch their torpedoes at long range. Only one destroyer, H.M.S. *Worcester*, came within 3,000 yards; she was badly damaged and set on fire, limping back to Harwich with four of her crew dead and nineteen wounded. She came close to being attacked by a Beaufort *en route*. Once again, the German warships were unharmed.

The Brest Squadron slipped away into the darkness. Just before 20.00 the *Gneisenau* struck a mine, but sustained no very serious injury. Ninety minutes later, however, the *Scharnhorst* was mined a second time and came to a stop, but by that time the British had lost touch with the enemy and were unable to take advantage of this development. On 13 February, the *Scharnhorst* limped to safety in Wilhelmshaven while the other two cruisers went on to the Elbe Estuary.

The Channel Dash had been an undisputed success for the Germans, and for the British a woeful tale of incompetence, bad planning and humiliation for which not even the courage of the Royal Navy and R.A.F. could compensate. Yet for the enemy, the sequel to the operation was not a happy one. Ten days later, the *Prinz Eugen* was torpedoed and put out of action by the submarine

H.M.S. *Trident* (Cdr Sladen) while in passage from the Elbe to Norway with the *Admiral Scheer*. She was transferred to the Baltic Training Squadron, and in 1944 was used in support of the German Army against the advancing Russians. In 1945 she was taken over as war booty by the Americans and used as a target ship in the U.S. atomic bomb trials at Bikini Atoll in June 1946. Having survived that experience, was finally sunk at Kwajalein in 1947. The *Gneisenau* was hit by Bomber Command in Kiel harbour a fortnight after *Cerberus* and never went to sea again; her gun turrets were removed for coastal defence and she was sunk as a blockship at Gdynia, where she was seized by the Russians and broken up between 1947 and 1951. Only the *Scharnhorst*, as we shall see later, re-emerged to threaten Allied shipping on the high seas.

In March 1942, the Royal Navy participated in the biggest combined operation mounted so far by the British in the Second World War. Called Operation *Chariot*, it was born out of desperation. Behind it all lay the presence, in Norway, of the most powerful German naval force so far assembled: the *Admiral Scheer*, *Lützow* and four destroyers at Narvik, and the *Tirpitz*, *Hipper* and six destroyers at Trondheim. Of these, the principal threat was the *Tirpitz*, capable of wreaking awesome havoc on the Allied convoys should she be let loose in the North Atlantic.

One way of discouraging such a sortie was to make it impossible for the battleship to dock in western France, and that meant putting out of action the facilities at St-Nazaire, which featured the only dry dock capable of handling her. Known as the Normandie lock through its association with the famous French passenger liner, or more correctly the Forme Ecluse, it was over 1,100 feet in length; it was towards this haven that the *Bismarck* would have steered had she not been sunk.

The principal objective of the plan to raid St-Nazaire was to ram and destroy the lock gates of the Forme Ecluse using the old ex-American destroyer H.M.S. *Campbeltown*, her bows filled with explosives. The destruction of the smaller South Lock gates and their installations, pumping machinery for the outer dock, and any U-boats or

By 1943 the Royal Navy had denied the English Channel to Germany's blockade runners, one of which is seen here ablaze after an attack by British Coastal Forces

shipping present, were to be subsidiary objectives in that order of priority.

The Naval Force comprised the *Cambeltown* (formerly U.S.S. *Buchanan*), two escorting Hunt class destroyers, *Atherstone* and *Tynedale*, a motor gunboat, a motor torpedo-boat and fifteen motor launches, four of which carried torpedoes and the remainder the Military Force, consisting of 44 officers and 224 other ranks of No. 2 Commando and detachments from others. The naval force commander was Commander R. E. D. Ryder, R.N., in peacetime an Arctic explorer and winner of the Polar Medal, while the military force was commanded by Lieutenant-Colonel A. C. Newman of the Essex Regiment.

The military plan of attack was based on landings at three places: from the bows of the *Campbeltown*, from motor launches on either side of the Old Entrance, and on the north side of the Old Mole. After demolition parties assigned to the three assault groups had done their work, in particular the destruction of the bridges that would effectively turn the area into an island, the force was to withdraw to the Old Mole for re-embarkation. Two hours was the maximum time allowed for the military force to complete its operation, by which time the naval force would have to leave in order to get clear before daybreak and rejoin the escorting destroyers.

The expedition sailed from Falmouth at 14.00 on Tuesday 26 March 1942, led by H.M.S. *Atherstone*, towing M.G.B. 314. Astern of her came H.M.S. *Campbeltown*, towing M.T.B. 74. Next in line was H.M.S. *Tynedale*, with the motor launchers (M.L.s) forming a column on each side of the destroyers.

The outward trip was not without incident. At 07.20 on 27 March *Tynedale* sighted a U-boat on the surface at 4,000 yards and opened fire as she closed, forcing the submarine to crash-dive. The U-boat's periscope was seen shortly afterwards and it appeared that she might have been damaged, but *Tynedale*'s captain, Lt-Cdr D. Tweedie, decided against ramming for fear of damaging his own ship and instead dropped a pattern of depth-charges. The U-boat's bow and conning tower emerged from the water and *Tynedale* engaged her with 4-inch and automatic weapons. The submarine assumed a 40-degree list to port and disappeared stern first. No further contact was made with the submarine, but it was by no means certain that it had been destroyed. (In fact, no U-boat was reported lost on this day at this location.) Later, two French trawlers were encountered and sunk by gunfire after their crews had been taken off.

Just after 17.00 on the 27th, the force received a signal from the C.-in-C. Plymouth, saying that five S-boats were believed to be operating in the area. (In reality this was the 5th Torpedo-boat Flotilla, comprising the T.B.s *Falke*, *Iltis*, *Kondor*, *Jaguar* and *Seeadler*.) Two hours later, another signal informed the force commander that two more Hunt class destroyers, the *Cleveland* and *Brocklesby*, were being sent at maximum speed as reinforcements.

During the afternoon the force had been following a decoy route across the Bay of Biscay towards La Pallice and La Rochelle, but now it turned north-east and headed for St-Nazaire at 15 knots. At 00.45 on 28 March, the force was within sight of the north bank of the Loire; by this time the two escorting destroyers had parted company and were patrolling to seaward.

The fact that the expedition arrived at exactly the right place at the right time was a tribute to the navigational skill of Lieutenant A. R. Green, R.N., the force navigation officer. The vessels now began their final approach, with three Coastal Force craft – M.G.B. 314 and two M.L.s – ahead of the *Campbeltown* and M.T.B. 74 and two columns of M.L.s astern. By now a small number of R.A.F. bombers had arrived overhead to create a diversion and the St-Nazaire flak defences were putting up a fine barrage.

As the force came abeam Les Morées Tower, three miles from the town, a single searchlight swept the estuary and a challenge came from a German shore station. M.G.B. 314 replied with a false identification, followed by a signal in German that she was 'proceeding up harbour in accordance with previous instructions'. The bluff seemed to have worked; then, with two miles to run, the searchlights came on again, fixing on the *Campbeltown*, and the defences opened up.

The force increased speed, returning fire as it forged ahead, and at 01.34 the bows of the *Campbeltown*, with their five tons of explosive, slammed into the lock gates and stuck fast. While the commandos on board her streamed ashore to carry out their demolition tasks, a party of naval engineers under Chief Engine Room Artificer H. Howard set about flooding the ship. This part of the operation had been accomplished with fine precision, and it later brought the award of the Victoria Cross to *Campbeltown*'s captain, Lieutenant-Commander S. H. Beattie, R.N.

The M.L.s, meanwhile, had been having a difficult time, some having been hit and set on fire as they struggled to land their troops. The port column, heading for the Old Mole, suffered particularly severely as gunfire ripped through their unarmoured hulls. The leading craft, M.L. 447, got to within ten feet of the jetty before she was set ablaze by machine-gun fire and grenades; her commander, Lt T. D. L. Platt, R.N.R., persisted in his attempts to land until M.L. 160 arrived. The latter's skipper, Lt T.W. Boyd, R.N.V.R., placed his craft between the Mole and M.L. 447 and took off some survivors, including Platt. Both officers were subsequently awarded the D.S.O. Some time later, M.L. 160 was joined by M.L. 443 and M.L. 446; they were the only three M.L.s to return to England under their own power and without escort.

Meanwhile, M.T.B. 74 had torpedoed the gates of the submarine pens and M.G.B. 314, with the force commanders on board, had been engaging enemy gun positions from a point midstream. Able Seaman W. A. Savage, the layer of the M.G.B.'s pom-pom, did excellent work amid all the fury and flying metal; he was killed by a shell splinter during the withdrawal, and was awarded a posthumous V.C. (The other posthumous V.C. went to Sergeant J. F. Durrant of the Royal Engineers.)

Many of the *Campbeltown*'s crew were also rescued by M.G.B. 314, and afterwards Commander Ryder – who also received a V.C. for his part in the night's work – gave the order to withdraw. It was a severely decimated force that fought its way out of the Loire estuary to make rendezvous with the escorting destroyers, H.M.S. *Tynedale* engaging incoming boats of the German 5th Torpedo-boat Flotilla outside the harbour; of the 62 naval officers and 291 ratings who had sailed from England, 34 officers and 151 ratings were killed or missing, and of the total of 44 officers and 224 other ranks of No. 2 Commando, 34 officers and 178 other ranks never returned. In fact, it was not until much later that the true casualty figures were etablished; 170 men killed or missing out of 621 committed. Given the nature of the operation, it was a remarkably light price to pay for the denial to the enemy of a major and threatening naval facility.

Shortly before noon on 28 March, *Campbeltown*'s demolition charges blew up with devastating effect. The lock gate was blown off its sill and seriously damaged, and the dock itself was put out of commission for the rest of the war.

British special forces mounted several more cross-Channel raids during the weeks that followed, often with destroyers carrying out diversionary bombardments. As the summer progressed there were frequent skirmishes between opposing coastal forces, with destroyers and light craft carrying out hit-and-run attacks on enemy coastal traffic. One notable action took place on the night of 14/15 May, when the German raider *Stier* passed through the Channel *en route* for the Gironde, escorted by the destroyers *Kondor*, *Falke*, *Iltis*, and *Seeadler* and sixteen motor minesweepers. The force was heavily shelled by the Dover batteries and attacked by M.T.B.s, the *Iltis* and *Seeadler* both being sunk with heavy loss of life. The rest escaped, despite attempts by British destroyers to intercept them *en route*; the British naval forces lost M.T.B. 220 in this action.

On 19 August 1942 Operation *Jubilee*, the ill-fated expedition to Dieppe, required a maximum effort on the part of British naval and air forces in the Channel area. The aim of the plan was, in the words of Winston Churchill, to carry out 'a reconnaissance in force to test the enemy defences on a strongly defended sector of coast, and to discover what resistance would have to be met in the endeavour to seize a port'. It involved a frontal seaborne assault on the beaches of the small peacetime holiday resort by 4,961 Canadian troops, supported by a tank battalion, while gun batteries on the headlands east and west of the town were to be silenced by 1,057 British Commandos.

As a prelude to the operation, the assault area was extensively photographed from the air and minesweepers cleared a way through the German minefield in mid-Channel ahead of the main force, which sailed from Portsmouth, Newhaven and Shoreham on the evening of 18 August. The naval forces supporting the operation totalled 237 craft of all types, including landing craft, the principal units being: the destroyers *Calpe* (acting as H.Q. ship), *Fernie* (reserve H.Q. ship), *Albrighton*, *Berkeley*, *Bleasdale*, *Brocklesby*, *Garth* and *Slezak*, the latter Polish; the gunboat *Locust* of Dunkirk fame; and the landing ships infantry (L.S.I.) *Duke of Wellington*, *Glengyle*, *Invicta*, *Prins Albert*, *Princess Astrid*, *Princess Beatrix*, *Prince Charles*, *Prince Leopold* and *Queen Emma*. Thirty-eight small craft of the Coastal Forces were also committed.

All seemed set to achieve surprise when, just

before 04.00 on the 19th, the landing craft on the eastern flank encountered a German convoy. In the brief and confused battle that followed, the German escort UJ1404 was sunk and the British steam gunboat S.G.B. 5 badly damaged. The engagement delayed the assault on this flank, which crumbled into total disaster under intense fire. On the western flank the attack achieved better results, but even so the Germans were not dislodged from the batteries and strongpoints commanding the beaches where the main assault was to take place. When this went in at 05.20, therefore, it encountered a murderous and devastating enfilading fire that pinned down the troops on the beaches, while the supporting Churchill tanks failed to penetrate the town.

Too much has been written about the desperate gallantry of the Canadian infantry, tankmen and commandos in the hours that followed to bear repetition here. Suffice to say that the Canadians lost 215 officers and 3,164 men and the Commandos 24 officers and 223 men killed, wounded or prisoners – 68 per cent of the attacking force.

The naval forces offshore did what they could to lend fire support, but since none of the warships mounted guns of more than 4-inch calibre the degree of help from this quarter was limited. Only about 1,000 men were brought away in the assault craft that moved inshore to evacuate them at 11.00, an operation as desperate in its way as the fighting on land. Many craft were lost in the process, including the destroyer H.M.S. _Berkeley_, hit by bombs from a Dornier 217.

Without doubt, the most important lesson learned at Dieppe was the absolute need for massive fire support from both sea and air in amphibious operations. Another lesson learned was the need to devise special equipment to overcome defensive obstacles, the realisation of which resulted in a formidable array of specially equipped tanks being available to the forces that went ashore in Normandy two years later. For all three services, the overall lesson of Dieppe was how not to do it, and it was better learned in 1942 than in 1944.

CHAPTER TWELVE
The Arctic Convoys, 1941–42

During the last week of July 1941 the aircraft carriers *Victorious* and *Furious* sailed from Seidisfjord in Iceland, where they had stopped to refuel on the way out from Scapa Flow, and set course north-westwards, heading deeper into Arctic waters with their escort of two cruisers and six destroyers. Five weeks earlier, on 22 June, the German armies had invaded the Soviet Union. The event brought great relief to Britain, which at last had an ally, but it also brought problems for the Home Fleet, which had a new theatre of war to contend with. Russia desperately needed war supplies, which had to be channelled through the northern ports of Murmansk and Archangel; and the merchant ships carrying those supplies had to be escorted by the Royal Navy, which meant diverting warships from elsewhere.

At the core of the July operation was the minelaying cruiser *Adventure*, tasked with making a fast supply run to Murmansk while carrier aircraft attacked shipping in the north

Nightmare conditions: naval aircrews on Arctic convoy duty had to contend with the added perils of ice and fog

Russian icebreaker in the White Sea

Norwegian harbour of Kirkenes and Petsamo in north Finland. The hope that the attacks would come as a complete surprise to the Germans, however, vanished when a lone Junkers 88 reconnaissance aircraft located the British force, which had now split into two groups, shortly before the carriers reached their flying-off positions on 30 July. Nevertheless, the attack went ahead as planned. In the early afternoon *Victorious* flew off her striking force of 20 Albacores from 827 and 828 Squadrons, escorted by nine Fulmars of 809 Squadron, for the raid on Kirkenes; while nine Albacores of 817 Squadron, nine Swordfish of 812 and six Fulmars of 800 Squadron left the *Furious* and headed for Petsamo.

The attacks ended in disaster. Of the Kirkenes force, eleven Albacores and two Fulmars were shot down by A.A. fire and the Me 109s of 6/J.G. 5, and only light damage was inflicted on the gunnery training ship *Bremse* and one or two other vessels in the harbour. In terms of losses the Petsamo force fared a little better; only one Albacore and a Fulmar were lost, but there was no shipping in the harbour and the aircraft attacked shore installations, again causing little damage.

The following day, a Dornier 18 flying boat was seen shadowing the force and two Sea Hurricanes of No. 880 Squadron, piloted by Lt-Cdr Judd and Sub-Lt Howarth, were launched from *Furious* to intercept it. After a short chase they shot it down – the first victory to be scored by a Hurricane at sea. On 4 August, on the way home, *Victorious* – which had taken on the other carrier's remaining aircraft – lost another Fulmar in an attack on Tromsø.

On 21 August, the first experimental convoy to Russia, code-named *Dervish*, left Hvalfjord in Iceland. It comprised seven merchant ships and the carrier *Argus* escorted by the cruisers *Devonshire* and *Suffolk*, the carrier *Victorious* and six destroyers, the latter providing close escort for the *Argus*, under the command of Rear-Admiral W. F. Wake-Walker. The merchantmen reached Archangel without incident on 31 August, and the *Argus* flew off 24 Hurricane fighters of the R.A.F.'s No. 151 Wing, destined for operations in north Russia. A further 15 crated Hurricanes were offloaded from the merchant liner *Llanstephan Castle*. While this operation was in progress, warships of Force K from Scapa Flow under Rear-Admiral Sir Philip Vian evacuated Norwegian and Russian nationals from the island of Spitzbergen and destroyed shore installations, afterwards making a sortie to the Norwegian coast, where they sank the gunnery training ship *Bremse* and narrowly missed sinking two troop transports, which escaped into a fjord in bad visibility.

Dervish seemed to prove the concept of convoys to north Russia, and on 29 September the first of the regular convoys, PQ1 (designated QP1 on the return trip), left Iceland for Archangel with fourteen merchantmen, and by the end of 1941, 55 merchant ships had been dispatched in eight separate convoys. Murmansk was now the destination port, the passage to Archangel having been closed by ice. All the convoys so far had been unmolested by the enemy.

Between 22 December and 1 January units of

the Home Fleet operated in support of commando raids on the Lofoten Islands (Operations *Anklet* and *Archery*), the principal objectives being to destroy fish processing plants and telecommunications facilities. The raids were successful, and in addition to the damage caused ashore three German patrol boats and a number of transports were sunk, beached or captured; several hundred Norwegian volunteers were also brought out. The cruisers *Arethusa* and *Kenya* were damaged, the former by near misses in an air attack and the latter by shells from a shore battery. The propaganda of this, the first large-scale combined operation, far outweighed its material results; but it paved the way for greater efforts in the years to come.

In October 1941 Britain and the U.S.A. had agreed to supply the Soviet Union with 400 aircraft, 500 tanks, 200 Bren-gun carriers, 22,000 tons of rubber, 41,000 tons of aluminium, 3,860 tons of machine tools and large quantities of food, medical supplies and other materials every month. It was an input that the Germans could not ignore, and on 25 December the German Navy C.-in-C., Admiral Raeder, ordered the deployment of the U-boat group *Ulan* (U-134,

The cruiser H.M.S. Kenya served with the Home Fleet 1940–3, and afterwards with the Eastern Fleet

U-454 and U-584) to the passage south of Bear Island to lie in wait for the convoys. Their first success came on 2 January 1942, when U-134 (*Kapitänleutnant* Schendel) sank the British freighter *Waziristan* of convoy PQ7A, and on 17 January U-454 (*Kapitänleutnant* Hacklander) sank the destroyer *Matabele*, escorting convoy PQ8, as well as damaging the freighter *Harmatris*.

On 21 February, a new but not unexpected threat to the Arctic convoys developed when the pocket battleship *Admiral Scheer* and the heavy cruiser *Prinz Eugen* were transferred from the Elbe to Norway, accompanied by the destroyers Z25, *Friedrich Ihn* and *Hermann Schoemann*. The warships were shadowed by R.A.F. reconnaissance aircraft (one of which was shot down) during their northward passage, and on 27 February the *Prinz Eugen* was damaged by the submarine *Trident* and forced to return home. Before the end of the month, however, an even bigger threat materialised when the new battleship *Tirpitz* slipped out of the Baltic and arrived at Trondheim, bearing the flag of *Admiral* Ciliax.

On 6 March, the *Tirpitz*, accompanied by three destroyers, set out to intercept convoys PQ12 and QP8, the first bound for Murmansk, the second on its way home. PQ12 had been detected by a Fw 200 the day before 70 nautical miles south of Jan Mayen Island, and the submarines U-134, U-377, U-403 and U-584 were also deployed to intercept it. The movements of the *Tirpitz* and her escorts, meanwhile, had been reported by the submarine *Seawolf* (Lt Raikes), and units of the Home Fleet, comprising the battleships *King George V*, *Duke of York* and *Renown*, the carrier *Victorious*, the cruiser *Kenya* and 12 destroyers placed themselves between the threat and the convoys, which passed one another off Bear Island at noon on 7 March. Ciliax detached some of his destroyers to search for the convoys and they sank one straggling Russian freighter, but apart from that no contact was made and the German commander turned southwards again.

Thanks to intercepted radio signals, Admiral Tovey knew of the Germans' intentions and ordered his forces towards the Lofoten Islands in an attempt to cut them off. At daybreak on the 9th, a reconnaissance Albacore from the *Victorious*

A welcome sight at the end of an Arctic run: the Kola Inlet. The Russian welcome on shore was not so good

spotted the *Tirpitz*, and twelve torpedo-carrying Albacores took off soon afterwards to attack the warship. The attack, unfortunately, was carried out in line astern, which gave the *Tirpitz* ample room to avoid all the torpedoes, although one passed within 30 feet of her. Two Albacores were shot down. The failure of this attack was a bitter pill for the Royal Navy to swallow, but it did have one result; on Hitler's orders, the *Tirpitz* never put to sea again if carrier-based aircraft were known to be in the vicinity.

On 20 March 1942 German naval strength in Norway was further augmented with the arrival at Trondheim of the heavy cruiser *Admiral Hipper*, accompanied by the destroyers Z24, Z26 and Z30 and the torpedo-boats T15, T16 and T17. The enemy now had a formidable striking force of aircraft, warships and submarines in the theatre, and convoy losses inevitably began to mount.

Between 27 March and 31 March, PQ13 became split up due to bad weather; two of its ships were sunk by the Ju 88s of III/K.G. 30, operating from Banak, three by the U-376, U-435, U-436, and one by the destroyer Z26, which was herself sunk by the cruiser *Trinidad*. The cruiser was then hit and disabled by one of her own torpedoes, which went out of control; the U-585 closed in to attack her, but was sunk by the destroyer *Fury*. The remaining 13 ships of PQ13 reached Murmansk, but two were sunk by air attack on 3 April.

Convoy PQ14 (8–21 April) found that the ice, not the Germans, was the main enemy; it ran into ice floes in thick fog and 16 of its 24 vessels had to return to Iceland. One was sunk by the U-403. PQ15 (26 April–7 May), a large convoy of 50 ships under heavy Anglo-American escort, had two vessels sunk by air attack and one damaged (this ship, the *Jutland*, was later sunk by the U-251). QP11, a homeward-bound convoy, was attacked by destroyers and U-boats; the U-456 hit the escorting cruiser *Edinburgh* with two torpedoes and she was finished off later by other British warships after sustaining further damage from a destroyer's torpedo. Two British destroyers, the *Forester* and *Foresight*, were badly damaged in an engagement with the German destroyers Z24 and Z25; the battleship *King George V* rammed and sank the destroyer *Punjabi* in a snowstorm and was herself damaged by the latter's exploding depth-charges; and, to add to a catalogue of woe, the Polish submarine *Jastrzab*, a long way from her position on the flank of the convoy, was sunk by the Norwegian-manned destroyer *St Albans* and the minesweeper *Seagull*.

Convoy PQ16 (25–30 May) was attacked by formations of Ju 88s and He 111s, which sank seven of its 35 ships with the loss of 43,205 tons of war stores, including 77 aircraft, 147 tanks and 770 vehicles. Then came the disaster of PQ17, which led to a complete revision of the Arctic

Clearing ice from the deck of an escort carrier during convoy protection duty in the Arctic

convoy system.

The 36 freighters of PQ17 sailed from Iceland on 27 June 1942 protected by a close-support force and a cover group of four cruisers and three destroyers. Additional long-range support was provided by a cover force from the Home Fleet, consisting of the battleships H.M.S. *Duke of York* and U.S.S. *Washington* (the latter attached to Admiral Tovey's command), the carrier *Victorious*, two cruisers and fourteen destroyers. As soon as they learned of PQ17's departure, the German Navy initiated Operation *Rosselsprung* (Knight's Move), its aim the total destruction of the convoy. In the afternoon of 2 July, Force I under *Admiral* Schniewind, comprising the battleship *Tirpitz* and the cruiser *Admiral Hipper*, with four destroyers and two torpedo-boats, set out from Trondheim, and the next day *Vizeadmiral* Kummetz's Force II, comprising the pocket battleships *Lützow* and *Admiral Scheer*, with five destroyers, sailed from Narvik and headed north to join Force I at Altenfjord. There they waited, the German commanders unwilling to risk their ships until they had more information about the strength of the enemy's covering forces.

Attacks by torpedo-bombers on the convoy began on 4 July, and that evening, the Admiralty received a completely false report that a Russian submarine had sighted the German warships heading on an interception course. This, in addi-

Arctic convoy: the cruiser H.M.S. Edinburgh *survives an air attack. She was lost in the Barents Sea in May 1942*

tion to reports that the convoy was being continually shadowed by enemy aircraft, led to one of the most tragic decisions of the war: to withdraw

the escorting cruisers and destroyers and to scatter the convoy, the merchantmen to make their way individually to the Russian ports. It was the signal for packs of enemy aircraft and U-boats to fall on the hapless transports and pick them off one by one. The slaughter began on 5 July and went on for five days, right up to the moment when the surviving ships entered Archangel. The convoy's losses were 24 ships out of 36, totalling 143,977 tons. The losses in equipment were astronomical: 3,350 vehicles, 430 tanks, 210 aircraft and 99,316 tons of other war equipment. German losses, in over 200 sorties flown by the *Luftwaffe*, were just five aircraft.

The next eastbound convoy was PQ18, its departure delayed until September because all the available aircraft carriers were engaged in escorting the desperately needed *Pedestal* convoy through to Malta – and, after the PQ17 fiasco, the dispatch of another convoy to Russia without a carrier escort could not be considered. When PQ18, 46 ships strong, finally sailed from Iceland on 9 September, its escort included the carrier H.M.S. *Avenger*, a 'utility' vessel converted from a merchant ship in the United States. The Royal Navy's first such escort carrier, *Audacity* – a captured and converted German merchant vessel, the *Hannover* – had proved her worth on the

Convoy escorts making smoke during an air attack in the Arctic

Arctic convoy under air attack

U.K.–Gibraltar run, her Martlet fighters destroying several enemy aircraft before she fell victim to a torpedo salvo from the U-751 on 21 December 1941. The *Avenger* was the second of her class; the first, H.M.S. *Archer*, had been in service for some time, and two more, the *Biter* and *Dasher*, were due to be commissioned in the coming months.

The *Avenger* carried Nos 802 and 883 Squadrons, each with six Sea Hurricanes, together with three Swordfish of A Flight 825 Squadron. Six more Hurricanes were carried in crates, as reserves. The fighters were in action almost from the moment the convoy left Icelandic waters. On 12 September, a Blohm und Voss Bv 138 flying boat appeared to the south, shadowing the convoy, and the Hurricanes were flown off to shoot it down. They failed, and while they were chasing it six Ju 88s of K.G. 30 dive-bombed the convoy. No ship was lost and the attackers were beaten off by A.A. fire, but soon afterwards 40 torpedo-carrying He 111s of K.G. 26 appeared and attacked the convoy's starboard column while the Hurricanes were still over the horizon chasing the Bv 138. In exactly eight minutes as many freighters were hit and sunk. All the German aircraft returned to base, but six of them

were so badly damaged that they had to be written off.

The next day, K.G. 26 was ordered to concentrate its attacks on the aircraft carrier, which had not been located on the 12th because she had stationed herself some distance from the convoy in order to be in a better tactical position. This time, the carrier was sighted to the north of the convoy and the German air commander ordered his formation to split up prior to making its attack when it was bounced by the Hurricanes. The Germans lost five Heinkels and of the remaining 17, nine were damaged beyond repair.

Subsequent attacks, later on the 13th and on the 14th, were broken up by the *Avenger*'s Sea Hurricanes. In all, the fighters and the A.A. from the escort – mainly the latter, which because of the fighters' efforts was able to concentrate on individual aircraft – accounted for 20 Heinkels and Junkers (the British claimed 41 at the time). Four Hurricanes were shot down, three of them by friendly fire.

Arctic convoy seen from the after 4-inch guns of an escort carrier. The nearer ship was sunk by a U-boat 24 hours after this photograph was taken

As PQ18 neared the end of its journey, it was attacked by U-boats on 15 September and 16 September, losing three more freighters. However, the U-457 and U-589 were sunk by escorting destroyers, the latter after it had been located by Swordfish of 825 Squadron. On the 18th, as the convoy entered the Kola Inlet, it was subjected to further air attacks, this time by Heinkel 115 floatplanes. Two more merchantmen were sunk, but two He 115s were destroyed by a Hurricane catapulted from the freighter *Empire Morn*. This was a Merchant Service Fighter Unit aircraft, piloted by Flying Officer A. H. Burr, who landed at an airfield near Archangel after the engagement.

There was no doubt that the carrier fighters had averted a disaster on the scale of PQ17; nevertheless, PQ18 had suffered the loss of 13 ships, and six more (including the destroyer *Somali* and the minesweeper *Leda*) were sunk by U-boats out of a homeward-bound convoy, QP14. Although the Russian convoys were now shielded from air attack by the onset of the Arctic night, the winter brought with it extremely bad weather, and Admiral Tovey was concerned that large convoys would be in danger of becoming split up. He therefore recommended that the next convoy, PQ19, should be divided in two and its designation changed to JW51 for security reasons.

The First Sea Lord, Admiral Sir Dudley Pound, agreed, albeit reluctantly, and on 15 December 1942 the 16 merchant ships of JW51A left Loch Ewe, escorted by seven destroyers and five small anti-submarine vessels. JW51B, of 14 ships with an escort of six destroyers and five small A.S. vessels, sailed a week later. Both were covered by the 6-inch cruisers *Sheffield* (Capt. A. W. Clarke, flying the flag of Rear-Admiral Bob Burnett) and *Jamaica* (Capt. J. L. Storey), with more distant cover provided by the new battleship *Anson* and the 8-inch cruiser *Cumberland*.

JW51A was not detected by the enemy and reached the Kola Inlet without incident on Christmas Day, accompanied by Burnett's cruisers. On 27 December, having refuelled, Burnett took his warships to sea again to cover JW51B, one of whose ships had become detached in a storm and was proceeding independently,

The Kola Inlet – the end of the Arctic run.

accompanied by an A.S. trawler. Unknown to Burnett, the convoy had already been sighted on 24 December by a German reconnaissance aircraft and the U-354 (*Kapitänleutnant* Herbschleb). The German Admiralty at once initiated Operation *Regenbogen* (Rainbow), its object the convoy's destruction.

On 30 December *Vizeadmiral* Oskar Kummetz took his flagship, the *Admiral Hipper* (*Kapt.* H. Hartmann), the *Lützow* (*Kapt.* R. Stange) and six destroyers out of Altenfjord. His tactical options were limited: he was under orders not to risk a night engagement against escorts which might make torpedo attacks on his ships, he was only to engage a force weaker than his own by day, and futhermore the *Lützow* was afterwards to make a sortie into the Atlantic, which meant that she would need to conserve fuel and ammunition, not to mention to avoid damage.

At 083.0 on 31 December the *Hipper* and her destroyers passed 20 miles astern of the convoy, while the *Lützow* and her escorts were 50 miles to the south and closing. Burnett's two cruisers were about 30 miles to the north. The approaching enemy force was sighted by the corvette *Hyderabad*, which, mistaking the German destroyers for expected Russian escorts, made no report. Ten minutes later, the German vessels were also detected by the destroyer *Obdurate*, whose captain, Lt-Cdr C. E. Sclater, reported them to the escort commander, Lt-Cdr R. St V. Sherbrooke, in the flotilla leader H.M.S. *Onslow* but did not identify them. Sherbrooke ordered Sclater to investigate and *Obdurate* closed to within four miles of the enemy ships, turning away when they opened fire.

Leaving the destroyer *Achates* and three smaller escorts to protect the convoy with a smokescreen, Sherbrooke headed to join *Obdurate* at full speed, accompanied by the *Obedient* and *Orwell* and transmitting an enemy report to Rear-Admiral Burnett. At 09.41 the *Scheer* opened fire on the *Achates* and was at once engaged by the *Onslow* and *Orwell*, Sherbrooke sending the other two destroyers to assist in protecting the convoy. At 10.20 the *Hipper* found *Onslow*'s range and set her on fire, putting half her armament out of

action and holing her engine room. Sherbrooke, badly wounded, was obliged to turn over command to Lt-Cdr D. C. Kinloch in the *Obedient*, refusing to leave the bridge until assured that his orders had been received. At the same time, the *Hipper* disappeared into a snow squall. Some minutes later, at 10.45, she encountered the little minesweeper *Bramble*, which was armed with only one 4-inch gun, and quickly destroyed her with the loss of her captain, Commander H. T. Rust, and all his crew.

As soon as the *Hipper* disappeared Lt-Cdr Kinloch instructed all the destroyers to rejoin the convoy, which was now threatened by the *Lützow*, only two miles away. Stange, however, decided to stand off while the weather cleared, so allowing a golden opportunity to wipe out the merchantmen to slip through his fingers. At 11.00, while Kinloch manoeuvred his destroyers between the convoy and the *Lützow* group, still making smoke, the *Hipper* suddenly reappeared to the north and opened fire on the *Achates*, inflicting many casualties and killing her captain, Lt-Cdr Johns; she sank early in the afternoon. The *Hipper* then turned her fire on the *Obedient*; the destroyer suf-

Russian destroyers leading the way into the Kola Inlet – a rare occurrence

fered only light damage but her radio was put out of action, so that Kinloch was compelled to turn over command to the *Obdurate*'s captain.

At 11.30, as Hartmann drew away to avoid the destroyers' torpedo attacks, the *Hipper* was suddenly straddled by 24 6-inch shells from the *Sheffield* and *Jamaica*, closing from the north. Burnett had been able to follow the action by means of *Sheffield*'s radar, but the radar picture was confused and it was not until he obtained a positive sighting that Burnett felt able to engage the German cruiser. Three shells hit the *Hipper*, reducing her speed to 28 knots, and faced with this new threat Kummetz ordered Hartmann and the destroyer captains to retire to the west. As they did so, the *Sheffield*'s guns turned on the destroyer *Friedrich Eckoldt* and quickly reduced her to a blazing wreck, but the other destroyer, the *Richard Beitzen*, followed the *Hipper* into a snow squall and got away.

At about 11.45 the *Lützow* also opened fire on the convoy from a range of 18,000 yards, then she too withdrew as the British destroyers began an attack. There was a further brief engagement between Burnett's cruisers and the enemy force at 12.30, in which neither side suffered damage; the Germans continued to retire to the west and contact was lost at 14.00. Three days later, JW51B reached the Kola Inlet without further harm. That it did so was due in no small measure to the tactical skill, leadership and courage of Captain Sherbrooke, who survived his injuries to receive the Victoria Cross.

There was an important postscript to this action, which became known as the Battle of the Barents Sea. The *Lützow*, her sortie into the Atlantic cancelled, never sailed again against the Allied convoys; she was transferred to the Fleet Training Squadron in the Baltic, where, after action against the Russians, she was bombed and badly damaged at Swinemünde in April 1945, being blown up and scuttled a few weeks later. The *Admiral Hipper*, too, had made her last sortie; also transferred to the Baltic, she was bombed in Kiel in May 1945 and scuttled, being broken up in 1948–9. It may be said, with justification, that the Battle of the Barents Sea marked the beginning of the end of Germany's challenge on the oceans.

CHAPTER THIRTEEN
The Mediterranean Theatre, 1942–43

America's entry into the war in December 1941, although it gave Winston Churchill reason – in his own words – to 'sleep the sleep of the saved and the thankful', did not produce any overnight miracles. The Allied leaders quickly decided that the defeat of Germany was to be their first priority, but in the meantime the Americans were much too preoccupied with halting Japanese conquest in the Pacific to channel much in the way of immediate resources into the European theatre. The Americans advocated a cross-Channel assault in 1942; the British knew it would never work, and the subsequent tragedy of Dieppe proved them right. The British and Americans alike lacked the merchant ships, landing-craft and trained men to carry out such a venture, and Dieppe underlined the severity of the shortcomings.

Any large-scale invasion of enemy territory in 1942, therefore, would have to be in an area where defences were weak and opposition likely to be minimal. On 25 July the Allied leaders agreed that French North Africa was the logical objective, the landing of an expeditionary force to be timed to coincide with an offensive by the Eighth Army from Egypt. Although the final decision to go

ahead was not taken until October, the Admiralty immediately took steps to assemble the necessary merchant vessels and escorts, and to plan the convoys that would carry the invasion force. Convoys to Russia and North Africa were temporarily halted so as to provide the necessary resources and in August Admiral Sir Andrew Cunningham was appointed Allied Naval Commander Expeditionary Force for Operation *Torch*, as the venture was named.

The operational plan envisaged two assaults in the Mediterranean, at Algiers and Oran, and one on the coast of Morocco near Casablanca. The Anglo-American convoys bound for Algeria would sail from Britain and would be covered and supported by naval forces commanded by Vice-Admiral Sir Harold Burrough (Algiers) and Commodore T. H. Troubridge (Oran). The task of Vice-Admiral Sir Neville Syfret's Force H, reinforced by units of the Home Fleet, was to ensure that the Italian Navy was kept at bay during the operation. The naval force for Morocco, which would be all American, would sail direct from the United States under the command of Vice-Admiral H. K. Hewitt, U.S.N.

Attack and counterattack in the desert: the offensives of 1942.

The Allied landings in North Africa, November 1942: Operation Torch

After a number of delays D-Day for *Torch* was set for 8 November 1942, H-Hour being 01.00 at Algiers and Oran and 04.00 in Morocco. The 240 merchantmen needed to transport the forces from Britain were gradually assembled in various ports, mainly in the Clyde and Loch Ewe, while 160 warships were called in from other duties. Early in October a series of advance convoys carrying various stores began to sail for Gibraltar; these were followed, between 22 October and 1 November, by four big assault convoys carrying the troops. All the convoys were routed well to the west of Ireland, keeping well out into the Atlantic before turning east towards Gibraltar. Although they were sighted by U-boats, no ships were lost; the enemy submarines, in fact, were heavily engaged in attacking the homeward-bound convoy SL125 off the African coast. The convoy lost 13 of its 37 merchantmen, and there is little doubt that their sacrifice enabled the Gibraltar-bound convoys to reach their destination unmolested. (Indeed, it was suggested long after the war that SL125 was deliberately sacrificed in the interests of *Torch*, but there is no evidence at all to substantiate this.)

Inside the Mediterranean the invasion force divided into its various components, each being guided to its respective assault area by marker submarines. At Algiers the Eastern Task Force met with only slight resistance, and by daylight the troops were well established ashore with two local airfields captured. The destroyers *Broke* and *Malcolm* were assigned the task of penetrating the heavily defended harbour to land troops and also to prevent the French from scuttling their ships. The *Malcolm* was badly damaged and had to break off the attack, and although the *Broke* smashed through the boom and got inside the harbour to land her troops, she came under heavy fire from shore batteries and French warships and suffered heavy damage, sinking the next day.

At Oran, where the assault force was considerably larger, it encountered much stiffer opposition. An attempt by two sloops, the *Walney* and *Hartland*, to penetrate the harbour here was frustrated by heavy fire and both ships were sunk. Several French warships put to sea in an attempt to interfere with the invasion shipping, and in confused fighting the destroyers *Epervier*, *Tornade*, *Tramontane* and *Typhon*, a minesweeper and six submarines were sunk. The submarine *Fresnel* made an unsuccessful attack on the cruiser *Southampton* and escaped to Toulon, where she was joined by two submarines from Algiers, the *Caiman* and *Marsouin*. At Casablanca, the French also put to sea to try to intercept the American invasion force, losing a cruiser and six destroyers; the unfinished battleship *Jean Bart* was severely damaged by bombardment and air attack. There was a powerful French squadron at Dakar, from which the Americans had been expecting possible trouble, but it did not put to sea.

H.M. Submarine Tireless *was launched in March 1943. The T class boats had a complement of 65*

Careening H.M.S. Formidable *in Malta, summer 1943*

Resistance at Algiers ceased at 19.00 on 7 November, but at Oran the French continued to resist stubbornly until noon on 10 November, when British armoured vehicles penetrated the town. By this time the American assault forces were firmly consolidated ashore and were making ready to attack Casablanca, but a cease-fire was declared by Admiral Darlan, the French C.-in-C. The fighting had cost the Vichy French forces 462 dead, with over 1,000 wounded. German aircraft made sporadic appearances between 8 November and 14 November, sinking two troop transports, a landing-ship, two freighters and the gunboat *Ibis*; the aircraft carrier *Argus* was hit by bombs and the monitor *Roberts* was severely damaged.

The invasion of North Africa effectively sealed the fate of the Axis armies, and after over two years of bitter fighting, resistance in the theatre finally came to an end on 13 May 1943, when the last German troops in Tunisia capitulated. Two months later, British and American forces landed in Sicily.

Those two intervening months saw a great deal of naval activity in the Mediterranean, as the Allies consolidated their position in North Africa and built up port facilities. British submarines were particularly active, sinking thirty enemy merchant ships and the submarine U-303 during this period. The most important event prior to the Sicilian landings, however, was the capture of the Italian islands of Pantelleria and Lampedusa in the Mediterranean narrows early in June after a fierce air and naval bombardment (Operation *Corkscrew*). The islands had been used as a base by Italian M.T.B.s and submarines for attacks on the British Mediterranean convoys in 1942, and now that threat was removed.

Preparatory movements for the invasion of Sicily – which had been allocated the code-name *Husky* – began on 16 June with the trans-Atlantic passage of two American troop convoys to Oran and Algiers. Between 17 June and 23 June the British Force H, under Vice-Admiral Sir A. U. Willis, was transferred from Scapa Flow to Gibraltar, from where it sailed on to Oran; its assets comprised the battleships *Nelson*, *Rodney*, *Valiant* and *Warspite*, the carrier *Indomitable* and 18 destroyers. From Oran, the *Valiant*, *Warspite*, and *Formidable*, together with the cruisers *Aurora* and *Penelope* and six destroyers, moved on to Alexandria, which they reached on 5 July. In the meantime, the battleships *Howe* and *King George V* had also arrived at Gibraltar, having been relieved of Home Fleet duties by the deployment to Scapa of the U.S. battleships *Alabama* and *South Dakota*.

The operational plan for *Husky* envisaged landings by the British Eighth Army on five sectors of the east coast of Sicily stretching from just south of Syracuse to a point west of Cape Passero, while the U.S. Seventh Army was to land on three sectors on the south coast. The initial objectives were to capture the ports of Augusta and Syracuse, essential for subsequent resupply operations, and a clutch of airfields in the south west corner of the island for use by the Allied tactical air forces. The naval forces earmarked for the British assaults were to be commanded by Admiral Sir Bertram Ramsay, architect of the Dunkirk evacuation, while Vice-Admiral H. K. Hewitt U.S.N. was responsible for the American sectors.

In the British force, the troops earmarked for the three northern sectors, called *Acid North, Acid South* and *Bark East*, were to sail directly from the Middle East, while the *Bark South* force was to come from North Africa and Malta and the *Bark West* troops, comprising the 1st Canadian Division and Royal Marine Commandos, were to be transported from Britain. In all, some 115,000 British Empire and 66,000 American soldiers were involved.

D-Day for *Husky* was fixed at 10 July, and H-Hour at 02.45, about three hours before dawn. The operation featured a number of innovations, not least of which was that the troops allocated to the British *Bark South* sector would travel all the way from North Africa or Malta in their landing-ships and landing-craft, without recourse to troop transports; another was the appointment of a Beach Officer to each sector to control boat traffic, to maintain communications with the shipping offshore and generally to maintain order. The lessons of Dunkirk had been well learned.

The naval force involved in the operation was the largest yet assembled, comprising 2,590 warships and landing-craft – 1,614 of them British, 945 American and 31 from other nations. The force coming from the Middle East was commanded by Rear-Admiral T. Troubridge, the forces from North Africa and Malta were under the jurisdiction of Rear-Admiral R. R. McGrigor, while the convoys sailing from Britain came under the command of Rear-Admiral Sir Philip Vian. As mentioned earlier, Vice-Admiral Willis's Force H was charged with keeping the Italian Fleet at bay, while submarines patrolled off the enemy ports; and a cruiser and destroyer force under Rear-Admiral C. H. J. Harcourt was tasked with providing fire support for the land forces.

Despite delays caused by heavy seas, and some confusion that resulted when troops were landed on the wrong beaches, the operation unfolded

H.M. Submarine Seraph, *one of the more famous S class boats, operated as a beacon submarine during the Allied landings on Sicily*

Launched in 1941, the cruiser H.M.S. Newfoundland *survived the war to become the Peruvian Navy's* Almirante Grau *in 1959*

more or less to schedule under a heavy naval bombardment, and large vessels were able to clear the area before the first enemy air attacks developed in the afternoon. By dusk on D-Day, the Eighth Army's assault echelons were well established, Syracuse had been captured and the first resupply convoys were arriving. Best of all, losses had been insignificant.

The expected massive submarine assault on the invasion force never materialised, mainly because the German boats were operating off the coast of Algeria, and attacks by Italian submarines were not pressed home with determination, although the *Dandolo* succeeded in torpedoing the cruiser *Cleopatra* on 16 July. As the operation proceeded, the enemy suffered heavy submarine losses; six Italian boats were sunk, along with the German U-375, U-409 and U-561. The Italian submarine *Bronzo* was depth-charged to the surface in the middle of a British force off Syracuse on 12 July and captured intact. On 23 July the cruiser *Newfoundland* was damaged in a torpedo attack by the U-407, but between D-Day and the end of July the enemy submarines sank only four British merchantmen – one of which was torpedoed in Syracuse harbour by the U-81 – and two American L.S.T.s. Air attacks accounted for six British and one American merchantmen, two L.S.T.s, the destroyer U.S.S. *Maddox*, the minesweeper U.S.S. *Sentinel* and three smaller craft. A number of others were damaged, including the monitor *Erebus*, and on 14 July H.M.S. *Indomitable* was hit by an Italian aerial torpedo.

Despite overwhelming Allied air and naval superiority, the enemy succeeded in withdrawing over 100,000 troops (62,000 Italian, 40,000 German) together with large quantities of equipment, in more or less good order across the Straits of Messina to the Italian mainland early in August. This stretch of water, only two and a half miles across, was very well defended by coastal gun batteries, and the Allies were unable to establish naval domination there. Had the tactical air forces been unleashed against the enemy traffic in the straits as soon as the evacuation started they might have caused appalling havoc, but they were heavily committed to supporting Allied forces attacking the town of Troina, scene of some of the most bitter fighting of the campaign. It was not until 9 August that they were released from this task. By that time, the bulk of the enemy forces had got away, although 162,000 troops – mostly Italians – were taken prisoner on the island.

On 21 July, with the battle for Sicily still raging, the Combined Chiefs of Staff decided that an invasion of the Italian mainland should be launched at the earliest opportunity. As the Americans refused to allocate more fighters to the theatre – they were needed in western Europe to support the U.S.A.A.F's mounting daylight offensive against Germany – it was clear from the outset that naval aviation would have to play a key part in providing the necessary air cover over the invasion force. The Admiralty immediately dispatched the carrier *Illustrious* to join *Formidable* in Force H. In addition to these two fleet carriers, a Support Carrier Force (Task Force 88) was formed under the command of Rear-Admiral Vian; this comprised the light carrier *Unicorn*, the escort carriers *Attacker*, *Battler*, *Hunter* and *Stalker*, the cruisers *Euryalus*, *Scylla* and *Charybdis*, and nine destroyers (two of them Polish).

The plan that emerged called for General Montgomery's Eighth Army to cross the Straits of Messina (Operation *Baytown*) while a simultaneous amphibious assault was made on Salerno (Operation *Avalanche*) by the Fifth Army under the American General Mark Clark. Preparations had been completed by the beginning of September, and Admiral Cunningham named the 9th as D-Day, with H-Hour at 03.30, an hour before sunrise.

Montgomery's forces began their crossing of the Messina Straits on 3 September, and on the 7th the warships of Force H left Malta, sailing to the

With its narrow-track undercarriage the Seafire was not an easy aircraft to land on a carrier, as these photographs indicate. More were lost in deck landing accidents than through enemy action

The Fairey Barracuda first saw action during the Salerno landings in September 1943. It could carry six 250 lb bombs, four 450 lb depth-charges or one 1650 lb torpedo

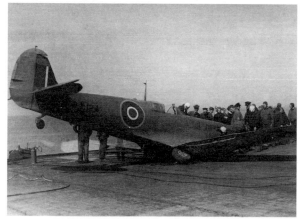

west of Sicily into the Tyrrhenian Sea. German torpedo-bombers attacked the force on the night of 8/9 September, but it escaped without damage, and on D-Day it was in position to cover the assault forces. Rear-Admiral Vian's Task Force 88 followed 24 hours later and took station off Salerno.

Meanwhile, there had been an important political development; on 8 September the Italian

government had accepted armistice terms tabled by the Allies, and this decision was publicly announced that evening. Admiral Cunningham at once ordered a powerful naval force to Taranto, where it landed the 1st Airborne Division (Operation *Slapstick*) and instructed the Italian fleet, whose transfer to the Allies had been agreed as part of the armistice terms, to sail south from Spezia by a specially designated route. The fleet, comprising the battleships *Roma*, *Vittorio Veneto* and *Italia* (formerly the *Littorio*), six cruisers and eight destroyers, accordingly put to sea in the early hours of the 9th, but that afternoon the ships were attacked by six Dornier 217s of III/K.G. 100, operating out of Marseille and carrying FX-1400 (*Fritz-X*) radio-controlled guided bombs. The battleship *Roma*, hit by two of these weapons, sank with the loss of 1,255 lives; the *Italia* was also hit, but reached Malta under her own steam. The destroyers *Da Noli* and *Vivaldi*, sailing to join the Allies from Castellamare, were shelled by German-manned coastal batteries in the Straits of Bonifacio and the latter was sunk; the *Da Noli* fell victim to a mine. At Taranto, meanwhile, the occupying British forces had taken over other Italian naval units, including the battleships *Andrea Doria*, *Caio Duilio* and *Giulio Cesare*.

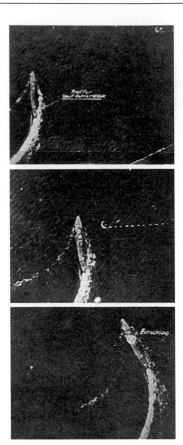

The Italian battleship Roma *manoeuvres desperately – and unsuccessfully – to avoid German glider bombs while en route to Malta after Italy's surrender*

The Italian Fleet at anchor off Malta after its surrender, September 1943

The Salerno landing was successful in the teeth of strong German opposition, but the troops at first failed to reach their initial objectives despite heavy naval fire support. Very slow progress was made on 10 September and that night three boats of the German 3rd M.T.B. Flotilla attacked a U.S. convoy and sank the destroyer *Rowan*. Naval aircraft continued to provide cover, as the Allied forces had not yet succeeded in capturing the key airfield of Montecorvino to permit the operation of tactical fighter-bombers, and there was a dangerous five-mile gap between the British X Corps, to the north, and the U.S. VII Corps.

On 13 September, the Germans launched a strong counter-attack, and for a time the Allied position was precarious. Cruisers were dispatched to Tripoli to embark reinforcements, and the battleships *Warspite* and *Valiant* were brought up from Malta to lend additional fire support. By nightfall on the 16th the enemy thrust had been halted, although not without cost to the naval forces involved: beginning on the 11th, Dornier 217s of K.G. 100 attacked with FX-1400 radio-controlled bombs and Hs 293 glider bombs, badly damaging the cruisers U.S.S. *Savannah* and H.M.S. *Uganda*, sinking the hospital ship *Newfoundland* and a supply ship and slightly damaging several other vessels. Then, on the 16th, H.M.S. *Warspite* took two Hs 293 hits and was so badly damaged that she had to be towed back to Malta.

On that day, troops of the Eighth Army, coming up from the south, broke through to the Salerno bridgehead. The advance inland began, and on 1 October the Allies entered Naples. In the meantime, the Germans were hastily evacuating Sardinia while French forces from North Africa occupied Corsica, an event that spelled the end of the enemy's presence in the western Mediterranean.

In Italy, there was a long and hard road to travel: just how hard, and how costly in terms of human suffering, no one at this stage could have envisaged. But the Allies were in undisputed control of the Mediterranean waters, and the task of Force H was at an end. For over three years, it had borne the brunt of the enemy onslaught by sea and air, its story one of terrible struggle and of gallantry unsurpassed; now it was disbanded, and its warships dispersed to other theatres of war.

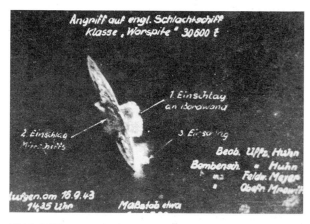

H.M.S. Warspite *dead in the water and leaking oil after being hit by glider bombs off Salerno, September 943*

With the crew drawn up on deck, H.M.S. Thane *passes the de Lesseps statue at Port Said en route to join the Eastern Fleet*

CHAPTER FOURTEEN
Naval Operations in the Indian Ocean, 1944–45

In October 1943, after a break of nine months, a British aircraft carrier was again deployed to the Indian Ocean. She was the escort carrier H.M.S. *Battler*, and she formed the nucleus of an anti-submarine group which, during the early months of 1944, began hunter-killer operations against the German and Japanese submarines which were preying on shipping in the area from their main base at Penang.

At the end of 1943, the British Eastern Fleet – apart from the carrier mentioned above – was reduced to the battleship *Ramillies*, eight cruisers, two auxiliary cruisers, eleven destroyers, thirteen frigates, sloops and corvettes and six submarines.

A Swordfish crumples after a bad landing on H.M.S. Battler in the Indian Ocean

It therefore came as a welcome event when, on 30 January 1944, the British naval presence in the Indian Ocean was strengthened by the arrival at Colombo of the battleships *Queen Elizabeth* and *Valiant*, the battlecruiser *Renown*, the carriers *Illustrious* and *Unicorn*, two cruisers and seven destroyers, the whole force having made a fast passage through the Mediterranean after leaving Scapa Flow and the Clyde a month earlier. The first operation by the strengthened Eastern Fleet was a sweep against enemy blockade runners and warships of the 7th Japanese Cruiser Squadron, two of which – the *Kuma* and *Kitakami* – were sunk by submarines in February.

Not long afterwards, on 12 March 1944, came the first success of *Battler*'s hunter-killer group, when the Fairey Swordfish of No. 842 Squadron located an enemy submarine supply ship off the Seychelles and steered destroyers to her position. The loss of this ship, together with another which had been destroyed a fortnight earlier, drastically reduced the time that could be spent at sea by enemy submarines, with a consequent reduction in the tonnage of Allied shipping sunk.

A British convoy en route from Aden to Bombay, with the escort carrier H.M.S. Battler

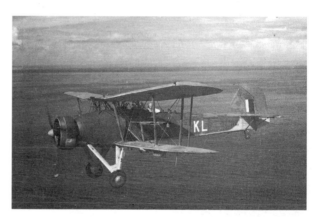

Fairey Swordfish on patrol over the Indian Ocean

Avengers being loaded on to H.M.S. Battler *at Suez*

Fairey Swordfish taking off from H.M.S. Battler *in the Indian Ocean*

In April 1944 the principal units of the Eastern Fleet made rendezvous with the American carrier *Saratoga*, loaned to the Royal Navy at Admiral Somerville's request to enable him to mount a big strike against Japanese targets in Sumatra. This operation, named *Cockpit*, began on 16 April, when the Eastern Fleet set out from Trincomalee in two groups: Task Force 69 with the battleships *Queen Elizabeth*, *Valiant*, *Richelieu* (French), the cruisers *Newcastle*, *Nigeria*, *Ceylon*, *Gambia* and *Tromp* (Dutch), the destroyers *Rotherham*, *Racehorse*, *Penn*, *Petard*, *Quiberon*, *Napier*, *Nepal*, *Nizam* (R.A.N.) and *Van Galen* (Dutch); and Task Force 70 with the carriers *Illustrious* and *Saratoga*, the cruiser *London*, the destroyers *Quilliam*, *Quadrant*, *Queenborough*, *Cummings*, *Dunlap* and *Fanning*, and the air-sea rescue submarine *Tactician*. On 18 April, the cruisers *Ceylon* and *Gambia* were detached from T.F. 69 to reinforce T.F. 70.

The aircraft carriers arrived at their flying-off position 100 miles south-west of Sabang Island shortly before dawn on 19 April, and at first light 83 aircraft – 17 Barracudas of 810 and 847 Squadrons covered by 13 Corsairs of 1830 and

The Fiji class cruiser H.M.S. Gambia *served with the Eastern Fleet and was transferred to the Royal New Zealand Navy in 1943. She took part in the final assault against Japan*

1833 Squadrons from the *Illustrious*, together with 18 Dauntlesses, 11 Avengers and 24 Hellcats from the *Saratoga*, headed for their primary target, Sabang Harbour. While the Corsairs and Hellcats strafed the enemy airfields in the neighbourhood, knocking out 25 Japanese aircraft, the bombers made a series of beautiful precision attacks on the harbour installations, causing severe damage and sinking two small freighters. Only one aircraft, a

The N class destroyer H.M.S. Nizam, *pictured here in the Indian Ocean from a F.A.A. Swordfish, served with the Royal Australian Navy throughout the Far Eastern War*

Hellcat, was lost, but its pilot was rescued by the *Tactician*. Later, a small formation of three Mitsubishi G4M *Betty* torpedo-bombers attempted to attack the Allied warships, and all were shot down by the Hellcats.

The Eastern Fleet's next operation was a strike – Operation *Transom* – on the big Japanese aviation fuel dump at Soerabaya in Java. The naval forces were designated Task Forces 65 and 66 and

Servicing a Royal Navy Grumman Avenger at Katakarunda, Ceylon

Towing a Barracuda from its dispersal at R.N.A.S. Katakarunda

comprised three battleships, two aircraft-carriers, five cruisers and 14 destroyers, the whole supported by six fleet tankers and two more cruisers (*London* and *Suffolk*). Since the strike aircraft had

to fly across the breadth of Java, 810 and 847 Squadrons temporarily exchanged their Barracudas for Avengers, the American aircraft having the greater range. Forty-five Avengers and Dauntlesses covered the 180-mile distance from the flying-off position to the target at daybreak on 17 May 1944, one wave attacking the fuel dump and the nearby refinery while the second wave dived on the harbour. The results were disappointing; the refinery was only lightly damaged and only one small ship was sunk. Japanese fighters failed to challenge the 40 Corsairs and Hellcats of the escort, and only one Allied aircraft – an Avenger – was lost. Twelve enemy aircraft were destroyed on the ground. After this attack, the *Saratoga*, having been ordered to return to the United States for a refit, left the main force and sailed for Pearl Harbor. The *Illustrious* returned to Trincomalee with the remaining warships.

On 22 June aircraft from the *Illustrious* raided targets on the Andaman Islands in the Bay of Bengal. The weather was poor, and the damage was limited to a few coastal vessels sunk and damaged by the Barracudas, and a dozen or so enemy aircraft destroyed on the ground at Port Blair airfield. It was the last operation before welcome reinforcements arrived in July, in the shape of the fleet carriers *Victorious* and *Indomitable*; in the weeks that followed the escort carriers *Shah*, *Begum*, *Atheling* and *Ameer* also joined the Eastern Fleet, permitting the formation of additional hunter-killer groups.

Between 22 July and 27 July 1944 the Eastern Fleet mounted Operation *Crimson*, a major attack on Sabang by air and surface forces. While Corsairs from the two fleet carriers strafed airfields and Barracudas attacked fuel facilities, the battleships *Queen Elizabeth*, *Valiant*, *Renown* and *Richelieu*, supported by five cruisers and five destroyers, fired 294 15-inch, 134 8-inch, 324 6-inch, 500 5-inch and 123 4-inch shells into Sabang. In the wake of this bombardment, the Dutch cruiser *Tromp* and the Australian destroyers *Quilliam*, *Quality* and *Quickmatch* penetrated the harbour and attacked shipping with torpedoes and close-range shellfire. The cruiser and two of the destroyers sustained damage, but got clear.

Ten enemy aircraft attempted to attack the raiding force, and seven were shot down by the combat air patrols. This was the last operation directed by Admiral Somerville; on 21 August he was relieved by Admiral Sir Bruce Fraser, who until recently had been C.-in-C. Home Fleet.

After the Sabang strike the *Illustrious* sailed to Simonstown for a refit. During the last week in August, Barracudas from the *Victorious* and *Indomitable* struck at two more targets in Sumatra: the port of Emmahaven and the cement works at Indaroeng. The latter target was badly hit, but the harbour was only lightly damaged. However, no strike aircraft were lost and the escorting Corsairs and Hellcats encountered no fighter opposition.

At the end of August 1944, the Eastern Fleet comprised the battleships *Howe, Richelieu, Queen Elizabeth*, the battlecruiser *Renown*, the carriers *Indomitable* and *Victorious*, eleven cruisers and 32 destroyers. The *Howe* had joined the fleet on 8 August; ironically, on the same day the *Valiant* was badly damaged in the collapse of the floating dock at Trincomalee. For the time being, then, the Eastern Fleet still had three battleships at its disposal instead of the planned four.

Between 16 September and 20 September 1944 the Eastern Fleet carried out Operation *Light*, an attack on the railway junction at Sigli in northern Sumatra by the carriers *Victorious* and *Indomitable* supported by the *Howe*, two cruisers and seven destroyers. Results might have been better; as in

The escort carrier H.M.S. Battler *in the Indian Ocean, 1943*

the earlier strikes, the Fleet Air Arm crews suffered from a lack of target intelligence, a consequence of the lack of very long range (V.L.R.) reconnaissance aircraft based in India and Ceylon.

On 19 October 1944, a huge armada of American warships approached Leyte, in the Philippines, on the eve of what was to be one of the most decisive battles of the Pacific War – the Battle of Leyte Gulf – as what was left of the Japanese naval forces in the area made an abortive attempt to draw off the U.S. fleet as a preliminary to smashing the invasion that was under way. As part of their plan, the Americans had asked Rear-Admiral Moody's Eastern Fleet Carrier Squadron to mount a series of strikes on the Nicobar Islands in the hope that they would divert some of the Japanese forces from the main American objective.

The strikes, code-named Operation *Millet*, began early on 17 October with Barracudas from the *Victorious* and *Indomitable* mounting a series of softening-up attacks which, it was hoped, would convince the Japanese that an invasion of the Nicobars was imminent. The enemy, however, refused to rise to the bait, although Japanese fighters came up in strength to meet the attackers. On the 19th, Corsairs of 1834 Squadron from the *Victorious* shot down four Nakajima Ki.43 *Oscar* fighters in two engagements, and an attempted attack by twelve torpedo-bombers cost the Japanese seven aircraft. During the three-day operation the Royal Navy lost only two aircraft, a Hellcat and a Barracuda.

The Nicobar Islands strike was the Fairey Barracuda's last operation. During the following weeks, the type was replaced in Nos 815, 817 and 831 Squadrons by Grumman Avengers. While the squadrons were working up with their new aircraft and undergoing intensive training at Trincomalee, two significant events occurred: first, the *Illustrious* returned from her refit in South Africa, and second, the carrier squadron got a new commander in the person of Rear-Admiral Sir Philip Vian.

The first operation under his command – Operation *Outflank* – began on 18 November, and involved a strike by 27 Avengers, escorted by as many Corsairs and Hellcats, from the carriers *Illustrious* and *Indomitable* on the port of Belawan Deli in Sumatra on 20 December. This was actually a secondary target; the strike had originally been flown off against Pangkalan Brandan, but low clouds and driving rain had prevented the attack on the primary target. The raid on Belawan Deli caused only light damage, and no British aircraft were lost. The Corsairs and Hellcats strafed several airfields in the vicinity, destroying a number of enemy aircraft, and two of No. 1839 Squadron's Hellcats from the *Indomitable* caught a Mitsubishi Ki.21 *Sally* twin-engined bomber slipping along just under the clouds and shot it down in flames. The carriers were supported by the cruisers *Newcastle*, *Black Prince* and *Argonaut* and seven destroyers.

At the end of November 1944 the Eastern Fleet was reorganized, part of it becoming the British East Indies Fleet under Vice-Admiral Sir Arthur Power. It comprised the battleship *Queen Elizabeth*, the battlecruiser *Renown*, five escort carriers, eight cruisers and 24 destroyers. The more modern warships were assigned to the British Pacific Fleet under Admiral Sir Bruce Fraser and included the battleships *King George V* and *Howe*, the carriers *Indefatigable*, *Illustrious*, *Indomitable* and *Victorious*, the cruisers *Swiftsure*, *Argonaut*, *Black Prince*, *Ceylon*, *Newfoundland*, *Gambia* and *Achilles*, and three destroyer flotillas.

On 17 December the First Aircraft Carrier Squadron (*Illustrious* and *Indomitable*, supported by four cruisers and seven destroyers) carried out Operation *Robson*, a second raid on Belawan Deli. After this attack Rear-Admiral Vian returned to Trincomalee, staying only long enough to refuel and rearm before taking the First Aircraft Carrier Squadron to sea again for another strike on Pangkalan Brandan, this time with the *Indomitable*, *Victorious* and *Indefatigable* supported by four cruisers and eight destroyers, the whole being designated Task Force 63. The strike – Operation *Lentil* – took place on 4 January 1945 in fine weather, and was highly successful. While the Avengers inflicted severe damage on the refinery, the British fighters had something of a field day; the Corsairs of *Victorious*'s No. 1836 Squadron shot down five *Oscars*, while No. 1834 Squadron destroyed a *Sally* and a Mitsubishi Ki.46 *Dinah*. Total claims in air combat amounted to 12, with 20 more enemy aircraft destroyed on the ground. Only one Avenger was lost, its crew being rescued.

On 16 January 1945, under the mantle of Operation *Meridian*, the British Pacific Fleet, as Task Force 63, sailed from Trincomalee for Sydney in the first stage of its planned deployment to the Pacific Theatre. It comprised the battleship *King George V*, the carriers *Illustrious*, *Indefatigable*, *Indomitable* and *Victorious*, three

Rear-Admiral Moody, commanding the Eastern Fleet's carrier force, inspecting a ship's company in Colombo, 1944

H.M.S. Begum, one of the Eastern Fleet's escort carriers

cruisers and nine destroyers. Four days later the fleet made rendezvous with its support force, Task Force 69, comprising the tankers *Arndale*, *Echodale*, *Empire Salvage* and *Wave King*, which had sailed from Fremantle in Western Australia.

On the way to Australia, Rear-Admiral Vian planned to carry out an operation which, as well as dealing a severe blow to the Japanese war effort, would also help to convince the Americans that the British Pacific Fleet meant business: an air strike on the enemy oil refineries at Pladjoe and Soengi Gerong, north of Palembang, which supplied a large part of Japan's aviation fuel.

The strike was originally scheduled to take place on the 22nd, but because of torrential rain at the flying-off point 200 miles off the south-west coast of Sumatra it had to be postponed for 48 hours. At dawn on 24 January, however, the four carriers launched 43 Avenger bombers of Nos 820, 849, 854 and 857 Squadrons and 12 rocket-armed Fireflies of No. 1770 Squadron. Top cover and strafing attacks on airfields in the area were to be the tasks of the Corsairs and Hellcats, while the Supermarine Seafires of Nos 887 and 894 Squadrons, because of their restricted range, were to carry out fleet defence.

The Japanese defences were taken by surprise and, although anti-aircraft fire was heavy, the attackers left the refineries blazing fiercely. Only about 20 Japanese fighters took off to intercept the raid; 14 were shot down, and a further 34 destroyed on the ground. The British lost seven aircraft due to enemy action, but no fewer than 25 were destroyed or damaged in crash-landings on returning to the carriers.

Meanwhile, following the end of the monsoon season in October 1944, the East Indies Fleet had been involved in supporting the British Fourteenth Army's offensive in Burma. Between 11 December and 20 December 1944, the newly formed Task Force 64, comprising the Australian destroyers *Napier* and *Nepal*, minesweepers, landing-craft and two motor-launch flotillas of the Indian Navy, operated in support of the coastal flank of the British XV Corps on the Arakan Front, and on 2 January T.F. 64 sailed from Chittagong to land 1,000 men of the 3rd Commando Brigade on the southern tip of the Akyab Peninsula (Operation *Lightning*). Originally, the Allied plan had been to capture the key port of Akyab by means of a seaborne assault in February, but when it was learned that the Japanese were withdrawing from the area the Marines were sent in, followed by the Indian 74th Brigade, and Akyab was won without serious opposition. The cruisers *Newcastle*, *Nigeria* and *Phoebe* (the latter a fighter-direction ship) which had been standing by to lend fire support were not called upon to do so. As a follow-up operation, T.F. 64 landed units of the 3rd Commando Brigade near Myebon, between Akyab and Ramree, on 12 January.

British and Dutch submarines were active throughout these operations. There were now 26 based on Ceylon, and in the last six months of 1944 they sank 16 merchantmen totalling 35,000 tons, together with two German U-boats and a Japanese submarine. Their main operating areas were the Malacca Straits, off Java and in the South China Sea. Many of their actions were against small craft, which they sank with gunfire; Japanese anti-submarine tactics were inefficient and their small submarine-chasers could sometimes be dispatched in this way. Large targets were rare, and warship targets even more so; it was a noteworthy achievement when Cdr A. R. Hezlet in *Trenchant* sank the Japanese heavy cruiser *Ashigara* on 8 June 1945 as the warship was heading for Singapore, laden with troops from Batavia. Hezlet fired a salvo of eight torpedoes at long range and five of them hit.

Three British and four Dutch submarines were lost on operations in the Far East. Their claim was two cruisers, two destroyers, five U-boats, 13 minor naval vessels, 47 sizeable merchant ships and many small merchant craft. Seven of these ships are known to have been sunk by some of the 640 mines laid by submarines in the course of 30 operations. The sinkings added up, in total, to some 130,000 tons by the end of the war.

The amphibious landings on the Burmese coast in January 1945 were supported by the Hellcats of No. 804 Squadron, from the escort carrier *Ameer*, but it was not until 1 March that 804's pilots had their first encounter with Japanese aircraft, shooting down two *Oscars* and a *Dinah*. During

Operation *Stacey*, from 24 February to 4 March, Hellcats of No. 888 Squadron, H.M.S. *Empress*, ranged over northern Sumatra, gathering a wealth of photographic intelligence on potential targets.

Armed with this information, the Avengers of 851 and the Hellcats of 808 Squadrons flew strikes against targets in Sumatra from the *Emperor* and *Khedive* during the second and third weeks in April, damaging several enemy vessels off Emmahavan and destroying a number of enemy aircraft. During this phase, destroyers of the East Indies Fleet also made frequent raids on the Andaman Islands and attacked Japanese convoys, sometimes in conjunction with long-range Liberator aircraft. Between 8 April and 18 April the East Indies Fleet carried out Operation *Sunfish*: this involved a sortie by the battleships *Queen Elizabeth* and *Richelieu*, the heavy cruisers *London* and *Cumberland*, and the destroyers *Saumarez*, *Vigilant*, *Verulam*, *Virago* and *Venus* against targets on the north coast of Sumatra, in the course of which Sabang was heavily shelled.

From 27 April to 7 May 1945 the East Indies Fleet participated in Operation *Dracula*, the Allied landings near Rangoon. The spearhead was Assault Force W under Rear-Admiral B. C. S. Martin, consisting of six convoys and the head-quarters ship *Largs*. The landing force, consisting mainly of the 26th Indian Division, was escorted by six Indian Navy sloops and supported by 22 minesweepers from the 7th and 37th M.S. Flotillas. Cover for the landing was provided by the 21st Carrier Squadron, consisting of the escort carriers *Hunter*, *Stalker*, *Emperor* and *Khedive*, the cruisers *Phoebe* and *Royalist*, four destroyers, eight frigates and two sloops. As a diversion, TF 63 carried out Operation *Bishop*, in which the battle-ships *Queen Elizabeth* and *Richelieu*, the cruisers *Ceylon*, *Cumberland*, *Suffolk* and *Tromp*, and six destroyers shelled Car Nicobar and Port Blair. This was carried out in conjunction with air strikes on airfields in the Nicobar and Andaman Islands by Avengers and Hellcats from the *Shah* and the *Empress*.

On 10 May 1945, the Japanese cruiser *Haguro* and the destroyer *Kamikaze* sailed from Singapore on a mission to evacuate Japanese forces from the Nicobars and Andamans. As they passed through the Malacca Straits, the warships were sighted by the British submarines *Statesman* and *Subtle*, which alerted Fleet H.Q. at Trincomalee. The response was immediate: Task Force 61 (Vice-Admiral H. T. C. Walker), comprising the battle-ships *Queen Elizabeth* and *Richelieu*, the cruisers *Cumberland*, *Royalist* and *Tromp*, the escort carriers *Hunter*, *Khedive*, *Shah* and *Emperor*, and eight destroyers converged on the north-west tip of Sumatra, intent on intercepting the enemy force in the Eleven Degrees Channel. *En route*, the escort carriers launched a Hellcat strike on Car Nicobar, which alerted the enemy to the task force's presence. The *Haguro* and her escort promptly reversed course, but Admiral Walker shrewdly guessed that she would make a second attempt, and on the night of 14/15 May he detached the escort carriers and the 26th Destroyer Flotilla, consisting of *Saumarez*, *Venus*, *Verulam*, *Vigilant* and *Virago* under Captain M. L. Power, to search the waters north of Sumatra.

The next day, the enemy ships were sighted by an Avenger from the *Shah* north-east of Sabang, and during the night the destroyer flotilla caught up with the *Haguro* 45 miles south-west of Penang. The destroyers attacked in a classic pincer movement and sent the cruiser to the bottom with many torpedo hits, but not before she had inflicted heavy damage on the *Saumarez*. The cruiser's escort, the destroyer *Kamikaze*, escaped with slight damage.

On 3 June, the *Kamikaze* was detailed for another escort mission, accompanying the cruiser *Ashigara* on a dash to Batavia, from where 1,200 Japanese troops were evacuated. On 8 June, however, as mentioned earlier, the *Ashigara* was attacked and sunk by the submarine *Trenchant*. Once again, the *Kamikaze* escaped.

During June and July 1945 the East Indies Fleet was engaged in operations against crumbling Japanese resistance in the Andamans, while carrier aircraft attacked airfields and rolling stock in Sumatra and southern Burma. Many enemy convoys in southern Thailand were also attacked by Corsairs and Hellcats, creating havoc on the tortuous roads.

On 26 July, seven Japanese aircraft swept low

over the sea towards the ships of the 21st Carrier Squadron in the Bay of Bengal. Three were shot down by fighters and two more by anti-aircraft fire, but another struck the minesweeper *Vestal*, which blew up and sank, and the other one narrowly missed the carrier *Ameer*. It was the 21st Carrier Squadron's first and only experience of a kamikaze attack; for the Imperial Japanese Army Air Force in South-East Asia, it was the last desperate act before the final collapse.

Meanwhile, firm plans had been laid for a large-scale amphibious landing on the west coast of Malaya, (Operation *Zipper*) and Admiral Lord Louis Mountbatten, the Supreme Commander in South-East Asia, now gave orders that this was to proceed. As part of the preliminaries, on 30 July, two midget submarines, the XE-1 (Lt J. E. Smart, R.N.V.R.) and XE-3 (Lt I. E. Fraser R.N.R.) made a very gallant attack on Japanese shipping in Singapore harbour, having been towed to the Johore Strait by the submarines *Spark* and *Stygian*. The heavy cruiser *Takao* was severely damaged by explosive charges and was only saved from sinking by shallow water. Lieutenant Fraser and his crewman, Leading Seaman Magennis, were each awarded the Victoria Cross for this exploit. On the following day, Lt M. H. Shean, R.A.N.V.R.,

in XE-4, cut both the Singapore–Saigon and Hong Kong–Saigon submerged telephone cables, virtually isolating the island base from the outside world.

But Operation *Zipper* never took place. On 6 August 1945, the first atomic bomb was dropped on Hiroshima, followed by a second on Nagasaki on the 9th, and two days later Japan accepted the Allied surrender terms. At this juncture the whole East Indies Fleet was on its way across the Bay of Bengal, with the object of occupying Penang and then sweeping the approaches to Singapore; but on 19 August General MacArthur, the Supreme Commander Allied Powers in the Pacific Theatre, ordered that no landings were to be made on Japanese-held territory until the instrument of surrender had been signed. So the East Indies Fleet, with all its accompanying troop transports, had to remain at sea off the Nicobars, short of supplies and in monsoon weather, until the restriction was lifted, and it was not until 2 September that forces were landed at Penang and also at Sabang in Sumatra. On the following day the Commander-in-Chief East Indies Fleet arrived at Singapore; and on 12 September 1945 Admiral Mountbatten accepted the surrender of all Japanese forces in the theatre.

CHAPTER FIFTEEN
The Battle of the Atlantic, 1942–44

The Atlantic battles of 1942 began with the dispatch, early in January, of twelve Type VIIC U-boats to operate in the area of the Newfoundland Bank. Between them, from 8 January to 12 February, they sank 21 ships. It was the beginning of the German submariners' second 'happy time', and the operations in Canadian waters were timed to coincide with the start of Admiral Dönitz's offensive against American mercantile traffic – Operation *Paukenschlag* (Drumbeat) – in the western Atlantic. Only five submarines were involved in this initial deployment, yet in operations from 11 January to 7 February 1942 they sank 26 ships, all of which were sailing independently, and

damaged several more. A second wave of five Type IX U-boats, operating off the U.S. east coast between 21 January and 6 March, sank a further 19 vessels, while off Canada another eight Type VII craft sank nine more, together with the destroyer H.M.S. *Belmont*.

For some time, the United States Navy had been actively participating in Atlantic convoy protection work, and this activity was stepped up considerably following a meeting between Winston Churchill and President Roosevelt off Argentia, Newfoundland, on 10 August 1941. From 17 September, the U.S. Navy's Task Force 4 assumed responsibility for escorting the fast convoys between Newfoundland and Iceland, while the slower convoys were escorted by the Canadian Newfoundland Escort Force as far as longitude 22° West, the so-called Mid-ocean Meeting Point, where the Royal Navy took over.

The destroyer H.M.S. Rocket *making 22 knots on convoy protection duty in the North Atlantic*

Ancient and modern: the escort carrier H.M.S. Ravager *passing an American river paddle-steamer as she leaves the United States to join the Royal Navy*

Voyages across the Atlantic to pick up a ship from the U.S.A. could be boring affairs – if no U-boats were in the vicinity

The growing American participation, the increase in overall Allied escort strength, and the availability of more long-range maritime aircraft – together with the contribution of *Ultra* – meant that the war in the Atlantic was being won by the beginning of December 1942. In November the U-boats sank only 13 ships, and in December the Allied shipping losses from all causes in the Atlantic amounted to just ten vessels. Eight U-boats were destroyed in December, five of them by warships escorting the Gibraltar convoy HG76. It was on passage with this convoy that the escort carrier *Audacity* was sunk by the U-751, but not before her Martlet fighters had shot down four Fw 200 *Kondor* maritime reconnaissance aircraft.

The high shipping losses suffered off the east coast of America between January and April 1942 gave the British Admiralty cause for concern, for some of the vessels were British and many were tankers, which were in short supply; and it must be said that the German successes during this period were attributable not so much to the skill and daring of their submariners, although they possessed both qualities in plenty, but to mistakes in strategy made by the Americans. They failed to institute an immediate convoy system, despite

British urging for them to do so, and as a result targets sailing independently, close to a coastline that was still often lit at night, were easy to sight, track and sink. The Americans advanced a number of reasons for not implementing a convoy system on British lines – lack of sufficient escorts, the danger of concentrating targets and so on – but there was a human factor involved as well. Admiral Ernest King, the Commander-in-Chief United States Fleet, believed that offensive tactics by patrol groups would produce better results. Apart from that, he was by no means an admirer of the British, and the idea of adopting a convoy system and naval control of shipping on the British pattern ran contrary to his nature. It was not until May 1942 that the Americans established a system of convoy on their east coast routes, and the result was immediately apparent: the U-boats were forced to switch their main area of operations to the Gulf of Mexico and the Caribbean. It was only there that they continued to register successes for the next three months or so, until the convoy system was extended to cover these sectors too.

It was at about this time that that anti-submarine aircraft began to make their mark. During their 'happy time' off the U.S. coast the U-boat crews had had practically nothing to fear from shore-based aircraft, as no experienced American A.S.W. squadrons were available. When Dönitz switched the weight of the U-boat offensive back to the North Atlantic convoy route in July 1942 most of the submarine operations took place in the 'air gap' outside the range of aircraft operating from Newfoundland, Iceland and Northern Ireland. To add to the Allies' problems, in February 1942 the Germans had introduced a new and more complex form of *Enigma* cypher solely for use with U-boats at sea, except for those in the Arctic and Mediterranean, and had tightened up security all round. Called *Triton* by the Germans, this new cypher defeated the experts at Bletchley Park for ten months and deprived the Allies (the Americans having been admitted to the *Ultra* secret well before Pearl Harbor) of their special knowledge of U-boat operations.

The one area in which *Ultra* was still useful was the Bay of Biscay, for Bletchley was able to

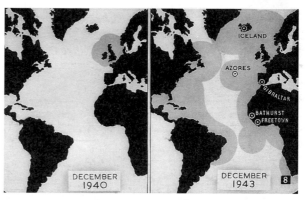

Atlantic air coverage in 1940 and 1943. By the latter year the Atlantic air gap was virtually closed by V.L.R. aircraft, and the introduction of escort carriers narrowed it even further

decrypt the *Hydra* cypher used by patrol vessels escorting the U-boats in and out. It was the custom of the submarines to traverse the bay submerged by day and to recharge their batteries on the surface at night, when there was minimal risk from the patrolling aircraft of Coastal Command's No. 19 Group. But on 6 July the cover of darkness was suddenly stripped away when the U-502 was attacked and sunk by a Wellington of No. 172 Squadron, equipped with a searchlight. Following more Leigh Light attacks the German U-boat Command changed its tactics; submarines were now directed to pass through the Bay at night submerged and surface to recharge their batteries in daylight, when aircraft could be detected visually in time for the boat to dive.

The Germans had good reason to be satisfied with the results obtained by their U-boats in the first half of 1942; in all waters they had sunk 585 merchantmen totalling more than three million tons. They had commissioned over a 100 new boats and lost 21, only six of which had been sunk in the western Atlantic.

From July to December 1942 many convoys were attacked in the air gap. The situation might have been alleviated by the provision of more very long range (V.L.R.) aircraft to Coastal Command (at this time, No. 120 Squadron, operating from Northern Ireland with detachments to

Iceland, was the Command's only V.L.R. unit, and it had only five Liberators). For some inexplicable reason, the 32 Liberators allocated to Coastal Command between July and September 1942 were not modified to V.L.R. standard, but instead were given to Nos 59 and 224 Squadrons, in south-west England, to strengthen the Bay patrols.

As for A.S.V. (Air-to-Surface Vessel) radar, the Mk II set had been used by Coastal Command since the end of 1940, but it had its drawbacks. Its range was limited to about twelve nautical miles on an operational target – a fully surfaced submarine – and then only when the boat was lying beam-on to an aircraft flying at 2,000 feet or more. The main disadvantages of the equipment were a strong back echo, excessive sea returns, bulky aerials and a rather high optimum search height. Nevertheless, A.S.V. Mk II was a proven success, and the number of U-boat sightings initially quadrupled after aircraft fitted with this equipment began operating at night to catch the enemy submarines on the surface.

In the summer of 1941 the first A.S.V. Mk II sets were supplied to the Americans, who were not yet at war, and these were installed in three PBY-5 Catalinas from Navy Patrol Squadrons VP-71, VP-72 and VP-73, one per squadron, and in two PBM-1 Mariners of VP-74. Additional aircraft

were equipped in September. The squadrons all belonged to Patrol Wing 7, which became the first unit in the U.S. Navy to be supplied with radar-equipped aircraft. The Catalinas and Mariners operated from Norfolk, Virginia, Quonset Point and advanced bases in Newfoundland and Iceland during the last months of America's 'neutrality patrol' prior to the attack on Pearl Harbor. Thereafter, Patrol Wing 7 joined the war against the U-boat.

In the spring of 1942, British A.S.V. operations suffered a setback when a Lockheed Hudson fitted with A.S.V. Mk II fell into enemy hands in Tunisia. Within a matter of months the Germans had produced a search receiver for installation in their U-boat fleet. Code-named *Metox*, the receiver gave warning of the approach of an aircraft using A.S.V. Mk II from about 30 nautical miles, which gave the U-boat ample time to evade. As a consequence, the number of U-boat sightings dropped dramatically in the latter half of 1942 as the tactical initiative was restored to the submarines.

One measure that did give the Allies a considerable advantage in the Atlantic battles of 1942,

The Strike Wings of R.A.F. Coastal Command wrought havoc on enemy shipping from the end of 1942. Photograph shows Beaufighters in action

The real enemy: both sides had to contend with often unpredictable Atlantic seas

made or lost contact with a convoy, and a single H.F./D.F. ship could provide reliable detection of a U-boat making a transmission on the frequency the ship was guarding when the latter was within 'ground wave' range (15–30 miles). Each H.F./D.F. report enabled the escort commander to send an escorting aircraft, if he had one, or anti-submarine ships to search for and attack the U-boat. The submarines needed their surface speed to keep up with or overtake a convoy, and even if the searching escorts failed to find and attack the U-boat, they could probably force it to submerge until the convoy was out of sight. By the end of January 1942, 25 escorts had been fitted with H.F./D.F., and the number increased steadily throughout the year. Next to centimetric radar, H.F./D.F. was probably the most important element in winning the Battle of the Atlantic. In combination with radar, it eventually made submarine attacks on convoys too hazardous to be attempted.

In 1942, though, despite the growing number of Allied surface and air escorts, and despite the introduction of new equipment, merchant shipping losses mounted to unprecedented levels, and in November they reached an all-time record of 700,000 tons. The Germans were now suffering severe reverses in Russia and North Africa, and the Atlantic seemed the one area in which they could inflict terrible damage on the Allies. With Allied shipping under immense strain the outlook was bleak, and the optimism of twelve months earlier had vanished. When the figures for 1942 were added up, they reached the appalling total of 1,664 merchantmen – nearly eight million tons – lost on the high seas. Unless this rate of loss could be reduced there seemed no prospect that the construction of new merchant tonnage could outstrip sinkings, and the gloomy economic news was that Britain's imports had fallen to two-thirds of the 1939 total.

In December 1942, in desperation, the Admiralty turned to Bletchley for help. It was not slow in coming, for in that very month, by an astonishing coincidence, documents from a U-boat sunk off Port Said enabled the experts at last to break into the *Triton* cypher. The decrypts revealed that Admiral Dönitz now had over 100

however, was the large-scale introduction of shipborne H.F./D.F. (High Frequency Direction Finding) equipment, known as 'Huff-Duff' to those who used it. The wolf-pack tactics employed by the U-boats required them to make radio reports to their shore stations when they

U-boats deployed; 50 were in the Atlantic, and 37 of them were operating in the air gap to the south of Greenland. The timely breaking of *Triton*, together with terrible weather conditions which hampered the U-boats as much as the convoys in the early weeks of 1943, meant that the Admiralty could once again adopt evasive routeing, which undoubtedly saved many ships in January. As an added bonus, the Germans' own cypher-breaking service, the *B-Dienst*, temporarily lost its ability to read the British convoy cypher, which robbed the U-boats of vital intelligence. As a result, sinkings dropped dramatically during this period, although from 3 January to 12 January the U-boats scored a notable success by sinking seven out of nine tankers in Convoy TM1, running from Trinidad to Gibraltar.

Then, in February, the *B-Dienst* restored its ability to read the convoy cypher, and the U-boats attacked in packs of unprecedented size. Between 2 February and 9 February, 20 boats of the *Pfeil* and *Haudegen* packs fell on the slow convoy SC118 between Newfoundland and Iceland and sank 13 of its 63 ships. Later in the month, 16 U-boats were directed to attack the outward convoy ON166, sinking 14 of its 40 ships, while other convoys were attacked in the central Atlantic by

Although not as effective as the Liberator in the A.S.W. role, the Boeing Flying Fortress scored a number of U-boat kills with Coastal Command

U-boats replenishing from *Milchkuh* supply submarines near the Azores. Allied losses for February amounted to 63 ships totalling 360,000 tons, and worse was to come. In March, Bletchley lost its grip on *Triton* for a fortnight, with the result that this month became the worst ever for convoy sinkings.

It began with an attack on the slow convoy SC121, which lost 13 ships between 7 March and 11 March. Then, from the 16th to the 20th,

Convoys SC122 (60 ships) and HX229 (40 ships), both outbound from New York, were attacked by 40 U-boats. The HX convoy lost 21 merchantmen totalling 141,000 tons; SC122 lost nine. In all theatres of war, in that terrible month, the U-boats sank 108 ships totalling 627,000 tons. Losses were so severe, in fact, that the naval staff later recorded that the enemy had come 'very near to disrupting communications between the New World and the Old'. Compounding the tragedy was the fact that the two convoys from New York had been re-routed from the northern to the southern route to avoid the *Raubgraf* U-boat pack, which was shadowing another convoy, ON170.

But the tide was about to turn. In March, as the Atlantic battles raged, representatives of the British, American and Canadian navies met in an 'Atlantic Convoy Conference' in Washington. It was agreed that the U.S. Navy should assume responsibility for the tanker convoys running between Britain and the West Indies, leaving the North Atlantic entirely to the British and Canadians. The Royal Canadian Navy, directed by a new North-West Atlantic Command H.Q. at Halifax, would be entirely responsible for the North Atlantic convoys as far as 47° West, where the Royal Navy would take over. March also saw the formation of the first Support Groups, which would provide rapid reinforcement for convoys under threat; two of the first five were composed of destroyers drawn from the Home Fleet, two of escort vessels from the Western Approaches Command, all with highly experienced crews.

The crew of a U-boat frantically man the guns as the craft is caught on the surface by patrolling aircraft from an escort carrier

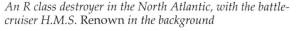

An R class destroyer in the North Atlantic, with the battle-cruiser H.M.S. Renown *in the background*

The fifth was formed around the escort carrier *Biter*.

In April 1943 the cryptanalysts at Bletchley once again made a partial inroad into the *Triton* cypher, with the result that evasive routeing could be re-established. It was not always a success, being often frustrated by *B-Dienst* countermeasures. The real Allied successes at this juncture came with new operational capabilities. By the end of March Coastal Command's slowly growing force of V.L.R. Liberators and Boeing Fortresses (the latter serving with Nos 206 and 220 Squadrons), together with aircraft from H.M.S. *Biter*, were closing the Greenland gap and forcing U-boat shadowers to submerge. Improved anti-submarine tactics and weapons began to make themselves felt. Shipborne H.F./D.F. maximised its exploitation of U-boat transmissions, often helping convoys to steer clear of danger and assisting air and surface escorts to seek out and kill the enemy. Above all, centimetric radar, now installed in surface escorts and (as A.S.V. Mk III) in aircraft, was turning them into deadly U-boat killers. The German Navy sought frantically for countermeasures, but it was not until September 1943 that the Germans realised that only 10 cm A.S.V. radar was being

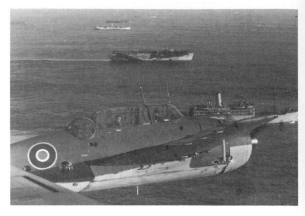

H.M.S. Biter *and an Atlantic convoy, seen from a No. 846 Squadron Avenger*

The view from H.M.S. Ravager *setting out on convoy protection; H.M.S.* Biter *is in the background*

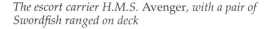

The escort carrier H.M.S. Avenger, *with a pair of Swordfish ranged on deck*

used. Their response was to modify the non-directional S-band *Naxos* night-fighter receiver, which the *Luftwaffe* used to home on transmissions from H2S radar sets, for U-boat use. Operating between 8 and 12 cm, *Naxos* was found to be capable of detecting A.S.V. Mk III transmissions out to about 10 nautical miles.

That, however, was in the future, and in the meantime, in the three months to the end of May 1943 the Allies sank 56 U-boats – 41 in May alone – compared with the 51 that left port, so that for the first time there was a net decrease in their operational number. The number lost in the period January – May was 96, of which 52 were sunk by aircraft. Signs of flagging morale now became apparent in the *Triton* decrypts, together with references to the U-boat crews' growing fear of air attack and the speed with which the escorts and Support Groups reacted to sightings. By 19 April, Dönitz was conceding that Allied reaction – in particular maritime air – was frustrating the U-boat pack concept, and on 25 May he withdrew his submarines to the central Atlantic, outside the radius of Allied land-based air cover and where convoys were less-well defended.

In this area the U-boats had already scored considerable success in April; on the 30th of that month a single submarine, the U-515, made three attacks on Convoy TS37 between Takoradi and Sierra Leone and sank seven of its 18 ships, totalling 43,255 tons. During this series of battles each side became aware that the other was learning of the movements and whereabouts of the opposing forces; the Allies, now convinced that the convoy cypher had been compromised, immediately brought a new one into force, and from June 1943 onwards the Germans were denied virtually all intelligence of Allied shipping movements. Adding to the Germans' problems was an order from Dönitz insisting that U-boats traversed the Bay of Biscay on the surface by day in the erroneous belief that they would be able to shoot it out with Allied aircraft. The maritime crews took every advantage of the order, and in the 94 days that it remained in force, from 1 May to 2 August 1943, they sank 28 U-boats in the Bay. But the success was not without its cost; 57 aircraft failed to return.

U-boat under air attack in the Bay of Biscay, 1943

From the end of July 1943 Bletchley and its American counterpart were able to break the *Triton* cypher until almost the end of the war with only very rare delays. Its recovery was ably demonstrated when, with its assistance, American escort carriers and Coastal Command between them sank almost the entire fleet of *Milchkuh* supply submarines (only ten were ever built). This reduced the U-boat campaign in distant waters to negligible proportions, and greatly diminished the effectiveness of the boats operating in the central Atlantic.

The success of the Allied achievement in the summer of 1943 may be judged by the fact that not one North Atlantic convoy was attacked in June, and in the central Atlantic U-boats were suffering from the attentions of U.S. carrier aircraft. The lack of activity now enabled the Admiralty to move from defence to offence, and on 20 June the 2nd Escort Group under Captain F. J. Walker was

ordered into the Bay to hunt U-boats in conjunction with aircraft. The *Milchkuh* tanker submarine U-119 was rammed and sunk by the sloop *Starling*, while the U-449 was depth-charged and sunk by *Wild Goose, Woodpecker, Kite* and *Wren.* Other escort and support groups also participated in these operations, relieving one another at intervals of five to eight days and sinking two more U-boats to bring the June total (in the Bay) to a somewhat disappointing four. Only 17 were sunk in all waters during the month.

In September 1943, Admiral Dönitz ordered group operations against the Atlantic convoys to resume, the U-boats now being equipped with search receiver equipment, eight 20 mm anti-aircraft guns and a new acoustic homing torpedo, the T5 *Zaunkönig* (Wren). Twenty submarines passed through the Bay of Biscay to operate against Convoys ON202 and ONS18 on the eastern side of the North Atlantic. The Admiralty

H.M.S. Wild Goose *(2nd Escort Group, pennant No. U45) participated in the sinking of two U-boats off Newfoundland in November 1943*

The sloop H.M.S. Woodpecker, *2nd Escort Group, seen here from an escort carrier*

was advised of the movement by *Ultra* and a Liberator of No. 10 Squadron R.C.A.F. sank the U-341 in the southern part of the patrol line on 19 September. However, because of grid reference problems the position of the first attack wave was miscalculated by 100 miles, and the U-boats were able to achieve a measure of surprise. In a five-day battle they sank three escorts and six merchantmen, losing three of their own number, but the U-boats were frustrated by the rapid reaction of Support Group B3 under Commander M. J. Evans, with 18 destroyers, corvettes and frigates, and by the V.L.R. Liberators which were constantly over the convoys when the weather permitted. German claims to have sunk twelve escorts with 24 T5 firings resulted in the effectiveness of the new torpedo being greatly over-

The escort carrier H.M.S. Trumpeter *in a heavy sea.*

Avengers of No. 846 Squadron, with H.M.S. Tracker *in the background*

estimated; in fact, many of the torpedoes failed to explode or detonated in the ships' wash.

Other operations against the Atlantic convoys culminated in a disaster for the U-boats. In an attack on Convoys ON206 and ONS20 between 15 October and 18 October, the submarines sank only one merchantman and lost six of their number, three to aircraft.

In all, Dönitz lost 25 U-boats in the Atlantic during September and October 1943, and they achieved nothing more than the sinking of nine merchant ships out of the 2,468 convoyed across the ocean.

More escort carriers were now available for operations in the Atlantic. H.M.S. *Tracker*, for example, was now working in conjunction with Captain Walker's 2nd Escort Group, and it was Walker who devised simple but effective tactics to make the U-boats' lives even more difficult. Once search aircraft from the carrier had made contact

Maritime air power: V.L.R. Liberators of Coastal Command at an unidentified airfield, 1943, and an aircraft of No 220 Squadron in flight

with a submarine and directed Walker's ships on to it, he would position a 'directing ship' astern of the enemy to maintain asdic contact. Meanwhile, two other escorts, not using their ASDIC, would creep up on either side of the submarine and release depth-charge patterns on the command of the director vessel, giving the U-boat no time to take avoiding action.

Such vigorous action by air and surface forces, together with evasive routeing, compelled Dönitz to abandon his wolf-pack tactics in November 1943 and to withdraw all but a few boats from the North Atlantic, where they continued for months to hunt for convoys with negligible success. The main U-boat forces were sent to operate against the Gibraltar convoys, where they had the advantage of air support, and during the ensuing months many battles were fought in Iberian waters and the south-western approaches. But here, too, frustrated by *Ultra*-directed air patrols, support groups and evasive routeing, they achieved little and suffered heavy losses. From 13 November to 21 November, for example, some 30 U-boats with strong maritime air support operated against the combined convoys MKS30 and SL140 on the Gibraltar route, but determined attacks by air and surface escorts fended the submarines off and the only two merchantmen (out of 66) lost were sunk by Hs 293 glider bombs launched by Heinkel 177s. Three U-boats were sunk.

From January to March 1944 only three merchant ships were sunk out of 3,360 convoyed, and in the whole of 1944 36 were sunk. Maritime air was the major factor in this, and by 1944, as *Ultra* revealed, the U-boats were reporting that air attacks in the central Atlantic were even more serious than those in the Bay of Biscay. Such was the background to the successful transport of U.S. forces to Britain, making it possible to launch the Normandy invasion on time.

The Allied victory in the Atlantic had been nothing short of incredible; and it had been made possible by the talent, courage and skill of the men who conducted it. Men such as Admiral Sir Percy Noble, Command-in-Chief Western Approaches, who in the crisis of the battle in 1942, recognised the need to form specialist support groups; and Admiral Sir Max Horton, that experienced submariner, who succeeded Noble and brought the Battle of the Atlantic to its successful conclusion. There were the men of R.A.F. Coastal Command, too, Air Marshals Bowhill, Joubert and Slessor, ceaselessly fighting the cause of maritime air and recognising the need for the fullest cooperation with the Royal Navy in order to prosecute a successful campaign.

And finally there were the men on the ships, merchant seamen and naval personnel; the sailors of the Merchant Navy, of whom 30,248 were lost at sea, mostly in the Atlantic, as were many of the 51,578 officers and men of the Royal Navy who never returned. They gave their utmost, and none more so than Captain F. J. Walker of the 2nd Escort Group, who on 9 July 1944 collapsed and died, the victim of the immense strain he had undergone in nearly five years of almost continuous anti-submarine operations.

The sloop H.M.S. Magpie *formed part of Captain F. J. Walker's successful 2nd Escort Group*

The escort carrier H.M.S. Ravager *became the merchant vessel* Robin Trent *after being returned to the U.S. in 1946*

CHAPTER SIXTEEN
Arctic Victory, 1943–45

As the mid-Atlantic struggle between the escorts and the U-boat packs continued, the battle flared up in Arctic waters once more. In September 1943, the *Tirpitz* and the *Scharnhorst* had made one sortie to bombard installations on the island of Spitzbergen before scurrying back to their Norwegian lair, and in December the *Scharnhorst* put to sea once more. After an interval of several months, when no convoys passed through to Russia because of the dangers involved, they had been resumed in November when Convoy RA54A sailed from Archangel to the U.K. without incident; two more outward-bound convoys, JW54A and JW54B, also made the journey from Loche Ewe to Russia unmolested. The next two convoys, however, were both reported by the *Luftwaffe*, and Admiral Dönitz issued orders that they were to be attacked not only by the 24 U-boats based on Bergen and Trondheim, but by available surface units, the largest of which was the *Scharnhorst*.

The convoys were JW55B, outward bound from Loch Ewe with 19 ships, and RA55A, homeward bound from Kola. The former sailed on 20 December 1943, the latter three days later. Each was escorted by ten destroyers and a number of smaller vessels.

At 14.00 on Christmas Day, the *Scharnhorst* (*Kapt.* F. Hintze, flying the flag of Admiral Bey) sailed from Norway accompanied by the destroyers Z29, Z30, Z33, Z34 and Z38 to intercept JW55B, which had been located by air reconnaissance on 22 December. The convoy had already been attacked by Ju 88s and by U-boats of the *Eisenbart* pack, but without success. On 26 December, Admiral Bey ordered his destroyers to form a patrol line to search for the convoy in heavy seas. He knew that a British cruiser covering force comprising the *Belfast*, *Norfolk* and *Sheffield* was operating in the Barents Sea; what he did not know was that there was also a distant covering force commanded by the C.-in-C. Home Fleet, Admiral Sir Bruce Fraser, comprising the battleship *Duke of York*, the cruiser *Jamaica* and four destroyers, which had sailed from Iceland.

Fraser, aware that JW55B had been located by enemy aircraft, was convinced that the *Scharnhorst* would make a sortie against it, and detached four destroyers from Convoy RA55A,

Convoy JW65 pictured in an Arctic sunset, March 1945

The battleship H.M.S. Duke of York *first saw operational service with the Arctic convoys in March 1942. Launched in 1940, she was scrapped at Faslane in February 1958*

which he did not consider to be under immediate threat, to reinforce JW55B's close escort. His hope was that this strengthened destroyer force would not only be sufficient to drive off the *Scharnhorst*, but might perhaps damage her enough for the *Duke of York* to come up and finish her off. At this point Fraser's ships were 200 miles south-west of North Cape and the cruiser force, under Admiral Burnett, 150 miles to the east.

Admiral Bey's five destroyers, meanwhile, had not only failed to locate the convoy; they had also, because of a signalling error, lost touch with the flagship and were subsequently ordered to return to base, so that they took no part in the coming events. At 08.40 on the 26th, the cruisers *Norfolk* and *Belfast* obtained radar contact with the *Scharnhorst* at 35,000 yards, and at 09.21 the *Sheffield* glimpsed her in the stormy darkness at 13,000 yards. A few minutes later all three destroyers opened fire on the battlecruiser and obtained three hits, one of which put her port 6-inch fire control system out of action. The *Scharnhorst* replied with a few harmless 11-inch salvoes, then Bey turned away to the south-east while Burnett placed his cruisers between the threat and the convoy, screened by four destroyers from the escort.

At 12.21 the three cruisers again sighted the *Scharnhorst* and opened fire with full broadsides at 11,000 yards, while the destroyers fanned out to attack with torpedoes. Before they were able to get into position the battlecruiser retired to the north-east, her gunfire having put one of *Norfolk's*

turrets and all her radar out of action; *Sheffield* also suffered some splinter damage. But the *Scharnhorst* had taken punishment too, including a hit abreast her A turret and one on her quarterdeck.

At 16.17, the *Duke of York*, now 20 miles away to the north north-east, obtained a radar echo from the *Scharnhorst*, and at 16.50 Fraser ordered *Belfast* to illuminate her with starshell, and immediately afterwards the *Duke of York* opened fire with her 14-inch armament. Admiral Bey was now trapped between Burnett's cruisers to the north and Fraser's warships to the south, and he had no choice but to fight it out. Once *Scharnhorst's* gunners had recovered from their surprise, their fire was accurate, but although they straddled the British battleship many times they failed to register a serious hit on her. The *Duke of York's* gunnery was excellent; she scored 31 straddles out of 52 broadsides, with enough hits to put the battlecruiser's A and B turrets out of action and to rupture some steam pipes, which reduced her speed so that Bey had no chance of outrunning his adversaries, even if the opportunity had arisen.

At 18.24 the third of *Scharnhorst's* turrets was put out of action, and Fraser, realising that the *Duke of York's* 14-inch shells, fired at short range with a flat trajectory, were unlikely to pierce the enemy's armour, turned away to let the destroyers finish the job. Two of them, the *Savage* and *Saumarez*, approached from the north-west under heavy fire, firing starshell, while *Scorpion* and *Stord* attacked from the south-east, launching their torpedoes at 18.49. As Hintze turned his ship to port to engage them, one of *Scorpion's* torpedoes struck home, closely followed by three more from the first two destroyers. As the small ships retired under cover of smoke, the *Duke of York* and the cruisers closed in to batter the enemy warship with merciless fire. As Lieutenant B. B. Ramsden, an officer of Royal Marines on H.M.S. *Jamaica*, later wrote, the *Scharnhorst*

> must have been a hell on earth. The 14-inch from the flagship were hitting or rocketing off from a ricochet on the sea. Great flashes rent the night, and the sound of gunfire was continuous, and yet she replied, but only occasionally now with what armament she had left.

By 19.30 the battlecruiser was a blazing wreck, her hull glowing red-hot in the Arctic night, and the destroyers closed in to finish her off with torpedoes. At 19.45, she blew up; only 36 of her crew of 1,968 officers and men were rescued from the freezing sea. Like their comrades of the *Bismarck* two and a half years earlier, they had fought their ship gallantly to the end; now, treated with great kindness by the destroyer men who pulled them from the oil-soaked water, they were transferred to the *Duke of York* for the voyage to England and captivity.

So ended the Battle of North Cape, and with it the last attempt by a German capital ship to challenge the supremacy of the Royal Navy. But there was still the *Tirpitz* to be reckoned with.

The *Tirpitz* had been damaged by X-craft (midget submarines) during a gallant attack on 18 September 1943, but it could only be a matter of months before she was made seaworthy again. Her continued presence in Norwegian waters constituted a permanent menace. In a bid to knock her out once and for all, the C.-in-C. Home Fleet planned a massive Fleet Air Arm strike against her. To simulate her anchorage in Altenfjord, a dummy range was built on Loch Eriboll in Caithness, and during March 1944 this was the scene of intense activity as aircraft from the *Victorious* and *Furious* rehearsed the attack plan.

The strike was to be carried out by the 8th and 52nd T.B.R. (Torpedo Bomber Reconnaissance) Wings, made up of Nos 827, 829, 830 and 831 Squadrons operating the Fairey Barracuda, a type that had first seen action with No. 810 Squadron during the Salerno landings eight months earlier. In addition to their T.B.R. Wings, the *Victorious* and *Furious* also carried Nos 1834 and 1836 Squadrons, equipped with American-built Vought Corsair fighters, and Nos 801 and 880 Squadrons equipped with Seafires. More fighter cover was to be provided by the Hellcats of Nos 800 and 804 Squadrons (H.M.S. *Emperor*) and the Martlet Vs of Nos 861, 896, 882 and 898 Squadrons (H.M.S. *Pursuer* and H.M.S. *Searcher*). Anti-submarine patrols were to be flown by the Swordfish of 842 Squadron on board H.M.S. *Fencer*. The carrier group was to be covered by warships of the Home Fleet, consisting of the battleships *Duke of York* and *Anson*, the cruisers *Belfast*, *Jamaica*, *Royalist* and *Sheffield*, and 14 destroyers. The strike was timed to coincide with the passage of a Russian convoy, JW58.

Altenfjord in Norway, refuge for the Tirpitz *and other heavy units of the German Navy's Norwegian Squadron*

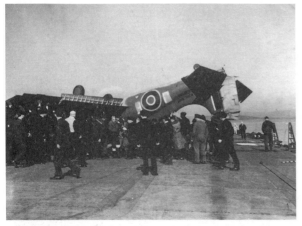

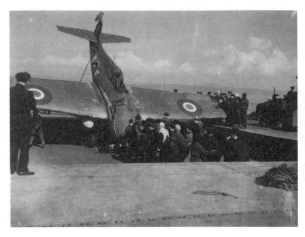

Deck landing problems were by no means confined to Seafires. Photos show Martlets of No. 881 Squadron, H.M.S. Ravager

Barracudas crossing the Norwegian coast en route *to attack the* Tirpitz *in Altenfjord, 24 August 1944*

On 30 March 1944, with the convoy well on its way, the Home Fleet units sailed from Scapa Flow in two forces, the first comprising the two battleships, the *Victorious*, one cruiser and five destroyers, and the second of the *Furious*, the four escort carriers and three cruisers. The actual attack on the *Tirpitz*, code-named Operation *Tungsten*, was to be conducted by Vice-Admiral Sir Henry Moore, second-in-command of the Home Fleet, flying his flag in the *Anson*.

The forces assembled in the afternoon of 2 April about 220 nautical miles to the north-west of Altenfjord and from there moved to the flying-off position, 120 miles north-west of Kaafjord, reaching it during the early hours of the following morning. At 04.30, 21 Barracudas of No. 8 T.B.R. Wing, escorted by 21 Corsairs and 20 Hellcats, took off from the *Victorious* and set course for the target. Fifty miles from their objective, the Barracudas, which had been flying low over the sea to avoid radar detection, went up to 8,000 feet and began their final approach, preceded by the fighters which went in at low level to suppress flak. The Germans were taken by surprise and the *Tirpitz*, lying virtually naked under the beginnings of a smokescreen, was hit by nine armour-piercing or semi-armour-piercing bombs. An hour later, a second attack was made by 19 Barracudas of No. 52 T.B.R. Wing, escorted by 39 fighters, and the performance was repeated. By

Martlets landing-on after escorting Barracudas over Norway, 1944

Naval aircrew on H.M.S. Indefatigable *prior to attacking the Tirpitz. The photograph well illustrates the typical FAA flying kit of late 1944*

this time the smokescreen was fully developed, but it hindered the German gunners far more than it did the Barracuda crews, who had no difficulty in locating their target. In all, the battleship was hit by 14 bombs, 122 of her crew being killed and 316 wounded; although the bombs failed to penetrate her heavy armour, they caused extensive damage to her superstructure and fire-control systems and put her out of action for three months. The British lost two Barracudas and a Hellcat.

Convoy JW58 – with 49 ships, the largest convoy so far to sail on the Arctic route – accompanied by the cruiser *Diadem*, the escort carriers *Tracker* and *Activity*, 20 destroyers, five sloops and

Battle damage to the escort carrier H.M.S. Tracker *near a 40mm A.A. gun mounting*

five corvettes, had meanwhile made steady progress. On 29 March, Captain F. J. Walker's 2nd Support Group scored an early success when it sank the U-961, *en route* to the Atlantic. During the next three days Martlets from the escort carriers shot down three Fw 200, two Ju 88 and one Bv 138 reconnaissance aircraft. Three U-boat groups, *Thor*, *Blitz* and *Hammer*, with twelve boats between them and assisted by five more bound for the Atlantic, made repeated attacks on the convoy, but without success; the U-355 was sunk by the destroyer *Beagle* following a rocket attack by one of *Tracker*'s Avengers, the U-360 was destroyed by the *Keppel*, and the U-288 was sunk by aircraft from the two carriers, all between 1 April and 3 April.

Further attempts to attack the *Tirpitz* in May were frustrated by bad weather, the naval aircraft instead turning their attention to enemy convoys off the Norwegian coast and scoring some successes. It was not until 17 July 1944 that another raid was carried out, this time by aircraft from the *Formidable*, *Furious* and *Indefatigable* under the command of Rear-Admiral R. R. McGrigor. The covering force, comprising the battleship *Duke of York*, the cruisers *Bellona*, *Devonshire*, *Jamaica* and *Kent*, was commanded by Admiral Moore, now C.-in-C. Home Fleet in place of Admiral Sir Bruce Fraser. Forty-five Barracudas of Nos 820 and 826 Squadrons (*Indefatigable*) and 827 and 830

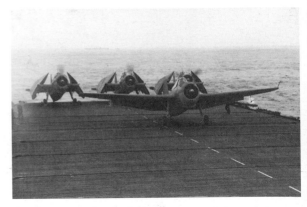

Avengers preparing for take-off

Grumman Avenger of No. 846 Squadron

An Arctic sunset, seen from H.M.S. Tracker

Squadrons (*Formidable*) set out to make the attack; the 50-strong fighter escort included the Fairey Fireflies of No. 1770 Squadron, making their appearance in combat for the first time. However, the enemy had plenty of warning on this occasion. The smokescreen obscured the warship, the A.A. defences were fully alerted, and the raid was unsuccessful.

The next attack, carried out on 22 August, was a disaster; the incoming aircraft were detected a long way from the target and were intercepted by Me 109s of J.G. 5, which shot down eleven of them, mostly Barracudas. The escort carrier *Nabob* was torpedoed off North Cape by the U-354 and damaged beyond repair; the U-354 was herself sunk by aircraft from the escort carrier *Vindex* three days later. Two minor bomb hits were obtained on the *Tirpitz* in an attack on 24 August, the Barracuda crews bombing blind through the smoke, and a further attack, on the 29th, was unsuccessful. Including a mission that had to be aborted because of the weather on 20 August, the Fleet Air Arm flew 247 sorties in this series of attacks.

As for the *Tirpitz*, she was moved south to Tromsø for repairs; and it was there, on 12 November 1944, that she was finally destroyed by the 12,000 lb Tallboy bombs dropped by the Lancasters of Nos 9 and 617 Squadrons, R.A.F.

His Majesty King George VI inspecting naval personnel on the carrier H.M.S. Indefatigable *at Portsmouth, 1 November 1944*

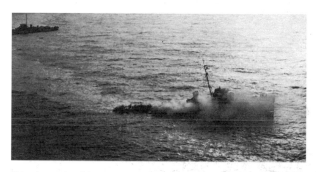

War loss: the frigate H.M.S. Bickerton *on fire and sinking after being torpedoed by the U-354 off Norway, 22 August 1944*

The escort carrier H.M.S. Nabob *after being torpedoed by U-354 off Norway, 22 August 1944. She reached Scapa Flow under tow*

During the last year of the war in Europe, with the U-boat packs decimated or immobilised by the capture of the Atlantic ports, the Royal Navy switched a major part of its task from convoy protection to offensive operations against enemy shipping in Norwegian coastal waters. The fleet carriers *Victorious*, *Indefatigable* and *Implacable* played a major part in these operations; the latter was the last carrier to enter service with the Home Fleet.

Most of the work in northern waters, however, was done by the escort carriers, equipped mostly now with Grumman Avengers. The *Emperor*, *Pursuer* and *Searcher* were fighter carriers; their aircraft covered all minelaying and strike missions so successfully that none of the Barracudas nor the Avengers was lost to enemy aircraft during any mission, while some 40 German aircraft were claimed as destroyed in the air or on the ground by the Fleet Air Arm pilots. Because most of the enemy fighters were by this time committed to the Battle of Germany, there were few

interceptions. The *Luftwaffe* made only one serious attempt to intervene, during a strike by Avengers on 26 March 1945, and the escorting Wildcats (Martlet Vs) shot down five Me 109s without loss to themselves.

Fairey Barracuda touching down on an aircraft-carrier. Note the huge flap area. The photograph was taken in the Firth of Clyde; Ailsa Craig is in the right background

Frigate carrying out a depth-charge attack in the Norwegian Sea, September 1944. The aircraft overhead with undercarriage down is a Seafire from H.M.S. Indefatigable

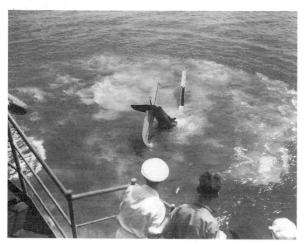

Missed approaches: Avengers of 846 Squadron come to grief during operations off Norway, 1944

H.M.S. Trumpeter *pictured from 'Q' deck of the escort carrier H.M.S.* Campania *in the Barents Sea*

The escort carrier H.M.S. Campania *on Arctic convoy duty, 1945*

The carrier H.M.S. Nairana *riding out an Arctic storm, 1944*

By the beginning of 1945, the only carriers still using Swordfish in the Norwegian operations were the *Campania* and *Nairana*. Their aircraft were engaged mainly in reconnaissance and minelaying duties, but on one memorable occasion – on 28 January 1945 – the Swordfish of *Campania*'s 813 Squadron carried out a night strike against shipping at Vaagsø. In brilliant moonlight, they attacked with rockets and sank three armed trawlers.

The achievement of the air and surface escorts accompanying the Arctic convoys in 1944 may be judged by the fact that of the nine JW/RA convoys that made the round trip to Russia during the year, only four merchantmen were sunk out of a total of 304 dispatched. The last escort mission by a carrier – H.M.S. *Queen* – in Arctic waters was carried out in May 1945, several days after the German surrender, in case of possible suicidal attacks by fanatical Nazi U-boat commanders (of whom, fortunately, there were very few).

On 4 May 1945, 44 Avengers and Wildcats from the carriers *Trumpeter*, *Searcher* and *Queen* swept down on the Norwegian port of Kilbotn, near Harstad, and destroyed the 5,000-ton submarine depot ship *Black Watch*, together with the U-711 lying alongside. It was the Fleet Air Arm's last

Grumman Martlet landing on H.M.S. Trumpeter

Avengers in flight

strike in European waters; four days later, the Germans surrendered. The enemy's plans to transfer most of their remaining forces from northern Germany and Denmark to Norway for a desperate last-ditch stand that might have prolonged the war by several months had not materialised. The combined efforts of the Fleet Air Arm and R.A.F. Coastal Command had tipped the scales against such a plan, which could not have succeeded without control of the air over Norway and the seas around it. The Norwegian fjords were littered with the sunken wrecks of ships, the Norwegian airfields littered with the charred remains of aircraft, in mute testimony to the fury that had descended from the skies. But it should not be forgotten that British submarines and M.T.B.s, many of the latter Norwegian-manned, also played their part in the dislocation of the enemy's seaborne traffic in Norwegian waters.

The S class destroyer H.M.S. Success *served on Arctic convoy protection; she became the Royal Norwegian Navy's* Stord *and was scrapped in 1959.*

Avengers in flight

Grumman Avengers attacking enemy shipping, Norway 1944

CHAPTER SEVENTEEN
Neptune

The preparations for the Royal Navy's contribution to the invasion of western Europe – Operation *Overlord* – were breathtaking in their extent and remarkable for their forward planning. An outline plan for an invasion in 1943, called *Roundup*, was actually drawn up in 1941; and another one, *Sledgehammer*, was drafted in 1942, its aim being to seize and hold a bridgehead in France to take some pressure off the Russians, who seemed in danger of collapse. In June that year, with the Allies suffering one reverse after another, the Admiralty appointed Admiral Sir Bertram Ramsay to be Naval Commander Expeditionary Force; two years later, with the invasions of North Africa and Sicily behind him, he was vastly experienced in the techniques of seaborne assault, and well aware of the naval fire-power requirement that accompanied it.

By 10 April 1944 Ramsay had completed his final plan for the naval participation in the forthcoming invasion, code-named *Neptune*. In a document that ran to over 700 foolscap pages, he stressed that the primary objective must be, in his own words, 'to secure a lodgement on the continent from which further offensive operations can be developed' and to achieve it he assigned the available naval forces to convoy escort, minesweeping, fire support for the invasion forces, and a multitude of other tasks that were likely to arise.

Two large amphibious task forces were assigned to the assault: an Eastern Task Force under Rear-Admiral Sir Philip Vian, and a Western Task Force under Rear-Admiral A. G. Kirk, U.S.N. The Eastern Task Force was to land three divisions of the British Second Army on three beaches, code-named *Gold*, *Juno* and *Sword*, on a 30-mile front west of the River Orne, while the Western Task Force was to land the U.S. First Army on two beaches, *Omaha* and *Utah*, on a 30-

mile front to the west of the British assault area. *Utah* beach lay at the base of the Cotentin peninsula, and the early capture of Cherbourg depended on how quickly it could be secured and the beachhead exploited. Immediately behind the assault forces were to come two follow-up forces, one British and the other American, which would relieve the assault troops and open the way for a steady flow of reinforcements and supplies that would be necessary to defeat any German counter-offensive.

To implement *Neptune*, Admiral Ramsay had a formidable array of 1,213 warships at his disposal, 79 per cent of them British or Canadian, 16½ per cent American and 4½ per cent supplied by other Allied navies. Of these, 107 were battleships, monitors and cruisers, representing the bombardment force; these assembled mainly in the Clyde and at Belfast, while the 286 destroyers, sloops, frigates and corvettes assigned to escort duty assembled at the south coast ports from which the invasion force would sail. The remainder of the force comprised all kinds of naval craft, down to the midget submarines that would approach the beaches well in advance of the assault force and act as pathfinders.

Then there were the combined operations craft, no fewer than 4,126 of them, ranging from big headquarters ships especially fitted out for the role, through large merchant vessels converted to landing-ships infantry (L.S.I.s), light assault craft (L.C.A.s) carried by the latter, landing ships tank (L.S.T.s), landing craft tank (L.C.T.s), A.A. defence vessels, rocket-firing craft, smoke-laying craft and obstacle clearance craft, down to repair and maintenance vessels. About three-quarters of the total were of American build.

In addition, hundreds of merchant ships were requisitioned to undertake such duties as channel marking, salvage and cable laying, for replen-

The tank landing-ship 3041, seen here at Malta, became the mercantile Empire Doric *in 1954*

The old D class cruiser H.M.S. Durban, *seen here in happier pre-war days on the China station, ended her days as a breakwater at Normandy in June 1944*

ishing the warships, for providing harbour facilities and for towing the special constructions that were vital to the success of the invasion. Foremost among these were the two artificial harbours, known as *Mulberries*, and five blockship breakwaters called *Gooseberries*. The creation of artificial harbours and breakwaters would involve the deliberate scuttling of 55 merchant vessels and

some obsolete warships, while 160 tugs would be needed to tow the sections of the *Mulberry* harbours across the Channel. About 400 units, totalling 1.5m tons, made up the two *Mulberries*; two of the 150 concrete *Phoenix* caissons that formed part of the breakwaters alone weighed 6,000 tons each. The *Mulberries*, with their miles of floating piers (called *Whale* units), were truly remarkable feats of engineering; when assembled, the British one – the larger of the two – would provide a sheltered anchorage for seven deep-laden ships of large tonnage, twenty coasters, 400 tugs and auxiliary vessels and 1,000 small craft.

In the planning of *Neptune*, much attention was paid to accurate fire-support procedures by the heavy bombardment ships. Each of the five assault forces was allocated a group of fire-support warships, their initial targets being the 23 German gun batteries that commanded the assault beaches. An elaborate spotting system was devised that included observation both from the air and from the surface. The lessons of Dieppe, and the subsequent Allied landings in Sicily and Italy, had been fully absorbed.

The Germans knew that the invasion was coming; but they did not know when and where the blow would fall. In the spring of 1944, however, they launched a series of air and sea attacks on the British coast in the hope of disrupting the build-up of invasion shipping. On 23/24 April, as part of the so-called 'little Blitz' on Britain (Operation _Steinbock_) the _Luftwaffe_ flew 100 sorties against Portsmouth, and two nights later 130 aircraft bombed the Poole and Swanage areas. Bombing accuracy was very poor, a reflection of the low quality of the crews that were now reaching the _Luftwaffe_'s operational units; in one attempted raid on Bristol no bombs at all hit the city, the majority falling on Weston-Super-Mare, 20 miles away. On 15 May the enemy bombers flew 106 sorties, of which 60 were directed at the Portsmouth area, and towards the end of these operations, during the last week of the month, fast fighter-bombers made a series of attacks on the south coast harbours, which by now were crammed with shipping. The damage caused was negligible, and _Steinbock_ cost the Germans over 300 aircraft between January and the end of May 1944, effectively spelling the end of the German bomber force in the west.

The early months of 1944 also saw an increase in German naval activity in the Channel area, the S-boat flotillas having been reinforced. On the night of 5/6 January, seven S-boats of the 5th Flotilla (_Kapitänleutnant_ Karl Muller) attacked Convoy WP457 off the south-west coast of England. The boats fired a total of 23 torpedoes, swamping the escort, which was led by the destroyer H.M.S. _Mackay_, and sank three freighters and the naval trawler _Wallasea_. The escorts proved more effective on 16/17 January, successfully driving off seven S-boats of the 5th Flotilla that tried to intercept a convoy off Lizard Point; the enemy fired eleven torpedoes, but all missed. On the last day of January, however, six boats of the 5th Flotilla attacked Convoy CW243 off Beachy Head, sinking two freighters and the

naval trawler _Pine_.

A few days later, on 5 February, there was a sharp engagement between the British destroyers _Brissenden_, _Talybont_, _Tanatside_ and _Wensleydale_ and the German minesweepers M156 and M206, escorted by the destroyer T29, off the coast of northern Brittany. The M156 was badly damaged and limped into L'Abervach, where she was destroyed later by air attack.

Some of the most intense actions during this period were fought in the North Sea, where S-boats were carrying out minelaying operations off Grimsby and Great Yarmouth. In the Channel itself, a combination of radar and rapid reaction by the escort forces were gradually getting the better of the S-boat forays towards the South Coast. There were, nevertheless, some frenetic actions in the Straits of Dover during March, beginning on the night of the 14th/15th, when British M.T.B.s attacked two groups of the German 36th Minesweeping Flotilla off Gravelines and sank the enemy leader, M3630, with a torpedo. Return fire was heavy and the British lost one boat, M.T.B. 417. On the following night, ten S-boats of the 5th and 9th Flotillas (_Kapt._ von Mirbach and _Kapt._ Klug) attempted to attack Convoy WP492 escorted by the corvettes _Azalea_ and _Primrose_ off Land's End. The German force was detected by air reconnaissance and other British warships in the area diverted to intercept – the cruiser _Bellona_, the Tribal class destroyers _Ashanti_ and _Tartar_, the Hunt class destroyers _Brissenden_ and _Melbreak_, two minesweepers and some M.T.B.s. Faced with this formidable weight of firepower the Germans had little choice but to disengage, but not before S143 had been damaged.

The value of the British coastal radar defences in combating the S-boat threat was again demonstrated on two nights in March, when the 5th and 9th Flotillas set out to attack shipping off the Lizard and Weymouth on the 16th/17th and 20th/21st. The boats' radar detection equipment alerted the crews that they were being tracked, and the sorties were abandoned. The British coastal forces were also in action on the night of 20/21 March, when five M.T.B.s attacked the German convoy _Hecht_, comprising the tanker _Rekum_ escorted by the 18th _Vorpostenboote_ Flotilla.

The M.T.B.s were beaten off, but the tanker was sunk by the Dover guns.

The real breakthrough in this phase of the naval war in the Channel came in April, when the British adopted new tactics. These involved the use of the cruisers *Bellona* and *Black Prince* in the role of command ships, using their radar to direct destroyers of the newly formed 10th Flotilla on to enemy targets and then maintaining a constant plot of the action, using their long-range guns to engage the enemy force while illuminating it constantly with starshell while the destroyers closed in. The tactics worked well, and on 26 April they resulted in the sinking of the Elbing class destroyer T28, two more destroyers – T24 and T27 – being badly damaged and forced to seek shelter in Morlaix. They broke out on the night of 28/29 April and were intercepted off Brieux by the Tribal class destroyers *Haida* and *Athebaskan*. The Germans fired twelve torpedoes at their pursuers and *Athebaskan* was hit, sinking at 04.42, but T27 was further damaged by shells from the *Haida* and ran aground, to be finished off later by M.T.B.s.

On the previous night – 27/28 April – the S-boats achieved their greatest victory since 1940, and it happened more or less by accident. On that night, nine boats of the 5th and 9th Flotillas (S100, S130, S136, S138, S140, S142, S143, S145 and S150) sailed from Cherbourg to attack a convoy that was reported to be off Selsey Bill. Instead, they encountered a convoy of landing-craft – eight U.S. L.S.T.s, escorted by the corvette *Azalea* – heading from Brixham and Plymouth for Slapton Sands in South Devon where they were to take part in Exercise *Tiger*, a dress rehearsal for the American landing on *Utah* Beach. The convoy should also have been escorted by the destroyer H.M.S. *Saladin*, but she had been damaged in a collision with a landing-craft in Plymouth harbour and no replacement had been assigned.

The S-boats fell upon the convoy as it entered Lyme Bay, and in the torpedo attack that followed L.S.T. 507 and L.S.T. 531 were sunk and another, L.S.T. 289, was damaged. The loss of life was severe: 441 soldiers and 197 seamen. The attackers were pursued by the destroyers *Onslow*, *Obedient*, *Ursa*, *Piorun* and *Blyskawica*, but escaped

unharmed. The incident was kept a closely guarded secret for a long time after the war, and even today there is controversy over the actual loss of life, some sources putting it as high as 749.

In the early hours of 6 June, 1944, as the invasion armada headed towards the Normandy coast, small ships of the Royal Navy – harbour defence vessels and motor launches – performed a vital task in the Pas de Calais. While R.A.F. Lancasters orbited overhead, dropping bundles of *Window*, the naval craft operated a device called *Moonshine*, which picked up enemy radar pulses, amplified them and retransmitted them, giving a 'solid' radar impression of a large concentration of ships forging slowly ahead. The boats also towed *Filberts*, 29-foot-long barrage balloons fitted with radar reflectors, each one producing a radar echo similar to that of a 10,000-ton ship. Near the enemy coast, the boat crews moored their *Filbert* floats and laid a smoke-screen, at the same time broadcasting recorded sounds of large vessels dropping anchor over powerful loudspeakers. The whole object of this joint R.A.F./R.N. exercise was to lead the enemy to believe that the invasion was taking place in the narrowest stretch of the Channel, and it succeeded admirably.

By 05.00 on 5 June the L.S.I.s had reached their lowering positions, some 7 or 8 miles off the Normandy coast, and the assault battalions embarked in their landing craft – no mean feat in itself, for a heavy swell was running and the craft were tossed up and down like corks. Nevertheless, the operation was accomplished with remarkably few mishaps. Visibility was poor as the assault craft and their supporting tank landing craft began their run-in to the beaches, with the coastline obscured by haze and smoke from the tactical air bombardment that had been in progress for some time. A fearful blanket of noise lay over the scene as the warships of the naval task forces hurled their broadsides at the enemy's positions. Opposite the British beaches, the bombardment was opened at 05.25 by the battleship H.M.S. *Warspite*, engaging the shore battery at Berneville; she was followed by another veteran battleship, H.M.S. *Ramillies*, and the monitor *Roberts*, which engaged other shore batteries. The cruisers *Ajax*, *Arethusa*, *Argonaut*, *Belfast*, *Danae*, *Diadem*, *Dragon* (the latter Polish-manned), *Emerald*, *Frobisher*, *Mauritius* and *Orion* also lent fire support to the British assault. Other British naval units, the cruisers *Bellona*, *Black Prince*, *Enterprise*, *Glasgow*, *Hawkins*, *Scylla*, and the monitor *Erebus*, as well as a number of Hunt class destroyers, were deployed in support of the assault on the American beaches. The battleships *Nelson* and *Rodney* and the cruiser *Sirius* formed a reserve force. The entire force of Allied warships committed to *Overlord* totalled seven battleships, 23 cruisers, three monitors, 105 destroyers and 1,073 smaller vessels; included among the latter were over 100 British and Canadian minesweepers, their vital task to clear the approaches to the landing areas, and 27 buoy-layers to mark the cleared lanes.

One major concern of the Allied Naval Command during *Overlord* was to prevent interference by U-boats, in particular those equipped with the new *Schnorchel* device which enabled them to stay submerged without the need to surface to recharge their systems. In fact, when *Overlord* began there was such a large concentration of Allied air power west of the Channel entrance, making radar searches by day and night, that it was impossible for U-boats without *Schnorchel* to come anywhere near the invasion area. All those that tried were heavily attacked by aircraft and either sunk or damaged so that they had to return to base or were recalled by the Commander U-boats. The *Schnorchel* boats were able to evade the air attacks, but they then had to face very strong naval anti-submarine groups concentrated in the Channel entrance, and only very few were able, after a fortnight or so, to enter the 'funnel', where they achieved minimal success.

Ten Support Groups of destroyers, sloops and frigates, in fact, formed a screen at either end of the Channel; six covered the Western Approaches and the Bay of Biscay, supported by the escort carriers *Activity*, *Tracker* and *Vindex*.

For some time, the Germans had been holding anti-invasion groups of U-boats at readiness in French and Norwegian harbours, and when *Overlord* began the Biscay group, together with all available S-boats and four destroyers from Le

Martlets and Avengers bearing black and white invasion stripes for operations off Normandy, June 1944

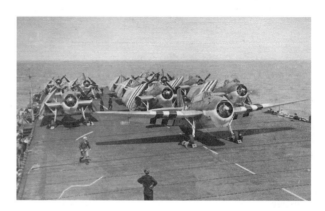

Avengers preparing for take off, Normandy, June 1944

Havre (the T28, *Falke*, *Möwe* and *Jaguar*) were ordered to proceed to the scene of the landings. The German destroyers sank the Norwegian destroyer *Svenner* on the first day of the invasion, but they were attacked constantly from the air and were soon forced to run for shelter. The S-boats sank a number of landing-craft, but in the main their attacks were beaten off.

On 6 June, 17 U-boats put to sea from Brest, 14 from St-Nazaire, four from La Pallice and one from Lorient. They were soon in trouble; the next day, aircraft of No. 19 Group Coastal Command sank the U-955 and U-70 in the Bay of Biscay, and four of the Brest boats, U-963, U-989, U-256 and U-415 were all damaged and forced to return to base. On 8 June, a Liberator of No. 224 Squadron sank the U-629 and U-373 in rapid succession, and on 9 June the U-740

Launched in May 1943, the escort carrier H.M.S. Vindex *was built by Swan Hunter on Tyneside and was operational on the North Atlantic convoys at the end of the war*

was also destroyed. A sortie from Brest by the German destroyers Z24, Z32, ZH1 and T24 on the night of 8/9 June was intercepted by the British 10th Destroyer Flotilla; ZH1 was sunk by torpedoes from H.M.S. *Ashanti*, and Z32 by gunfire from the Canadian destroyer *Haida*. Another Canadian destroyer, the *Huron*, was beached and blown up, while H.M.S. *Tartar* was severely damaged.

Only nine U-boats of the Biscay group were *Schnorchel*-equipped, and eight of these attempted to infiltrate the Channel area from 7 June. Between that date and 11 June three made abortive torpedo attacks, and U-821 was destroyed by an aircraft. It was not until 15 June that they enjoyed some success, the U-621 sinking the tank landing ship L.S.T. 280, the U-767 the frigate *Mourne*, and the U-764 the frigate *Blackwood*; the latter was taken in tow, but was a total loss. On 18 June, U-767 was sunk by destroyers of the 14th Support Group, and the U-441 by a Wellington of No. 304 (Polish) Squadron.

A second group of *Schnorchel*-equipped submarines penetrated the invasion area during the second half of June, and these suffered an early loss when U-971 was sunk in the western part of the Channel by the destroyers *Haida* and *Eskimo* on the night of 22nd/23rd. Two nights later, the destroyers *Affleck* and *Balfour* sank the U-1191, while the U-269 was destroyed by the *Bickerton*; the destroyer *Goodson* was torpedoed and damaged by the U-984. On 27/29 June, U-988 torpedoed the corvette *Pink*, which was a total loss, and sank two ships of 9,444 tons before she was sent to the bottom by the 3rd Support Group. The biggest German success came that same day, 29 June, when the U-984 attacked Convoy EMC17 and torpedoed four ships totalling 28,790 tons, three of which were sunk and the fourth beached. This attack showed what a *Schnorchel* boat could achieve under favourable circumstances, and it must be said that the U-boat operations in June 1944 had been dogged by technical failures; often, their torpedoes had detonated prematurely, or their motors had failed to work properly.

The frigate H.M.S. Bickerton *on Atlantic convoy escort duty, with a county class cruiser in the background*

On 26 June, after a heavy bombardment by naval forces, Cherbourg fell to the Americans, but the Germans destroyed the port facilities before surrendering; the port was out of action until September. *Ultra* now began to detect a steady movement of enemy submarines away from France to Norway; this transfer was accomplished with surprisingly few losses, because the U-boats could travel submerged and search aircraft were unable to locate the *Schnorchel*-heads in the sea clutter when they were raised above the surface at night for recharging the batteries. The S-boats continued to make gallant sorties against the cross Channel supply routes during July, but the back of their offensive had been broken; the majority of their missions were disrupted by British Coastal Forces craft, joined now by American P.T. boats and destroyers.

On the night of 5/6 July the Germans brought a new weapon into action: the *Neger* one-man torpedo, 26 of which were deployed against the invasion area from Villers-sur-Mer. On this occasion they sank the minesweepers *Cato* and *Magic*, and later in the month they sank the destroyer *Isis*, the minesweeper *Pylades* and disabled the Polish-manned cruiser *Dragon* so severely that she had to be scuttled as part of a *Gooseberry* harbour breakwater. *Neger* operations ceased in mid-August, their operating unit having suffered dreadful losses. Some success was achieved during this period by Small Battle Unit Flotilla 211, which used *Linsen* explosive boats to sink the

destroyer *Quorn* and the anti-submarine trawler *Gairsay* on the night of 2/3 August.

On 15 August 1944, with the breakout from Normandy in progress, the Allies launched Operation *Dragoon*, the invasion of the French Riviera between St-Raphaël and Fréjus. *Dragoon* was mainly an American and Free French operation, although the Royal Navy made a significant contribution to the escort carrier task force, T.F. 88, that had once again been mustered to provide the necessary air cover. Commanded jointly by Rear-Admiral Sir Thomas Troubridge and Rear-Admiral C. T. Durgin, U.S.N., it consisted of the British carriers *Attacker*, *Emperor*, *Khedive*, *Pursuer*, *Searcher*, *Hunter* and *Stalker*, and the American carriers *Tulagi* and *Kasaan Bay*. Only feeble resistance was encountered and the Allies swept rapidly inland, the carrier aircraft being used mainly for strafing and reconnaissance. The Royal Navy also provided warships for escort and fire support; these included the battleship *Ramillies*, the cruisers *Argonaut*, *Aurora*, *Ajax*, *Black Prince*, *Caledon*, *Colombo*, *Delhi*, *Dido*, *Royalist* and *Sirius*, 27 destroyers and two gunboats.

In September, the seven Royal Navy carriers that had taken part in *Dragoon* sailed for the Aegean, where their aircraft flew in support of the Allied forces engaged in recapturing Crete and the other German-occupied islands. The fighters wrought massive destruction among the fleets of small craft, packed with enemy troops. The *Searcher* and *Pursuer* joined the Home Fleet at the end of the month, but the other five remained in the area until the beginning of November, by which time all the major islands had been reoccupied. It was the last World War Two offensive operation mounted by carriers in the Mediterranean theatre.

By the end of August 1944, the Allied naval forces had secured the English Channel area, but for at least part of the bombardment force that had covered the Normandy landings there was still work to be done. In the first week of November 1944, a bombardment force led by H.M.S. *Warspite* and the monitors *Roberts* and *Erebus* shelled the island of Walcheren in the Scheldt estuary in support of a hard-fought and costly landing there by Canadian forces and the

Royal Marine Special Service Brigade. On 8 November the German commander and his 29,000-strong garrison surrendered, and the way was now open to the vital port of Antwerp, desperately needed to resupply the Allied armies advancing through north-west Europe.

During the winter of 1944–5 the *Schnorchel* U-boats launched their final offensive against Allied shipping in the Atlantic and in British home waters. Such was the weight of air and sea power ranged against them, however, that their freedom of movement was severely restricted and they virtually had to remain stationary, waiting for targets to come their way. Early in 1945 the British air and surface anti-submarine forces literally swamped the sea areas around the British Isles, inflicting such heavy losses on the U-boats that they were forced out of the coastal waters. Between 15 November 1944 and 27 January 1945 the U-boats sank 31 ships, including some naval escort vessels, but they also lost twelve of their number. At the end of January the new Type XXIII boats became operational, and in the following five-week period they sank 16 ships and damaged several others; but ten more U-boats fell victim to the anti-submarine forces.

The surviving S-boats, concentrated now in Holland, continued to make forays into the North Sea and English Channel. The last was on 22 March, when boats of the 2nd and 5th Flotillas set out from IJmuiden and Den Helder to attack shipping between the Thames Estuary and the Scheldt. The attack came to nothing, and the S-boats were driven off by the destroyer H.M.S. *Mackay.*

The U-boats fought on to the end, and on 5 April they suddenly returned to British coastal waters. In a desperate, last-ditch offensive lasting

a month they sank eight ships, but 15 submarines were destroyed. Yet they had the last word; on 7 May 1945, the day before Germany capitulated, the U-2336 (Lt Klusmeyer) sank the freighter *Avondale Park* in the Firth of Forth.

But perhaps R.A.F. Coastal Command had the last word, after all. That afternoon, a Catalina of No. 210 Squadron sank the U-320 (Lt Emmrich) off Bergen. It was the last U-boat to be destroyed in the Second World War.

Soon afterwards, one by one, the surviving U-boats – the menacing grey shapes that had terrorised the oceans for so long – rose from the depths and, under the Allied surrender terms, headed for the nearest Allied port, flying the black flags of defeat.

The frigate H.M.C.S. Teme *after being torpedoed in the Atlantic by the U-246, March 1945. She was damaged beyond repair*

CHAPTER EIGHTEEN

The Royal Navy in the Pacific, 1945

On 19 March 1945, the British Pacific Fleet, having assembled in Sydney, arrived at Ulithi Atoll in the Caroline Islands where – as Task Force 57 – it formed part of the U.S. Fifth Fleet. As well as the four British aircraft carriers, T.F. 57 consisted of the battleships *King George V* and *Howe*, the cruisers *Swiftsure*, H.M.N.Z.S. *Gambia*, *Black Prince*, *Euryalus*, *Argonaut* and eleven destroyers.

On 23 March the British warships sailed to take part in Operation *Iceberg* – the landings on Okinawa. Task Force 57's mission was to strike at six enemy airfields in the Sakishima Gunto island group, which lay to the south-west of Okinawa and the other Ryuku Islands. If these airfields, which were used as staging posts between Formosa and Okinawa, could be put out of action, the Japanese would be unable to fly in reinforcements and Okinawa would be isolated.

On 26 March, T.F. 57 had reached its flying-off position about 100 miles south of Sakishima Gunto and the first strike of forty Avengers was launched. While these attacked airfield installations with their 500 lb bombs, No. 1770 Squadron's twelve Fireflies went for the flak posi-

tions with their rockets. The attacks continued for two days, and in between the main Avenger strikes – of which there were eight – attacks were made by small formations of Corsairs and Hellcats. However, the strikes did comparatively little damage to the airfields themselves; the runways were made of crushed coral and were easily repaired during lulls in the bombing. Few enemy aircraft were destroyed on the ground, but 28 were shot down by the Corsairs and Hellcats for the loss of 19 Fleet Air Arm aircraft.

Late on the 28th, T.F. 57 withdrew for replenishment at sea, the operation being prolonged by unexpected bad weather. The carriers were back on station by the 31st, however, to renew their attacks on the enemy airfields. On 1 April, the Japanese appeared over the fleet in strength; first high-level bombers, and then the *kamikazes*. Most of the latter were splashed by the combat air patrol before they came within striking distance, but one managed to break through and hit the

The submarine depot ship H.M.S. Maidstone *served in all theatres, ending with the Pacific Fleet*

The A-class submarines were designed for long-range work in the Pacific but came too late for hostilities. The boat seen here is H.M. Submarine Artful

Indefatigable at the base of her island. If she had been an American carrier, with less armoured deck protection, the aircraft would have torn through and exploded in the hangar below. As it was, there was a delay of about 45 minutes while the wreckage was shovelled over the side, and then the *Indefatigable* carried on almost as if nothing had happened.

During the third series of operations against Sakishima, on 6 April, the *kamikazes* attacked again. This time, a burning *Zero* dived on the *Illustrious*, but only succeeded in hitting the carrier's island with its wingtip before plummeting into the sea. During this attack, the Corsairs of 1830 Squadron and the Hellcats of 1844 Squadron accounted for five Aichi D4Y *Judys* and one Nakajima P1Y *Frances*.

Allied intelligence had indicated that many of the *kamikaze* attacks were being launched from Formosa, and Admiral Spruance, the C.-in-C. U.S.

Fifth Fleet, asked Task Force 57 to mount a series of strikes on airfields in the northern part of the island. The first attack was carried out in poor weather on 11 April by 48 Avengers and 40 Corsairs. While the Avengers bombed the port of Kiirun, the fighters strafed airfields in the vicinity. The attacks continued on the 12th, when they were opposed by Japanese fighters. The Hellcats of 1844 Squadron shot down four *Oscars*, a *Zero* and a Kawasaki Ki 61 *Tony*, while the Corsairs of 1834 and 1836 claimed an *Oscar*, a *Zero* and a *Dinah*. The Fireflies of 1770 Squadron were particularly lucky; they ran into a formation of five Mitsubishi Ki 51 *Sonia* bombers heading for Okinawa and shot down four of them. A *kamikaze* attack later in the day, directed at the British carriers, was broken up by the combat air patrol, four Japanese aircraft being shot down and six more damaged. Eight more enemy aircraft were destroyed during the air strikes the following day.

After this operation, the *Illustrious* was withdrawn from the task force, suffering from an accumulation of technical troubles – the consequence of four years of combat operations. In addition, the pilots of her two Corsair squadrons, 1830 and 1833, had done far more than their normal tour and were long overdue for a rest. The carrier was replaced by the *Formidable*, which immediately went into action with the task force against Sakishima between 16 April and 20 April. By this time the fleet had spent over a month at sea on operations; the carriers required replacement aircraft and the tankers and supply ships of the fleet train badly needed replenishment. On the night of 20 April, the fleet sailed for Leyte in the Philippines, where it stayed until 1 May.

When Task Force 57 returned to operations on 4 May the target was once again the enemy airfields on Sakishima. While Avengers attacked Ishigaki, the 14-inch guns of the *King George V* and the *Howe* pounded the airfields and installations on the neighbouring island of Miyako. At 11.00, shortly before the first strikes returned to the carriers, T.F. 57 was attacked by a wave of 20 *kamikazes*. Almost every F.A.A. fighter squadron was involved in breaking up the attack; the Corsairs of 1834 and 1836 Squadrons shot down a Nakajima C6N *Myrt*, a *Judy* and two *Zeros*, the Seafires of 887 and 894 Squadrons destroyed a *Val* and four *Zeros* between them, while the Hellcats of 1839 and 184 Squadrons accounted for a Nakajima B6N *Jill* and two *Zeros*. Only two *kamikazes* penetrated the fighter screen and the A.A. barrage; the first struck the *Indomitable* aft, slid across the flight deck and went over the side, and the second hit the *Formidable* at the base of the island. The damage was quickly patched up and the carrier was fully operational again by the end of the day. Eleven aircraft were destroyed by the *kamikaze* on the *Formidable*'s deck; fortunately, most of her aircraft were airborne.

She was not so lucky on 9 May, when more *kamikazes* attacked T.F. 57 at 17.00, just after a strike had landed-on. This time, although a crashing *kamikaze* left no more damage than a long scar on *Formidable*'s armoured deck, 18 Corsairs and Avengers were destroyed when blazing fuel sprayed over them. Two *kamikazes* also hit the *Victorious*; the first damaged the forward lift and caused a sizeable blaze, and while this was being tackled by the crew a second Japanese aircraft

Avengers carrying out a dummy torpedo attack on H.M.S. Formidable *as the carrier passes through the Indian Ocean* en route *to join the British Pacific Fleet in 1945*

struck her and bounced overboard, destroying four Corsairs on the way.

The strikes against targets on Sakishima Gunto continued until 25 May, by which time Okinawa was in American hands. The *Formidable* had left the area for Sydney three days earlier, following an accidental hangar fire in which 30 of her aircraft were destroyed.

In two months at sea, the aircraft of T.F. 57 had flown 5,335 sorties, dropped 1,000 tons of bombs and fired 1,000 rocket projectiles. Their combined efforts had resulted in the 98 of them in air combat. But the Fleet Air Arm's losses had been far from light; 73 aircraft had been destroyed in the *kamikaze* attacks and the *Formidable*'s hangar fire, another 61 had been destroyed through accidents, and 26 had been lost to enemy A.A. and fighters. Eighty-five personnel had been killed, including 41 aircrew. Nevertheless, the carriers had survived a series of *kamikaze* hits which would have inflicted severe damage, if not total loss, on their American counterparts. The concept of the armoured deck, once criticised because of the extra weight penalty and sacrifice of speed that were its inevitable consequences, was amply vindicated in the Pacific.

Towards the end of June the fleet carrier *Implacable* joined the British Pacific Fleet at Manus anchorage, in the Admiralty Islands. The carrier had arrived in the Pacific three weeks earlier, and on 12 June, accompanied by the escort carrier *Ruler*, the cruisers *Swiftsure*, *Newfoundland*, *Uganda*, *Achilles* and five destroyers, she had carried out a two-day series of strikes against the badly battered Japanese base at Truk in the Carolines. Now, fully worked up to operational standards, she replaced the *Indomitable*, which departed for a refit.

The fleet, under Vice-Admirals Rawlings and Vian and now designated Task Force 37, sailed from Manus on 9 July to join the American Task Force 38 under Admiral J. S. McCain in Japanese waters. The *Indefatigable* did not join T.F. 37 until a fortnight later, having been held up by mechanical troubles. The first strikes were flown on 17 July, when Corsairs and Fireflies attacked airfields and marshalling yards in the northern part of Honshu, the main Japanese island, while the *King George V* and American warships shelled factories in the Hitachi area near Tokyo, the British battleship putting 267 rounds of 14-inch on the target. The destroyers *Quality* and *Quiberon* also took part in this action. The next British attacks were made on the 24th, after the arrival of the *Indefatigable*, with airfields and coastal shipping as the main targets. The most important strike was mounted by six Avengers, two Corsairs and two Fireflies against the escort carrier *Kaiyo*, which was left crippled and in flames.

At dusk the following day, the Japanese sent a formation of torpedo-bombers against T.F. 37. They were fast, powerful Aichi B7As, known to the Allies as *Grace* – one of the latest types to enter service with the Imperial Japanese Navy. They were intercepted by the Hellcats of No. 1844 Squadron; two were shot down and a third damaged by Lt W. H. I. Atkinson, bringing this pilot's score of Japanese aircraft to five, and another was destroyed by Sub-Lt R. F. Mackie.

More strikes were flown against enemy shipping between 28 July and 30 July, and on the night of 29/30 a British battle group comprising the *King George V* and the destroyers *Undine*, *Ulysses* and *Urania* shelled works and aircraft factories near Hamamatsu on south Honshu.

After the strikes at the end of July, operations were delayed for nine days because of bad weather and the dropping of the first atomic bomb on Hiroshima on 6 August. The attacks were resumed on the 9th, (the day a second atomic bomb obliterated Nagasaki), by a powerful British task force comprising the carriers *Victorious*, *Indefatigable*, *Formidable* and *Implacable*, the battleships *Duke of York* – flagship of Admiral Sir Bruce Fraser, C.-in-C. British Pacific Fleet – *King George V*, six cruisers and 17 destroyers.

This time, the main target was a concentration of shipping in Onagawa Wan. Shortly after sunrise, a strike of four Corsairs was flown off by the *Formidable*. Over Onagawa, the pilots sighted five enemy destroyers and escorts anchored around the fringes of the bay. While two of the fighter-bombers strafed enemy anti aircraft positions and a third provided top cover, the leader – Canadian-born Lieutenant Robert Hampton Gray, who had won the D.S.C. for his part in the *Tirpitz* strikes the year before – dived towards the escort sloop *Amakusa*. His aircraft was hit and was quickly enveloped in flames, but he pressed home his attack and his 1,000 lb bomb sank the enemy vessel. Gray was awarded a posthumous Victoria Cross, the last to be won in won in the Second World War.

On 10 August, in a series of strikes that lasted from dawn to dusk, the Fleet Air Arm brought the total of Japanese warships sunk during the two-day operation to six. Fifty aircraft were also destroyed on the ground for the loss of 13 F.A.A. machines. With the terms of the Japanese surrender being negotiated, the main body of the British Pacific Fleet returned to Sydney, leaving the *Indefatigable*, the *King George V*, two cruisers and ten destroyers in Japanese waters.

At dawn on 15 August, the Avengers of No. 820 Squadron were intercepted by *Zeros* during an attack on targets in the Tokyo area. The Japanese fighters were overwhelmed by the Seafires of 887 and 894 Squadrons, who shot down eight of them for the loss of one of their own number. Two hours later, all offensive operations against the

Japanese Home Islands were suspended.

On 2 September, the remaining British warships, designated Task Group 38.5, joined the massive Allied armada that assembled in Tokyo Bay to witness the Japanese surrender. The war was over, but for the Royal Navy in the Pacific much remained to be done; the reoccupation of Hong Kong, the acceptance of the surrender of Japanese forces in New Britain, and a hundred humanitarian tasks, including the repatriation of prisoners of war.

But for the officers and men who watched the sun go down over Fujiyama on that September day in 1945, amid the most awesome demonstration of naval power the world had ever seen, this was the supreme moment. Few could have envisaged that within a few years, the Royal Navy would be facing a vastly different role in a much altered world, a world menaced by the very weapons that had brought Japan to the brink of surrender.

Principal Royal Navy Ship Losses, 1939–45

(Note: the appendices do not list warship losses of the British Commonwealth navies and do not include foreign-manned British vessels.)

Abbreviations C.V.E. Escort Carrier, D.B.R. Damaged Beyond Repair

Battleships

Barham sunk by U-331, Mediterranean, 25 Nov. 1941

Prince of Wales sunk by Japanese air attack off Malaya, 10 Dec. 1941

Royal Oak sunk by U-47 in Scapa Flow, 14 Oct. 1939

Battle-cruisers

Hood sunk by *Bismarck* in Denmark Strait, 24 May 1941

Repulse sunk by Japanese air attack off Malaya, 10 Dec. 1941

Aircraft-carriers

Ark Royal sunk by U-81, Mediterranean, 13 Nov. 1941

Audacity (C.V.E.) sunk by U-751, north Atlantic, 22 Dec. 1941

Avenger (C.V.E.) sunk by U-155, central Atlantic, 15 Nov. 1942

Courageous sunk by U-29 W. of Ireland, 17 Sept. 1939

Dasher (C.V.E.) destroyed on Clyde as result of petrol explosion and fire, 27 March 1943

Eagle sunk by U-73, Mediterranean, 11 August 1942

Glorious sunk by *Scharnhorst* and *Gneisenau*, Norwegian Sea, 8 June 1940

Hermes sunk by Japanese air attack, Indian Ocean, 9 April 1942

Nabob (C.V.E.) D.B.R. by U-354, Arctic, 22 Aug. 1944

Thane (C.V.E.) D.B.R. by U-482 off Clyde, 15 Jan. 1945

Cruisers

Bonaventure sunk by Italian submarine *Ambra*, Mediterranean, 31 March 1941

Cairo abandoned after attack by Italian submarines *Dessie* and *Axum*, Mediterranean, 12 Aug. 1942

Calcutta sunk by air attack N. of Alexandria, 1 June 1941

Calypso sunk by Italian submarine *Bagnolini* S. of Crete, 12 June 1940

Carlisle D.B.R. in air attack off Rhodes, 9 Oct. 1943

Charybdis sunk by German destroyers off French coast, 23 Oct. 1943

Cornwall sunk by Japanese air attack, Indian Ocean, 5 April 1942

Coventry sunk by air attack off Tobruk, 14 Sept. 1942

Curacao sank after collision with *Queen Mary*, N. Atlantic, 2 Oct. 1942

Curlew sunk by air attack off Harstad, Norway, 26 May 1940

Dorsetshire sunk by Japanese air attack, Indian Ocean, 5 April 1942

Dunedin sunk by U-124 off St Paul's Rocks, S. Atlantic, 24 Nov. 1941

Edinburgh sank after attacks by U-456 and German destroyer Z24, Arctic, 30 April 1942

Effingham damaged in air attack and sunk by R.N. destroyers, Norway, 21 May 1940

Exeter sunk by Japanese destroyer *Inazuma*, Java Sea, 1 March 1942

Fiji abandoned after air attack off Crete, 22 May 1941

Galatea sunk by U-557 off Alexandria, 15 Dec. 1941

Gloucester sunk by air attack S.W. of Crete, 22 May 1941

Hermione sunk by U-205 S. of Crete, 16 June 1942

Manchester abandoned after attack by Italian M.T.B.s off Tunisia, 13 Aug. 1942

Naiad sunk by U-565, Mediterranean, 11 March 1942

Neptune sunk by mines, Mediterranean, 17 Dec. 1941

Penelope sunk by U-410 off Anzio, 18 Feb. 1944

Southampton damaged in air attack and abandoned, Mediterranean, 10 Jan .1941

Spartan sunk by air attack, Mediterranean, 29 Jan. 1944

Trinidad sunk by R.N. destroyer after sustaining torpedo and bomb damage, Arctic, 15 May 1942

York D.B.R. in attack by Italian explosive craft, Suda Bay, 26 March 1941

Destroyers

Acasta sunk by *Scharnhorst* and *Gneisenau*, Norwegian Sea, 8 June 1940

Achates sunk by *Admiral Hipper*, Arctic, 31 Dec. 1942

Acheron sunk by mine off Isle of Wight, 17 Dec. 1940

Afridi lost in air attack, Norwegian Sea, 3 May 1940

Airedale sunk by destroyer *Aldenham* after suffering damage in air attack S. of Crete, 15 June 1942

Aldenham sunk by mine off Pola, Italy, 14 Dec. 1944

Ardent sunk by *Scharnhorst* and *Gneisenau*, Norwegian Sea, 8 June 1940

Arrow D.B.R. in explosion of adjacent ammunition ship, Algiers, 4 Aug. 1943

Basilisk sunk in air attack, English Channel, 1 June 1940

Bath sunk by U-204 S.W. of Ireland, 19 Aug. 1941

Bedouin sunk by Italian aircraft while under tow, Mediterranean, 15 June 1942

Belmont sunk by U-82, N. Atlantic, 31 Jan. 1942

Berkeley sunk by destroyer *Albrighton* after sustaining damage in air attack, English Channel, 19 Aug. 1942

Beverley sunk by U-188, N. Atlantic, 11 April 1943

Blanche sunk by mines, Thames Estuary, 13 Nov. 1939

Blean sunk by U-443, Mediterranean, 11 Dec. 1942

Boadicea sunk by air attack, English Channel, 13 June 1944

Brazen sunk by air attack, English Channel, 20 July 1944

Broadwater sunk by U-101, N. Atlantic, 18 Oct. 1941

Broke sunk by French coastal artillery, Algiers, 9 Nov. 1942

Cameron wrecked in dry dock during air attack, Portsmouth, 15 Dec. 1940

Campbeltown destroyed in St-Nazaire raid, 28 March 1942

Codrington sunk in air attack on Dover Harbour, 26 July 1940

Cossack sunk by U-563, N. Atlantic, 23 Oct. 1941

Dainty sunk by air attack off Tobruk, 24 Feb. 1941

Daring sunk by U-23, North Sea, 19 Feb. 1940

Defender sunk by air attack, Mediterranean, 12 July 1941

Delight sunk by air attack, English Channel, 29 July 1940

Diamond sunk by air attack, Mediterranean, 27 April 1941

Duchess sank after collision with H.M.S. *Barham* off Scotland, 12 Dec. 1939

Dulverton sunk by Hs 293 glider bomb off Kos, 14 Nov. 1943

Eclipse sunk by mine E. of Kalymnos, 24 Oct. 1943

Electra sunk by Japanese destroyers, Java Sea, 27 Feb. 1942

Encounter sunk by Japanese destroyer *Inazuma*, Java Sea, 1 March 1942

Eridge D.B.R. in Italian M.T.B. attack, Mediterranean, 29 July 1942

Escort sank under tow after attack by Italian submarine *Marconi*, Mediterranean, 11 July 1940

Esk sunk by mine, North Sea, 31 Aug. 1940

Eskdale sunk by S-boats, English Channel, 14 April 1943

Exmoor sunk by mine, North Sea, 25 Feb. 1941

Exmouth sunk by mine, North Sea, 21 Jan. 1940

Fearless abandoned after air attack, Mediterranean, 23 July 1941

Firedrake sunk by U-211, N. Atlantic, 17 Dec. 1942

Foresight sunk by air attack, Mediterranean, 12 Aug. 42

Fury D.B.R. by mine off Normandy, 21 June 1944

Gallant D.B.R. by air attack, Malta, 5 April 1942

Glowworm sunk by *Admiral Hipper*, Norwegian Sea, 8 April 1940

Goathland D.B.R. by mine off Normandy, 24 July 1944

Grafton sunk by U-62, English Channel, 29 May 1940

Grenade sunk by air attack, English Channel, 29 May 1940

Grenville sunk by mine, North Sea, 19 Jan. 1940

Greyhound sunk by air attack S.W. of Crete, 22 May 1941

Grove sunk by U-77, Mediterranean, 12 June 1942

Gurkha (1) sunk by air attack off Norway, 9 April 1940

Gurkha (2) sunk by U-133, Mediterranean, 17 Jan. 1942

Gypsy sunk by mine, North Sea, 21 Nov. 1939

Hardy (1) sunk by German destroyers, Ofotfjord, 10 April 1940

Hardy (2) damaged by U-278 and sunk by destroyer *Venus* off Bear Island, 30 Jan. 1944

Harvester sunk by U-432, N. Atlantic, 11 March 1943

Hasty sunk by S-55, Mediterranean, 14 June 1942

Havant sunk by air attack, English Channel, 1 June 1940

Havock sunk by Italian submarine *Aradam* after running aground, Cap Bon, 6 April 1942

Hereward sunk by air attack S. of Crete, 29 May 1941

Heythrop sunk by U-652, Mediterranean, 20 March 1942

Holcombe sunk by U-593, Mediterranean, 12 Dec. 1943

Hostile sunk by mine, Mediterranean, 23 Aug. 1940

Hunter sunk by German destroyers, Ofotfjord, 10 April 1940

Hurricane sunk by U-415 N.E. of the Azores, 24 Dec. 1943

Hurworth sunk by mines off Kalymnos, 22 Oct. 1943

Hyperion abandoned after being torpedoed by Italian submarine *Serpente* and sunk by R.N. warships, Mediterranean, 2 Dec. 1940

Imogen blew up and sank after collision with cruiser *Glasgow*, Pentland Firth, 16 July 1940

Imperial sunk by air attack off Crete, 28 May 1941

Inglefield sunk by air attack off Anzio, 25 Feb. 1944

Intrepid sunk by air attack off Leros, 27 Sept. 1943

Isis sunk by *Neger* human torpedo, English Channel, 20 July 1944

Ithuriel D.B.R. by air attack, Bougie, 28 Nov. 1942

Ivanhoe sunk by mine, North Sea, 31 Aug. 1940

Jackal sank under tow following air attack, Mediterranean, 11 May 1942

Jaguar sunk by U-652, Mediterranean, 26 March 1942

Janus sunk by air attack off Anzio, 23 Jan. 1944

Jersey sunk by mine, Malta, 2 May 1941

Juno sunk by air attack, Crete, 21 May 1941

Jupiter blew up, cause uncertain, Java Sea, 27 Feb. 1942

Kandahar abandoned after hitting mine, Mediterranean, 19 Dec. 1941

Kashmir sunk by air attack, Crete, 23 May 1941

Keith sunk by air attack, English Channel, 1 June 1940

Kelly sunk by air attack, Crete, 23 May 1941

Khartoum beached after gun battle with Italian submarine *Torricelli*, Indian Ocean, 23 June 1940

Kingston wrecked in air attacks, Malta, April 1942, and sunk as blockship

Kipling sank after air attack S. of Crete, 11 May 1941

Laforey sunk by U-223, Mediterranean, 29 March 1944

Lance wrecked by air attacks, Malta, April 1942

Legion beached after air attack and destroyed, Malta, 26 March 1942

Lightning sunk by German S-boat, Mediterranean, 12 March 1943

Limbourne sunk by German torpedo boat T22, English Channel, 23 Oct. 1943

Lively sunk by air attack S. of Crete, 11 May 1942

Loyal D.B.R. by mine in Adriatic, 12 Oct. 1944

Mahratta sunk by U-990, Arctic, 25 Feb. 1944

Maori sunk by air attack, Malta, 12 Feb. 1942

Martin sunk by U-431, Mediterranean, 10 Nov. 1942

Mashona sunk by air attack W. of Ireland, 28 May 1941

Matabele sunk by U-454, Arctic, 17 Jan. 1942

Mohawk sunk by Italian destroyer *Tarigo*, Mediterranean, 15 April 1941

Nestor sank after sustaining air attack damage S. of Crete, 16 June 1942

Pakenham abandoned after battle with Italian M.T.B.s, Mediterranean, 16 April 1943

Panther sunk by air attack off Rhodes, 9 Oct. 1943

Partridge sunk by U-565, Mediterranean, 18 Dec. 1942

Pathfinder D.B.R. in *kamikaze* attack off Ramree Island, Burma, 11 Feb. 1945

Penylan sunk by S115, English Channel, 3 Dec. 1942

Porcupine D.B.R. in torpedo attack by U-602, Mediterranean, 9 Dec. 1942

Puckeridge sunk by U-617 E. of Gibraltar, 6 Sept. 1943

Punjabi sank after collision with H.M.S. *King George V*, Arctic, 1 May 1942

Quail D.B.R. by mines off Brindisi, 15 Nov. 1943 (sank under tow 18 June 1944)

Quentin sunk by air attack, Mediterranean, 2 Dec. 1942

Quorn sunk by *Linsen* explosive craft, English Channel, 2 Aug. 1944

Rockingham sunk by mine off Aberdeen, 27 Sept. 1944

Rockwood D.B.R. in air attack, Aegean Sea, 11 Nov. 1943

Sikh sunk by coastal battery, Tobruk, 14 Sept. 1942

Somali sank under tow after being torpedoed by U-703, Arctic, 20 Sept. 1942

Southwold sunk by mine, Malta, 23 March 1942

Stanley sunk by U-574 W. of Lisbon, 19 Dec. 1941

Stronghold sunk by Japanese warships E. of Java, 2 March 1942

Sturdy wrecked in storm on Tiree, 30 Oct. 1940

Swift sunk by mine off Normandy, 26 June 1944

Tenedos sunk by air attack, Ceylon, 5 April 1942

Thracian beached in Hong Kong harbour, 24 Dec. 1941

Tynedale sunk by U-593, Mediterranean, 12 Dec. 1943

Valentine sunk by air attack, Scheldt Estuary, 15 May 1940

Venetia sunk by mine, Thames Estuary, 19 Oct. 1940

Veteran sunk by U-404, N. Atlantic, 26 Sept. 1942

Vimiera sunk by mine, Thames Estuary, 9 Jan. 1942

Vortigern sunk by S-104, English Channel, 15 March 1942

Wakeful sunk by S-30, English Channel, 29 May 1940

Walpole sunk by mine, North Sea, 6 Jan. 1945

Warwick sunk by U-413 off Trevose Head, 20 Feb. 1944

Wessex sunk by air attack, English Channel, 25 May 1940

Whirlwind sunk by U-34, N. Atlantic, 5 July 1940

Whitley beached after air attack, Nieuport, 19 May 1940

Wild Swan sunk by air attack, Bay of Biscay, 17 June 1942

Worcester D.B.R. by mine, North Sea, 23 Dec. 1943

Wren sunk by air attack, English Channel, 27 July 1940

Wryneck sunk by air attack, Mediterranean, 27 April 1941

Zulu sunk by air attack off Tobruk, 14 Sept. 1942

Submarines

Cachalot sank after being rammed by Italian M.T.B. *Papa* off Benghazi, 30 July 1941

Grampus sunk by Italian M.T.B.s *Circe* and *Clio* off Syracuse, 24 June 1940

H-31 Missing, Bay of Biscay, Dec. 1941

Narwhal sunk by air attack, North Sea, 23 July 1940

Odin sunk by Italian destroyer *Strale*, Mediterranean, 13 June 1940

Olympus sunk by mine off Malta, 8 May 1942

Orpheus sunk by Italian destroyer *Turbine* off Tobruk, 19 June 1940

Oswald rammed and sunk by Italian destroyer *Vivaldi*, Mediterranean, 1 Aug. 1940

Oxley accidentally sunk by H.M.S. *Triton* off Norway, 10 Sept. 1939

P-32 sunk by mine off Tripoli, 18 Aug. 1941

P-33 sunk by Italian M.T.B.s off Pantellaria, 23 Aug. 1941

P-36 sunk in air attack, Malta, 31 March 1942

P-38 sunk by Italian patrol vessels off Tunisia, 25 Feb. 1942

P-39 sunk in air attack, Malta, 26 March 1942

P-48 sunk by Italian patrol craft off Tunis, 25 Dec. 1942

P-222 sunk by Italian patrol craft off Naples, 12 Dec. 1942

P-311 missing off Maddalena, 8 Jan. 1943

Pandora sunk in air attack, Malta, 31 March 1942

Parthian lost in Adriatic, Aug. 1943

Perseus sunk by Italian submarine *Enrico Tati*, Mediterranean, 6. Dec. 1941

Phoenix sunk by Italian M.T.B. *Albatros* off Augusta, 17 July 1940

Porpoise sunk by Japanese aircraft in Malacca Straits, 19 Jan. 1945

Rainbow sunk off Calabria, 15 Oct. 1940

Regent lost in Adriatic, April 1943

Regulus missing, Mediterranean, Dec. 1940

Sahib sunk by Italian corvette *Gabbiano* off N. Sicily, 24 April 1943

Salmon sunk by mine of S. Norway, 9 July 1940

Saracen sunk by Italian corvette *Minerva* off Bastia, 18 March 1943

Satyr sunk by U-987 W. off Narvik, 15 June 1944

Seahorse missing, North Sea, 30 Jan. 1940

Seal forced to surface by mine damage and captured by seaplane, Kattegat, 5 May 1940; in German service as UBA

Shakespeare D.B.R. by Japanese aircraft in Nankauri Strait, 3 Jan. 1945

Shark sunk by German minesweepers, North Sea, 6 July 1940

Sickle lost in Aegean, June 1944

Simoon sunk by U-565, Dardanelles, 15 Nov. 1943

Snapper missing, Bay of Biscay, 11 Feb. 1941

Spearfish sunk by U-34 off Norway, 2 Aug. 1940

Splendid sunk by German destroyer *Hermes* off Capri, 21 April 1943

Starfish sunk by minesweeper, Heligoland Bight, 9 Jan. 1940

Sterlet sunk by A.S. trawlers, Skagerrak, 18 April 1940

Stonehenge missing off Nicobar Islands, March 1944

Stratagem sunk by Japanese patrol craft off Malacca, 22 Nov. 1944

Sunfish sunk in error by R.A.F. W. of Norway during passage to Russia, 27 July 1944

Swordfish sunk by mine off Isle of Wight, 7 Nov. 1940

Syrtis sunk by mine off Bodo, Norway, 28 March 1944

Talisman lost in Sicilian Channel, Sept. 1942

Tarpon sunk by German minesweeper M6, North Sea, 14 April 1940

Tempest sunk by Italian M.T.B. *Circe*, Gulf of Taranto, 13 Feb. 1942

Terrapin D.B.R. by Japanese surface forces, S. Pacific, 19 May 1945

Tetrarch missing, W. Mediterranean, 2 Nov. 1941

Thames missing, Norwegian Sea, July 1940

Thistle sunk by U-4 off Norway, 10 April 1940

Thorn sunk by Italian M.T.B. *Pegaso* off Tobruk, 6 Aug. 1942

Thunderbolt sunk by Italian corvette *Cicogna* off Sicily, 13 March 1943

Tigris missing, Gulf of Naples, 10 March 1943

Traveller lost in Gulf of Taranto, Dec. 1942

Triad missing, Mediterranean, 20 Oct. 1940

Triton sunk by air attack, Mediterranean, 18 Dec. 1940

Triumph lost in Aegean, Jan. 1942

Trooper lost in Aegean, Oct. 43

Turbulent sunk by Italian patrol vessels off Bastia, 11 March 1943

Umpire sank after collision with A.S. trawler *Peter Hendricks* off the Wash, 19 July 1941

Unbeaten sunk in error by R.A.F. aircraft, Bay of Biscay, 11 Nov. 1942

Undaunted missing off Libya, 13 May 1941

Undine sunk by minesweeper, Heligoland Bight, 6 Jan. 1940

Union sunk by Italian M.T.B.s off Tunisia, 22 July 1941

Unity sank after collision, North Sea, 29 April 1940

Unique missing W. of Gibraltar, Nov. 1942

Untamed lost in accident off Campbeltown, 30 May 1943 (later salvaged and renamed *Vitality*)

Upholder sunk by Italian M.T.B. *Pegaso* off Tripoli, 14 April 1942

Urge sunk by Italian M.T.B. *Pegaso*, E. Mediterranean, 28 April 1942

Usk sunk by mine off Cap Bon, 3 May 1941

Usurper lost in Bay of Genoa, Oct. 1943

Utmost sunk by Italian M.T.B. *Groppo* off Sicily, 24 Nov. 1942

Vandal lost in Firth of Clyde, 24 Feb. 1943

Monitors

Terror sunk as a result of bomb damage, Mediterranean, 23 Feb. 1941

Sloops

Auckland sunk by air attack, Mediterranean, 24 June 1941

Bittern sunk by air attack, Norwegian Sea, 30 April 1940

Culver sunk by U-105 W. of Bay of Biscay, 31.1.42

Cornflower Sunk in air attack, Hong Kong 15 Dec. 1941

Chanticleer D.B.R. by U-238 off Azores, 18 Nov. 1943

Dundee sunk by U-48, N. Atlantic, 15 Sept. 1940

Egret sunk by Hs 293 glider bombs, Bay of Biscay, 28 Aug. 1943

Herald Scuttled at Seletar, Singapore, Feb. 1942; salvaged by Japanese and renamed *Heiyo*. Mined in Java Sea, 14 Nov. 1944

Hartland destroyed by shore batteries, Oran, 8 Nov. 1942

Ibis sunk by air attack off Algiers, 10 Nov. 1942

Kite sunk by U-344, Arctic, 21 Aug. 1944

Lapwing sunk by U-968, Kola Inlet, 20 March 1945

Laburnum lost at Singapore, Feb. 1942

Penzance sunk by U-37, N. Atlantic, 24 Aug. 1940

Pintail sunk by mine, Humber Estuary, 10 June 1941

Stork D.B.R. by U-77, Mediterranean, 12 Nov. 1942

Woodpecker sank under tow after being damaged by U-256, N. Atlantic, 27 Feb. 1944

Walney destroyed by shore batteries, Oran, 8 Nov. 1942

Frigates

Bickerton sunk by U-354, Arctic, 22 Aug. 1944

Blackwood sunk by U-764, English Channel, 15 June 1944

Bullen sunk by U-775, N. Atlantic, 6 Dec. 1944

Cuckmere D.B.R. by U-223, Mediterranean, 11 Dec. 1943

Capel sunk by U-486, Western Approaches, 26 Dec. 1944

Duff D.B.R. by mine off Dutch coast, 30 Nov. 1944

Ekins D.B.R. by mine, North Sea, 16 April 1945

Goodall sunk by U-968, Arctic, 29 April 1945

Goodson D.B.R. by U-984 off Cherbourg, 25 June 1944

Gould sunk by U-358, N. Atlantic, 1 March 1944

Halsted D.B.R. by S-boats off Normandy, 11 June 1944

Itchen sunk by U-260, N. Atlantic, 22 Sept. 1943

Lawford sunk by air attack off Normandy, 8 June 1944

Mourne sunk off Normandy by U-767, 15 June 1944

Manners D.B.R. by U-1172 S. of Isle of Man, 26 Jan. 1945

Redmill D.B.R. by U-1105 off W. coast of Ireland, 27 April 1945

Trollope D.B.R. by S-boats and beached at Arromanches, 5 July 1944

Tweed sunk by U-305, N. Atlantic, 7 Jan. 1944

Whitaker D.B.R. by U-483, N. Atlantic, 1 Nov. 1944

Corvettes

Arbutus sunk by U-136, N. Atlantic, 5 Feb. 1942

Asphodel sunk by U-575, N. Atlantic, 9 Feb. 1944

Auricula damaged by mine off Madagascar and sank next day, 5 May 1942

Bluebell sunk by U-711, Arctic, 16 Feb. 1945

Denbigh Castle D.B.R. by U-992, Kola Inlet, 13 Feb. 1945

Erica sunk by mine off Benghazi, 9 Feb. 1943

Fleur de Lys sunk by U-206, N. Atlantic, 14 Oct. 1941

Gardenia lost in collision off Oran, 9 Nov. 1942

Gladiolus missing in N. Atlantic, 17 Oct. 1941

Godetia sank after collision off N. Ireland, 6 Sept. 1940

Hollyhock sunk by air attack, Indian Ocean, 9 April 1942

Hurst Castle sunk by U-482, N. Atlantic, 1 Sept. 1944

Marigold sunk by air attack off Algiers, 9 Dec. 1942

Mimosa sunk by U-124, W. Atlantic, 9 June 1942

Montbretia sunk by U-262, N. Atlantic, 18 Nov. 1942

Orchis D.B.R. by mine off Normandy, 21 Aug. 1944

Picotee sunk by U-68, N. Atlantic, 12 Aug. 1941

Pink D.B.R. by mine, Bay of Biscay, 27 June 1944

Polyanthus sunk by U-952 S. of Iceland, 20 Sept. 1943

Rose lost in collision with frigate *Manners*, N. Atlantic, 27 Nov. 1944

Salvia sunk by U-568, Mediterranean, 24 Dec. 1941

Samphire sunk by Italian submarine *Platino* off Bougie, 30 Jan. 1943

Snapdragon sunk by air attack, E. Mediterranean, 19 Dec. 1942

Vervain sunk by U-1208 S. of Iceland, 20 Feb. 1945

Windflower lost in collision with merchant ship, N. Atlantic, 12 Dec. 1941

Zinnia sunk by U-564, N. Atlantic, 23 Aug. 1941

Fleet minesweepers

Abingdon wrecked in air attacks, Malta, April 1942

Algerine sunk by Italian submarine *Ascianghi*, Mediterranean, 15 Nov. 1942

Banka missing off Malaya, 10 Dec. 1941

Bramble sunk by German destroyers, Arctic, 31 Dec. 1942

Britomart sunk in error by R.A.F. aircraft off Cap d'Antifer, 27 Aug. 1944

Cato sunk by *Neger* human torpedo, English Channel, 6 July 1944

Clacton sunk by mine off Corsica, 31 Dec. 1943

Cromarty sunk by mine, Strait of Bonifacio, 23 Oct. 1943

Cromer sunk by mine off Mersa Matruh, 9 Nov. 1942

Donoon sunk by mine, North Sea, 30 April 1940

Dundalk sank under tow off Harwich after mine damage, 16 Oct. 1940

Fantome D.B.R. by mine, Mediterranean, 20 May 1943

Felixstowe sunk by mine off Sardinia, 18 Dec. 1943

Fermoy wrecked in air attack, Malta, 4 May 1941

Fitzroy sunk by mine off Great Yarmouth, 27 May 1942

Gossamer sunk by air attack, Kola Inlet, 24 June 1942

Hebe sunk by mine off Bari, 28 Nov. 1943

Huntley sunk by air attack off Mersa Matruh, 31 Jan. 1941

Hussar sunk in error by R.A.F. aircraft off Cap d'Antifer, 27 Aug. 1944

Hythe sunk by U-371, Mediterranean, 13 Oct. 1943

Jarak sunk by air attack off Singapore, 17 Feb. 1942

Jeram lost at Singapore, 15 Feb. 1942

Klias scuttled off Pelambang, 15 Feb. 1942

Leda sunk by U-435, Arctic, 20 Sept. 1942

Loyalty sunk by U-480, English Channel, 15 Aug. 1944

Magic sunk by *Neger*, human torpedo, English Channel, 6 July 1944

Mercury sunk by mine off Ireland, 25 Dec. 1940

Minnie Moller   lost at Hong Kong, 31 Dec. 1941

Niger   sunk by mine in Denmark Strait, 5 July 1942

Pylades   sunk by _Neger_, human torpedo, English Channel, 8 July 1944

Prompt   D.B.R. by mine, 9 May 1945

Regulus   sunk by mine off Corfu, 12 Jan. 1945

Salamander   D.B.R. in attack by R.A.F. aircraft, Cap d'Antifer, 27 Aug. 1944

Skipjack   sunk by air attack, English Channel, 1 June 1940

Sphinx   sank under tow after air attack, Moray Firth, 3 Feb. 1940

Squirrel   D.B.R. by mine off Phuket and sunk by R.N. destroyers, 24 July 1945

Stoke   sunk by air attack, Tobruk, 7 May 1941

Sunset   wrecked in air attack, Malta, 1 April 1942

Texas   lost in collision off Jamaica, 19 July 1944

Vestal   sunk by _kamikaze_ attack off Phuket, 26 July 1945

Waverley   sunk by air attack, Dunkirk, 29 May 1940

Widnes   beached at Suda Bay after air attack, 20 May 1941. (later salvaged by Germans and used as escort vessel Uj2109; sunk 17 Oct. 1943)

Minelayers

Abdiel   sunk by mine, Taranto, 10 Sept. 1943

Corncrake   sank in N. Atlantic, 25 Jan. 1943

Latona   sunk by air attack off Bardia, 26 Oct. 1941

Peterhead   D.B.R. by mine off Normandy, 8 June 1944

Redstart   sunk in Hong Kong harbour, Dec. 1941

Rhu   lost at Singapore, 15 Feb. 1942

Shepperton   sunk by air attack, Belfast, 5 May 1941

Welshman   sunk by U-617, Mediterranean, 1 Feb. 1943

Armed merchant cruisers

Andania   sunk by German submarine U-A., S. Atlantic, 14 June 1940

Asturias   sunk by Italian submarine _Cagni_, S. Atlantic, 25 July 1943

Aurania   sunk by U-123, N. Atlantic, 21 Oct. 1941

Carinthia   sunk by U-46, N. Atlantic, 6 June 1940

Comorin   lost as result of fire, N. Atlantic, 6 April 1941

Dunvegan Castle   sunk by U-46, N. Atlantic, 28 Aug. 1940

Forfar   sunk by U-99, N. Atlantic, 1 Dec. 1940

Jervis Bay   sunk by _Admiral Scheer_, N. Atlantic, 5 Nov. 1940

Laurentic   sunk by U-99, N. Atlantic, 3 Nov. 1940

Patroclus   sunk by U-99, N. Atlantic, 3 Nov. 1940

Rawalpindi   sunk by _Scharnhorst_, N. Atlantic, 23 Nov. 1939

Rajputana   sunk by U-108, N. Atlantic, 13 April 1941

Salopian   sunk by U-98, N. Atlantic, 13 May 1941

Scotstoun   sunk by U-25, Bay of Biscay, 13 June 1940

Transylvania   sunk by U-56, N. Atlantic, 10 Aug. 1940

Voltaire   sunk by German auxiliary cruiser _Thor_, central Atlantic, 4 April 1941

River gunboats

Cicala   sunk by air attack, Hong Kong, 21 Dec. 1941

Dragonfly   sunk by Japanese aircraft off Singapore, 14 Feb. 1942

Grasshopper   driven ashore at Sianpend Island, Sumatra, 14 Feb. 1942

Ladybird   sunk by air attack off Tobruk, 12 May 1941

Moth   scuttled at Hong Kong, 12 Dec. 1941; salved by Japanese as _Suma_; lost 19 March 1945.

Peterel   sunk by Japanese destroyer _Idzumo_ and shore batteries, Shanghai, 8 Dec. 1941

Scorpion   sunk by Japanese warships in Banka Strait, 13 Feb. 1942

Tern   scuttled at Hong Kong, 19 Dec. 1941

Auxiliary Trawler Losses 1939–45

Anti-submarine trawlers

Arctic Pioneer   lost off Portsmouth, 15 May 1942

Argyllshire   sunk by S-34, English Channel, 1 June 1940

Arsenal   lost in collision with Polish destroyer *Burza*, Clyde, 16 Nov. 40

Aston Villa   sunk by air attack, Norway, 3 May 1940

Birdlip   sunk by U-547 off Liberia, 14 June 1944

Blackburn Rovers   sunk by mine, Dunkirk, 2 June 1940

Bradman   sunk by air attack, Norway, 25 April 1940 (later raised by Germans for service as patrol vessel *Friese*)

Bredon   sunk by U-521, central Atlantic, 7 Feb. 1943

Cape Chelyuskin   sunk by air attack, Norway, 29 April 1940

Cape Finisterre   sunk by air attack off Harwich, 2 Aug. 1940

Cape Passaro   sunk by air attack, Narvik, 21 May 1940

Cape Siroteko   sunk by air attack, Norway, 29 April 1940 (later raised by Germans for service as patrol vessel *Gote*; sunk by Allied air attack, 11 May 1944)

Cayton Wyke   sunk by S-boat, English Channel, 8 July 1940

Daneman   sank after hitting ice, N. Atlantic, 8 May 1943

Erin   destroyed by explosion (sabotage), Gibraltar, 18 Jan. 1942

Evelina   sunk by mine, North Sea, 16 Dec. 1939

Force   sunk by air attack, Great Yarmouth, 27 June 1941

Gairsay   sunk by *Linsen* explosive boat, English Channel, 3 Aug. 1944

Ganilly   sunk by U-390, English Channel, 5 July 1944

Gaul   sunk by air attack off Norway, 3 May 1940

Hammond   sunk by air attack, Norway, 25 April 1940 (later raised by Germans for service as patrol vessel *Salier*)

Horatio   sunk by S-58, Mediterranean, 7 Jan. 1943

James Ludford   sunk by mine, North Sea, 14 Dec. 1939

Jardine   sunk by air attack, Norway, 30 April 1940 (later raised by Germans for service as patrol vessel *Cherusker*; sunk by mine, 6 Dec. 1942)

Jasper   sunk by S-81, English Channel, 1 Dec. 1942

Juniper   sunk by German warships, Norwegian Sea, 8 June 1940

Jura   sunk by U-371 off Algiers, 7 Jan. 1943

Kingston Alalite   sunk by mine off Plymouth, 10 Nov. 1940

Kingston Beryl   sunk by mine off Skerryvore, 25 Dec. 1943

Kingston Cairngorm   sunk by mine, English Channel, 18 Oct. 1940

Kingston Galena   sunk by air attack off Dover, 27 April 1940

Kingston Jacinth   sunk by mine off Portsmouth, 12 Jan. 1943

Kingston Sapphire   Sunk by Italian submarine *Nani*, Gibraltar, Oct. 1940

Lady Lilian   sunk by air attack W. of Ireland, 16 March 1941

Lady Shirley   sunk by U-374 off Gibraltar, 11 Dec. 1941

Larwood   sunk by air attack, Norway, 25 April 1940 (later raised by Germans as patrol vessel *Franke*)

Leyland   sunk in collision off Gibraltar, 25 Nov. 1942

Lincoln City   sunk by air attack off Faeroes, 21 Feb. 1941

Lord Hailsham   sunk in S-boat attack, English Channel, 27 Feb. 1943

Lord Stamp   sunk by mine, English Channel, 14 Oct. 1940

Lord Stonehaven   sunk by S-112, English Channel, 2 Oct. 1942

Lord Wakefield   sunk by air attack off Normandy, 29 July 1944

Manor   sunk by S-boat, English Channel, 9 July 1942

Mastiff   sunk by mine, Thames Estuary 20 Nov. 1939

Melbourne   sunk by air attack, Narvik, 22 May 1940

Northern Isles   ran aground and wrecked off Durban, 19 Jan. 1945

Notts County   sunk by U-701 S. of Iceland, 8 March 1942

Orafsay   sunk by U-68 off W. Africa, 22 Oct. 1943

Peridot   sunk by mine, English Channel, 15 March 1940

Recoil   sunk by mine, English Channel, 28 Sept. 1940

Roche Bonne   sunk by air attack off the Lizard, 7 April 1941

Rosabelle   sunk by U-374, N. Atlantic, 11 Dec. 1941

Rubens   sunk by Fw 200 off Ireland, 13 Feb. 1941

Rutlandshire   beached after air attack, Namsos, 20 April 1940 (later raised by Germans for service as patrol vessel _Rubier_; sunk by mine, 6 Dec. 1942)

St Achilleus   sunk by mine off Dunkirk, 31 May 1940

St Apollo   sunk in collision with destroyer _Sardonyx_ off the Hebrides, 22 Nov. 1941

St Goran   sunk by air attack off Norway, 3 May 1940

Sedgefly   sunk by mine, North Sea, 16 Dec. 1939

Sindonis   sunk by air attack off Tobruk, 29 May 1941

Stella Dorado   sunk by air attack, English Channel, 1 June 1940

Stella Capella   sunk by U-701 off Iceland, 11 March 1942

Stronsay   sunk by Italian submarine _Avorio_, Mediterranean, 5 Feb. 1943

Syvern   sunk by air attack, Mediterranean, 27 May 1941

Tervani   sunk by Italian submarine _Accacio_, Mediterranean, 7 Feb. 1942

Thuringia   sunk by mine, North Sea, 28 March 1940

Ullswater   sunk by S-boats, English Channel, 19 Nov. 1942

Warwickshire   sunk by air attack off Norway, 30 April 1940 (later raised by Germans for service as patrol vessel _Alane_; sunk by Soviet submarine, 19 July 1943)

Westella   sunk by mine, Dunkirk, 2 June 1940

Minesweeping trawlers

Akranes   sunk by air attack, Bridlington Bay, 4 July 1941

Alouette   sunk by U-552 off Portugal, 19 Sept. 1942

Aragonite   sunk by mine, English Channel, 22 Nov. 1939

Arley   sunk under tow following mine damage, North Sea, 3 Feb. 1945

Asama   sunk by air attack off Plymouth, 21 March 1941

Avanturine sunk by S-142 off Beachy Head, 2 Dec. 1943

Ben Gairn   sunk by air attack off Lowestoft, 4 May 1941

Benvolio   sunk by mine, North Sea, 22 Feb. 1940

Botanic   sunk by air attack, North Sea, 18 Feb. 1942

Calverton   sunk by mine off Humber, 29 Nov. 1940

Calvi   sunk by air attack, Dunkirk, 29 May 1940

Cap d'Antifer   sunk by S-boats, North Sea, 13 Feb. 1944

Cape Spartel   sunk by air attack off Humber, 2 Feb. 1942

Capricornus   sunk by mine, English Channel, 7 Dec. 1940

Caroline   sunk by mine off Milford Haven, 29 April 1941

Caulonia   foundered after running aground, Rye Bay, 31 March 1943

Charles Boyes sunk by mine, North Sea, 25 May 1940

Cloughton Wyke   sunk by air attack off Humber, 2 Feb. 1942

Computator   sank after collision with destroyer _Vanoc_, Seine Bay, 21 Jan. 1945

Conquistador   lost in collision, Thames Estuary, 25 Nov. 1940

Crestflower   sank after air attack, Portsmouth, 19 July 1940

Darogah   sunk by mine, Thames Estuary, 16 Jan. 1941

Dervish   sunk by mine, North Sea, 9 Sept. 1940

Desiree   sunk by mine, Thames Estuary, 16 Jan. 1941

Dromio   lost in collision, North Sea, 21 Dec. 1939

Drummer   sunk by mine, English Channel, 4 Aug. 1940

Ebor Wyke   sunk by U-979 off Iceland, 2 May 1945

Eileen Duncan   sunk by air attack, North Shields, 30 Sept. 1941

Elizabeth Angela   sunk by air attack, English Channel, 13 Aug. 1940

Emilion   sunk by mine, Thames Estuary, 24 Oct. 1941

Fifeshire   sunk by air attack, North Sea, 20 Feb. 1940

Fleming   sunk by air attack, Thames Estuary, 24 July 1940

Fontenoy   sunk by air attack off Lowestoft, 19 Nov. 1940

Fort Royal   sunk by air attack, North Sea, 9 Feb. 1940

Gulfoss   sunk by mine, English Channel, 9 March 1941

Hayburn Wyke   lost off Ostend, 2 Jan. 1945

Henriette   sunk by mine off Humber, 26 Dec. 1941

Irvana   sunk by air attack off Great Yarmouth, 16 Jan. 1942

James Ludford sunk by mine, North Sea, 14 Dec. 1939

Joseph Button sunk by mine off Aldeburgh, 22 Oct. 1940

Kennymore sunk by mine, Thames Estuary, 25 Nov. 1940

Keryado sunk by mine, English Channel, 6 March 1941

Kurd sunk by mine off Cornwall, 10 July 1945

Loch Assater sunk by mine, North Sea, 22 March 1940

Loch Doon sunk by mine, North Sea, 25 Dec. 1939

Loch Inver sunk by mine off Harwich, 24 Sept. 1940

Lorinda sank after fire off Freetown, 28 Aug. 1941

Luda Lady sunk by mine off the Humber, 22 Jan. 1941

Manx Prince sunk by mine off Humber, 28 Nov. 1940

Marconi sunk by air attack off Harwich, 20 Sept. 1941

Marmion sunk by air attack off Harwich, 9 April 1941

Marsona sunk by mine off Cromarty, 4 Aug. 1940

Meror sunk by mine off the Humber, 3 Oct. 1943

Milford Earl sunk by air attack off E. coast of Scotland, 8 Dec. 1941

Mollusc sunk by air attack off N.E. coast, 17 March 1941

Murmansk lost after grounding, Brest, 17 June 1940

Nogi sunk by air attack off Cromer, 23 June 1941

Nordhav sunk by U-714 off Dundee, 10 Feb. 1945

Northcoates sank under tow, English Channel, 2 Dec. 1944

Ormond sunk by air attack off Scotland, 16 Feb. 1941

Ostwaldian sunk by mine, Bristol Channel, 4 Aug. 1940

Pelton sunk by S-28 off Great Yarmouth, 24 Dec. 1940

Phineas Beard sunk by air attack off E. coast of Scotland, 8 Dec. 1941

Polly Johnson sunk by air attack, Dunkirk, 29 May 1940

Red Gauntlet sunk by S-86, North Sea, 4 Aug. 1943

Refundo sank under tow after being mined, 18 Dec. 1940

Relonzo sunk by mine off Liverpool, 20 Jan. 1941

Resmilo sunk by air attack off Peterhead, 20 June 1941

Resparko sunk by air attack off Falmouth, 20 Aug. 1940

Rifsnes sunk by air attack off Ostend, 20 May 1940

Rinovia sunk by mine off Falmouth, 2 Nov. 1940

River Clyde sunk by mine off Aldeburgh, 5 Aug. 1940

Robert Bowen sunk by air attack, North Sea, 9 Feb. 1940

Rodino sunk by air attack off Dover, 24 July 1940

Rosemonde sunk by U-203, N. Atlantic, 22 Jan. 1942

Royalo sunk by mine off Cornwall, 1 Sept. 1940

Sarna sunk by mine in Suez Canal, 25 Feb. 1941

Sea King sunk by mine off Grimsby, 9 Oct. 1940

Silicia sunk by mine off the Humber, 8 May 1941

Sisapon sunk by mine off Harwich, 12 June 1940

Solomon sunk by mine off Cromer, 1 April 1942

Star of Deveron sunk by air attack, North Shields, 30 Sept. 1941

Stella Orion sunk by mine, Thames Estuary, 11 Oct. 1940

Strathborne sunk by mine off the Humber, 6 Sept. 1941

Tervani sunk by Italian submarine *Accacio* off Algeria, 7 Feb. 1943

Thomas Bartlett sunk by mine off Calais, 28 May 1940

Tilburyness sunk by air attack, Thames Estuary, 1 Nov. 1940

Tranio sank under tow after air attack, North Sea, 26 June 1941

Tranquil Valdora sunk by air attack off Dover, 12 Nov. 1940

Washington sunk by mine, North Sea, 6 Dec. 1939

Waterfly sunk by air attack off Dungeness, 17 Sept. 1942

Waveflower sunk by mine off Aldeburgh, 21 Oct. 1940

William Hallett sunk by mine, North Sea, 6 Dec. 1939

William Stephen sunk by S-boats off Cromer, 25 Oct. 1943

William Wesney sunk by mine off Orfordness, 7 Nov. 1940

Wyoming sunk by mine off Harwich, 20 May 1944

In addition to the above, many other naval trawlers and other auxiliary vessels were lost between 1939 and 1945. The total number of auxiliary craft and minor war vessels – coastal craft, M.T.B.s, M.G.B.s and M.L.s – lost from all causes was 1,035.

General Index

Index of Ships (Main Text)